"Structural adjustment" has been a central part of the development strategy for the "third world." Loans made by the World Bank and the IMF have been conditional on developing countries pursuing rapid economic liberalization programs as it was believed this would strengthen their economies in the long run. M. Rodwan Abouharb and David Cingranelli argue that, conversely, structural adjustment agreements usually cause increased hardship for the poor, greater civil conflict, and more repression of human rights, therefore resulting in a lower rate of economic development. Greater exposure to structural adjustment has increased the prevalence of anti-government protests, riots, and rebellion. It has led to less respect for economic and social rights, physical integrity rights, and worker rights, but more respect for democratic rights. Based on these findings, the authors recommend a human rights-based approach to economic development.

M. RODWAN ABOUHARB is an Assistant Professor of Political Science at Louisiana State University. His research examines human rights and civil and international conflict.

DAVID CINGRANELLI is a Professor of Political Science at Binghamton University, SUNY, co-director of the CIRI Human Rights Data Project, and former President of the Human Rights Section of the American Political Science Association.

Human Rights and Structural Adjustment

M. Rodwan Abouharb
and
David Cingranelli

CAMBRIDGE
UNIVERSITY PRESS

CAMBRIDGE UNIVERSITY PRESS
Cambridge, New York, Melbourne, Madrid, Cape Town, Singapore, São Paulo, Delhi

Cambridge University Press
The Edinburgh Building, Cambridge CB2 8RU, UK

Published in the United States of America by Cambridge University Press, New York

www.cambridge.org
Information on this title: www.cambridge.org/9780521676717

First published 2007

Printed in the United Kingdom at the University Press, Cambridge

A catalogue record for this publication is available from the British Library

ISBN 978-0-521-85933-2 hardback
ISBN 978-0-521-67671-7 paperback

This book is dedicated to Margaret Elizabeth Barker and Therese Cingranelli

Contents

Figures

Tables

Acknowledgments

We are indebted to a number of people who have assisted us in this project, which began when Rod Abouharb was a graduate student at Binghamton University, of the State University of New York and David Cingranelli was a member of the faculty there. During the final year and a half of the book's writing, Rod Abouharb took a faculty position at Louisiana State University. Faculty members and graduate students at both institutions spent considerable time reading, thinking about, and making suggestions concerning early drafts of the book. In particular, we benefited from the criticisms offered by the participants in the International Relations Reading Group at Binghamton University and the participants in the Brown Bag series at Louisiana State University who patiently read and listened to various aspects of the project that would later become chapters in the book. Special thanks go to David Clark, Ben Fordham, Sol Polachek, Patrick Regan, David Richards, David Sobek, and Brandon Zicha who provided many helpful suggestions.

We are also very grateful to the thoughtful comments and generosity of Jim Vreeland who committed a great deal of intellectual energy and happily shared his data and ideas as the project progressed. He has greatly improved the quality of the work generated by this research agenda. Susan Aaronson and Armand Pereira also read several chapters of the book and provided detailed substantive comments and editing suggestions. Our editor, John Haslam, and members of the production staff at Cambridge University Press, including Carrie Cheek and Joanna Breeze, were also encouraging and helpful throughout the execution of this project. The comments of several anonymous reviewers recruited by John Haslam improved the quality of the book as well.

Just as the final manuscript was about to be sent to Cambridge University Press in December of 2006, Nancy Alexander, Director of Citizens' Network on Essential Services (CNES), offered to give the entire book a final careful reading designed to make the book more readable and relevant to the policy-making community. The CNES is an NGO that monitors the activities of the World Bank, IMF, and WTO affecting the quality of basic services in poor countries: water, power, education, and health care. We accepted her generous offer, and, after about a week, she produced editing suggestions and/or critical comments on almost every page. We carefully reviewed all of her suggestions and accepted many of them. In some cases, we added new sections, substantially rewrote sections of the book, and cited more research by others to clarify or to elaborate on our arguments.

The research project on which the book is based would not have been possible without the Cingranelli and Richards (CIRI) Human Rights Data. These data were collected and made available to the public with the generous financial support of the National Science Foundation, Political Science Division, and the World Bank. Any opinions, findings, and conclusions or recommendations expressed in this book are those of the authors and do not reflect the views of these organizations. Any errors or oversights remain our own.

On a personal note, Rod would like to thank his mum, Margaret Elizabeth Barker, and her husband, Les, for their support, interest, willingness to read drafts of various quality over innumerable cups of coffee, and dinners. They provided space to work on this project each time Rod returned to the United Kingdom for the "holidays." David would like to thank Therese, his wife, and his children, Nicholas, Tyler, and Leah, for enduring his lack of proper attention to family affairs, especially during the final year of the book's writing.

Part I

The argument

1 Structural adjustment programs undermine human rights

Introduction

In 1981, the Reagan administration in the US, the Thatcher administration in the UK, and their allies compelled the International Monetary Fund (IMF) and World Bank Group (known as the "International Financial Institutions" [IFIs]) to launch an ideological assault against the state and promote a shift in power from the state to the market.[1] From 1981 to the present, the IFIs have financed structural adjustment agreements (SAAs) in developing and transition countries to achieve that goal.[2] Structural adjustment agreements call upon recipient governments to liberalize and privatize economies in the context of strict budget discipline. Adjustment lending facilitates economic integration – the hallmark of globalization – on terms that are advantageous to corporate and finance capital. The policy conditions associated with adjustment loans have accelerated transnational corporate penetration and expansion of markets in developing countries and lowered risks of portfolio investment and foreign direct investment. The role of the state has been reshaped to serve market liberalization, as governments have downsized, decentralized, and privatized (or "contracted out") their functions. Such measures were intended to jump-start economic growth and free up resources for debt service. However, in most countries, public investment in critical areas (health care, education, infrastructure) foundered, growth rates were disappointing, and debts mounted to unsustainable levels (Pettifor 2001).

This volume explores the relationship between adjustment and respect for human rights. Importantly, as governments in developing

---

[1] At that time, the UK and New Zealand were implementing the model that they proposed for developing countries. This model, called "New Public Management," contains the basic elements of public sector reform, as understood by the IFIs. These include: decentralization, privatization or commercialization of services, improved efficiency, and results-oriented approaches.

[2] For simplicity, this text uses the term "developing countries" to include low- and middle-income countries including the transition economies of the former Soviet Bloc.

3

countries implemented World Bank and IMF-financed structural adjustment programs (SAPs), respect for human rights diminished. World Bank and IMF structural adjustment programs usually cause increased hardship for the poor, greater civil conflict, and more repression of human rights, resulting in a lower rate of economic development. Based on an analysis of outcomes in 131 developing countries between 1981–2003, we show that, on average, structural adjustment has led to less respect for economic and social rights, and worker rights. The poor, organized labor, and other civil society groups protest these outcomes. Governments respond to challenges to their authority by murdering, imprisoning, torturing, and disappearing more of their citizens. Paradoxically, long exposure to structural adjustment conditionality is also associated with some democratic reforms. This work is one of the few global, comparative studies to focus on the manner in which SAPs have affected human rights.

Previous research by others has shown that respect for some human rights is necessary for, or at least facilitates, rapid and robust economic development. Thus, to the extent that structural adjustment programs diminish respect for human rights, robust economic development is less likely to occur. For now, we use the term "equitable" economic development to refer to a pattern of economic growth which improves the living conditions of the poorest people in society.

Based on previous research – especially case studies and small-scale comparisons – we expected to find that long-standing relationships between the governments of developing countries, on the one hand, and the World Bank or the International Monetary Fund, on the other, had worsened all types of human rights practices of the governments of developing countries. Our findings confirm that the implementation of structural adjustment agreements leads to less respect for most but not all human rights we examined. More specifically, we show that governments undergoing structural adjustment for the longest periods of time have murdered, tortured, politically imprisoned, and disappeared more of their citizens. In addition, the execution of structural adjustment programs has caused governments to reduce their levels of respect for economic and social rights, created higher levels of civil conflict, and more abuse of internationally recognized worker rights.

Our main argument linking structural adjustment policies to worsened human rights protection is that the policy changes implicitly or explicitly required in most structural adjustment agreements have hurt the poorest off in developing societies the most. Compliance with structural adjustment conditions causes governments to lessen respect for the economic and social rights of their citizens, including the rights to decent jobs, education, health care, and housing. This problem is compounded, because pressures from the World Bank and IMF to create a more business-friendly climate have encouraged the leaders of developing countries to reduce protections of workers from exploitation by employers.

Such protections include the internationally recognized core worker rights to freedom of association at the workplace, collective bargaining, and protection of children from exploitation.[3] Greater hardships for workers and the poor have led to increased civil conflict, itself an impediment to economic growth. The need to implement unpopular policies and the need to counter increased civil conflict, in turn, cause the governments of developing countries to reduce their respect for other human rights.

However, the results of our study show that structural adjustment has not led to a worsening of protections of all human rights in developing countries. We did not examine the effects of structural adjustment on all internationally recognized human rights, but we did examine the impact of structural adjustment on the degree of respect for a variety of procedural democratic rights in developing countries. We found that longer exposure to structural adjustment conditions was associated with more democracy in developing countries – one of the human rights also found to be associated with rapid economic growth (Kaufmann 2005; Isham, Kaufmann, and Pritchett 1977). Governments involved with structural adjustment the longest have better-developed democratic institutions. They have elections that are freer and fairer. Their citizens have more freedom to form and join organizations, and they have more freedom of speech and press.

We present the findings regarding the positive impacts of structural adjustment agreements on democratic institutions and respect for civil liberties in Chapter 10. For now, let us simply say that these findings are very important. First, they contradict the prevailing view in the case study literature. Second, they illustrate that our mostly negative findings do not result from our choice of methods. Finally, they demonstrate that the World Bank and the IMF can have a positive effect on the human rights practices of developing countries. Future research may show that greater involvement in structural adjustment is also associated with stronger protections of the human rights to private property including intellectual property, to adjudication of their rights through an independent judiciary,

---

[3] More precisely, our study shows that protections of worker rights in developing countries with long-standing involvement in structural adjustment of their economies are not as strong as they would have been had there been less involvement with the IMF and World Bank.

to stronger protection of women's economic rights, and to stronger protections of people's freedom to travel domestically and internationally.

Important previous research

Amartya Sen (1999), in *Development as Freedom*, made two major arguments. The ability for citizens to exercise their full range of internationally recognized human rights according to Sen is the litmus test for determining the level of economic development. Second, respect for human rights also facilitates economic development. He argued that traditional economic indicators used to measure development such as GDP per capita are incomplete and inadequate. Rather, development occurs when economic growth generates the freedoms associated with human rights.[4] Further, he contended that increasing people's ability to exercise their fundamental human rights was also critical, in an instrumental way, to the promotion of economic growth.

At the time Sen wrote his book, there already were suspicions that structural adjustment policies were not producing economic growth in most developing countries. Moreover, in the few cases where economic growth had occurred, it was not at the same time alleviating poverty. Perhaps the most influential book on this subject was Joseph Stiglitz's *Globalization and its Discontents* (2002). Stiglitz won the Nobel Prize in Economics in 2001. He had served as Chairman of President Clinton's Council of Economic Advisers and as Chief Economist for the World Bank. The main problem with structural adjustment policies, Stiglitz felt, was that they relied too heavily on the power of an unregulated free market to produce efficient outcomes. They did not allow for government interventions that could guide economic growth, especially economic policies that ensured a more equitable distribution of the benefits of growth.

In addition to the comprehensive critiques of structural adjustment such as the one offered by Stiglitz (2002), there have been many studies of one, two, or a few countries that have described the consequences of structural adjustment programs on those countries (e.g., SAPRIN 2004). Not many of these case studies focus explicitly on the human rights effects of structural adjustment, but most of them describe hardships that structural adjustment conditions caused for the poorest people. There are many websites maintained by human rights nongovernmental organizations that also detail the harmful effects of structural adjustment policies

---

[4] The United Nations Committee on Economic, Social, and Cultural Rights (2001) has echoed this view arguing for a better integration of human rights in development strategies.

on the least well off in developing countries. We cite the scholarly literature and activist arguments throughout the book, but especially in
Chapter 6. Work by David Pion-Berlin (1983; 1984; 1989; 1997; 2001)
explains the linkages between structural adjustment programs and
repression of human rights in Argentina and Peru. His work led us to
expect that governments seeking to make major economic changes that
hurt the poorest members of society would be likely to resort to coercion.
Thus, we hypothesized that governments implementing structural
adjustment programs the longest would be more willing to torture,
politically imprison, disappear, and murder their citizens.

To us, James Vreeland's book, *The IMF and Economic Development*
(2003), developed the most persuasive scientific case showing the negative economic impacts of structural adjustment. He concluded that
structural adjustment programs produced less growth in developing
countries than would have occurred without any IMF intervention.
Further, he noted that structural adjustment did the most damage to the
least well off in society. It usually reduced the size of the "economic pie" to
be distributed, and resulted in a more unequal distribution of the pie itself.

Vreeland's work is also important because he noted that few previous
studies of the effects of structural adjustment policies had controlled for
the effects of selection. Perhaps, he reasoned, the countries the IMF had
worked with had failed because they were intrinsically difficult cases. We
needed to determine the counterfactual – namely, what would have
happened to developing countries if the IMF had never intervened. In
his own study, Vreeland (2003) used estimation methods that corrected
for the effects of selection. His 2003 book and his earlier work with
Adam Przeworski (Przeworski and Vreeland 2000) convinced us to use
two-stage selection models to establish the consequences of structural
adjustment programs.

The few previous scientific studies of the impacts of structural adjustment programs on human rights used different research designs, but all
agreed that the imposition of structural adjustment conditions on less
developed countries had worsened the human rights practices of governments (Franklin 1997; Keith and Poe 2000; McLaren 1998). However,
those studies that explicitly addressed the effects of structural adjustment
on human rights practices only examined impacts on a government's willingness to murder, disappear, torture, and politically imprison its citizens.
These types of rights are generally referred to as "personal integrity" or
"physical integrity" rights.[5] The case study literature suggested that

---

[5] Physical integrity rights are sometimes called "life rights," "civil rights," or "personal
  integrity rights."

structural adjustment programs had worsened other types of human rights practices such as respect for economic and social rights, worker rights, and procedural democratic rights as well. In addition, no previous study of the human rights impacts of structural adjustment had controlled for the effects of selection.

Sen (1999) had made his case for a human rights-based development strategy using many good examples and some systematic analysis of evidence. However, he left some questions unanswered. What human rights protections are necessary for equitable economic growth to occur? In Chapter 2, we suggest that respect for some human rights is necessary if equitable economic development is to occur. There may even be a third category of human rights where the level of respect is not relevant to equitable economic growth.[6] The research program to investigate these issues is in its early stages.

Daniel Kaufmann (2005), an economist who heads the Governance Project at the World Bank, made an important contribution to this research program in his paper titled "Human Rights and Governance." His global, comparative, scientific study showed that respect for physical integrity rights and procedural democratic rights led to faster economic growth and more respect for economic and social rights of citizens. These are important findings, because, as noted, this combination of growth and increased respect for economic and social rights is the proper goal of economic development strategies.

We began this study, then, accepting the following premises. First, the World Bank and International Monetary Fund, as specialized agencies of the United Nations, have a responsibility to promote respect for human rights by governments around the world (Chapter 2). Second, the structural adjustment programs that have been jointly promulgated by the International Monetary Fund and the World Bank since about 1980 have not been successful in stimulating economic growth in most developing countries. Third, a relatively high level of respect for some human rights is a necessary precondition for equitable economic development (Chapter 2).

Measuring human rights

Measuring human rights practices is the first step towards *building theories to explain the causes and consequences of government respect for human rights*. It is also necessary for the *development and implementation*

---

[6] For example, the human right to travel internationally without any constraints may fuel a "brain drain" in developing countries that actually impedes equitable economic growth.

of evidence-based policies. Both types of research are necessary steps in the effort to attain human dignity for all persons worldwide. This research would not have been possible without the availability of a new data set measuring government respect for a broad array of human rights in every country in the world annually from 1981 to the present. Now covering 24 years, 13 separate human rights practices, and 195 countries, the CIRI Human Rights Data Set is the largest human rights data set in the world. It contains standards-based measures of the human rights practices of governments around the world (Cingranelli and Richards 2006). The CIRI Human Rights Data Set includes measures of many human rights recognized in the 1948 Universal Declaration of Human Rights. Activists, scholars, and policy-makers need a human rights profile for countries around the world that better reflects the range of human rights recognized in the Universal Declaration.

The critique of structural adjustment in a nutshell

This volume focuses on the mostly negative impact of structural adjustment agreements on a wide variety of human rights, but there are many other criticisms of structural adjustment in the policy community.[7] In many instances, the staff of the Bank and the Fund have made public statements or issued research papers refuting their critics.[8] We address the main points of their defense as they relate to human rights impacts later in this chapter and in several other chapters of this volume where the arguments are most relevant. Here, we briefly review their main points.

As already noted, there are mounting research results showing that, although SAPs were intended to jump-start economic growth, growth rates were negative or disappointingly low in most countries which implemented SAPs. The Center for Economic Policy Research (Weisbrot *et al.* 2001) has documented how growth rates in the 1960 to 1980 time frame exceeded growth rates when SAPs were prevalent – the 1980 to 2000 time frame. With the collapse of the USSR in 1989, laissez-faire capitalism was triumphant. Western governments and Western-led creditor institutions, particularly the IMF and World Bank, sought to make state ownership and "command and control" economies of the former Soviet Union things of the past. They

---

[7] See, for example, Alexander (2001; 2006a; 2006b) and SAPRIN (2004).

[8] For example, the Bank was very critical of the conclusions of the SAPRIN (2004) study of the impacts of structural adjustment. Kapil Kapoor (2001), Lead Economist, Poverty Reduction and Economic Management, World Bank IBRD and IDA, wrote a critical report titled "Comments on the Draft Synthesis Report on the Bangladesh SAPRI Research."

orchestrated "big bang" liberalization and privatization in the former Soviet Union, which led to a concentration of wealth and power among the oligarchs, high levels of poverty, and dramatically lowered life expectancy. Lawrence King (2002) analyzed policies of twelve countries in Eastern Europe using an index that measures the intensity with which each country has embraced neoliberal policies. He found an inverse relationship between the intensity with which these policies were embraced and economic performance. In other words, one finds a correlation between the fervor with which a country embraces neoliberalism and its declining economic performance.

Thus, it is not surprising that, after decades of SALs, there is deeper debt for developing countries. The required policies did not produce the returns – otherwise known as sustained economic growth – necessary to repay. This occurred uniformly across almost all borrowing countries and not in just a few. The repayment of SALs has funneled scarce resources from developing country governments to their creditors, including the IMF and World Bank. As is well documented, soaring levels of interest payments have crowded out public investment in basic services and infrastructure, among other things.

One of the reasons why the SALs may have been ineffective is that, over the years, structural adjustment programs have been invitations to corruption. Some leaders of developing countries have enriched themselves and left their citizens to pay the bills. In 1992 the President of Brazil was impeached for massive corruption and the thirty-eighth President, Cardoso, narrowly avoided a broad Congressional probe into central bank insider trading. The primary defense against corruption is openness in the borrowing and the repayment process. Any loan operation should provide factual, quantitative, and qualitative information to the public throughout the loan cycle. How much is to be borrowed? What does it pay for? What is the interest rate? From whom is it borrowed? How much is owed? To whom is it owed? The answers to these questions allow the representatives of the public to determine whether it is reasonable to conclude that borrowed funds will be effectively used and that investments using borrowed funds can produce the returns necessary for a sound repayment program. Structural adjustment (or "policy-based lending") evades these basic considerations (Alexander 2006c).

Structural adjustment lending breaks the link between the loan and its repayment. It makes the most relevant question about any loan – What does it pay for? – a moot point. Through structural adjustment lending, the banks simply require that certain policies be implemented as a condition for budget support in hard currency. No one is responsible for producing any proof that the policies implemented have produced the returns necessary to repay the loan. Nor do adjustment loans need to generate hard currency for debt repayment. For example, the World Bank claims that it is fighting poverty by requiring the protection of certain social programs as a condition of a structural adjustment loan (SAL), but the social programs are financed with local currency. In addition, the funds lent as structural adjustment programs become "pork barrel" spending because they are not tied to concrete objectives. Funds can disappear in bogus contracts and consultancies, or corrupt privatization schemes. To reduce corruption and politically motivated legal spending on activities that do nothing to stimulate development, the banks should eliminate the grace period attached to borrowing. With a grace period on repayment of three to five years, the administration that negotiates the loan is almost never responsible for repaying it. In the terminology of the Bank, this is a "perverse incentive" (Alexander 2006c).

Many groups argue that SAPs impose harsh economic measures that deepen poverty, undermine food security and self-reliance, and lead to unsustainable resource exploitation, environmental destruction, and population dislocation and displacement. These groups, which include nongovernmental organizations (NGOs), grassroots organizations, economists, social scientists and United Nations agencies, have rejected the narrow conception of economic growth as the means to achieve social and environmental objectives. They believe SAP policies have increased the gap between rich and poor in both local and global terms.

Structural adjustment policies generally have a negative impact on poor and marginalized people as, among other things, 1) Variants of privatization of public services – health care, education, and water – raise the fees that people must pay for them (sometimes to unaffordable levels) while at the same time resulting in significant layoffs; 2) Subsidies for farming, education, health care, and water are often cut or eliminated; 3) Trade liberalization subjects domestic businesses, industries, and agricultural production to stiff international competition. If liberalization opens markets too rapidly, domestic enterprises wither, particularly if international competitors are subsidized. For instance, West African cotton farmers cannot successfully compete against subsidized US cotton farmers; 4) With trade liberalization, trade taxes (which constituted a third to a half of national revenue in many countries) are cut; 5) "Flexible" labor policies cause deterioration of worker rights and working conditions; 6) Programs that subsidize credit and direct credit to particular groups (often needy groups) are ended; 7) Under some circumstances, liberalization of financial and capital accounts can lead to capital flight, as occurred in the Asian crisis of 1996–1997; and 8) Macroeconomic policies have often led to high interest rates and low inflation rates that stifle domestic enterprises and lead to unemployment.

Despite claims to the contrary, World Bank-imposed SAPs have paid little or no attention to their environmental impact. SAPs call for increased exports to generate foreign exchange to service debt. The most important exports of developing countries include timber, oil and natural gas, minerals, cash crops, and fisheries products. The acceleration of resource extraction and commodity production that results as countries increase exports is not ecologically sustainable. Deforestation, land degradation, desertification, soil erosion and salinization, biodiversity loss, increased production of greenhouse gases, and air and water pollution are but among the long-term environmental impacts that can be traced to the imposition of SAPs.

Finally, some argue that women are bearing a disproportionate share of the burdens imposed by SAPs. The macroeconomic thinking on which SAPs are based, takes little account of the gender-based division of labor (Sadasivam 1997). For example, SAPs promote export-oriented crops, which tend to be grown by men. This leaves women with little support, marginal land, and fewer resources to grow food crops to feed their families. In addition, cutbacks to public services result in a greater workload for women as they struggle to pay extra fees to secure health care and education for the family. Often, these cutbacks simply place such services out of reach.

Policy implications: towards a human rights-based strategy of development

Many alternatives to structural adjustment have been suggested that address both the economic model upon which SAPs are based, and the nondemocratic and excessively harsh method by which SAPs are imposed. For example, the UN Economic Commission for Africa (1989) proposed the African Alternative Framework. It called for "adjustment with transformation" which entailed a reduction in the continent's reliance on external trade and financing, the promotion of food self-sufficiency, and greater popular participation in economic planning and decision-making.

Many international NGOs including the SAPRIN, Third World Network, and Freedom from Debt Coalition have proposed their own alternative policies in the areas of international trade and sustainable development. National nongovernmental organizations (NGOs), grassroots organizations, economists, political scientists, other social scientists, and other UN agencies have also offered suggestions for alternative approaches to development. Specific alternatives for economic reform include promoting diversification in the products that Southern countries export, providing some protection to infant industries, and promoting more regional trade. Most alternatives to structural adjustment recognize the need for governments to play a strong role in facilitating the diversification away from traditional commodities, in determining and promoting investment priorities, and in making general economic policies including long-term economic planning. A few strongly recommend gendered analyses of the various economic policy options (Sadasivam 1997). Others advocate policies that take into account environmental impacts and promote sustainable natural resource use that benefits local communities. Finally, some reform proposals emphasize non-price structural reforms such as land reform, and institutional reforms to increase democratic practice and accountability. Many critics of the current system of international finance note the need to take further measures to reduce the debt problems of poorer countries (Pettifor 2001), regulate capital markets, and address unfair trading practices.

The results of our work, when combined with the ideas of Sen (1999) noted above, suggest that equitable economic development efforts would be more efficient and many of the negative impacts of World Bank and IMF loans and grants would be mitigated or eliminated if the IFIs pursued a human rights-based strategy of development assistance. A human rights-based strategy of development assistance by the IFIs would also be morally preferable, since the IMF and World Bank are agents of the United Nations. As agents of the UN, the IFIs are bound by the UN Charter to uphold human rights (Clapham 2006; Darrow 2003; Skogly 1993; 2001). In practice, implementation of a human rights-based strategy would consist of four elements (expanded in Chapter 11).

1) Equitable economic development, defined as the simultaneous achievement of economic growth and advancement in protections of economic and social rights of citizens, should be the goal of the IMF and the World Bank.
2) Some minimal level of respect for human rights should be a necessary condition before the World Bank and IMF even enter into negotiations that might result in provision of financial assistance.
3) The Bank and Fund should develop and issue regular human rights impact assessments of their activities.

4) The government of every developing country should be expected to make progress (or at least not to regress) in the protection of all human rights and especially those that have been shown to facilitate equitable economic development.

Theoretical implications

The main theoretical implication of this work is that if one seeks to build theory explaining why some governments respect the human rights of their citizens while others do not, one must examine the effects of transnational forces. Most previous theory building has focused on country characteristics such as the level of economic development, democracy, or internal conflict. Several scholars have carefully examined the effects of the human rights regime including the activities of both intergovernmental and nongovernmental international organizations. However, this study and others suggest that other regimes – including the international financial, world trade, labor, and property rights regimes – may also be having important human rights consequences around the world (Aaronson and Zimmerman forthcoming; Monshipouri and Welch 2001). All of the international regimes likely to affect the human rights practices of governments except for the labor regime and the human rights regime, itself, have substantial ability to enforce their rules. All but the international labor and human rights regimes promulgate neoliberal economic policies throughout the developing world. We develop these ideas further in Chapter 3.

Background: World Bank and International Monetary Fund

The World Bank and International Monetary Fund, created as agencies of the United Nations in 1948, now work closely together to assist the process of economic development in low- and middle-income countries (Leite 2001). Judging by the reports they issue and the public statements they make, the leaders of the Bank, and to a lesser extent the IMF, recognize that they should encourage recipient governments to give equal weight to the pursuit of economic growth and greater respect for internationally recognized economic and social human rights. Unfortunately, despite rhetoric to the contrary, the Bank and Fund do not do much to remedy the negative impacts of structural adjustment programs on human rights (Bradlow 1996; Clapham 2006; Tomasevski 1993).

In 1981, the Reagan administration in the US, the Thatcher administration in the UK, and their allies used the World Bank and International Monetary Fund to launch "structural adjustment" programs ostensibly to promote economic growth in developing countries, while ensuring that countries serviced their debts. The Bank and Fund require that recipient governments implement policy conditions attached to their financing (loan or grant) agreements.[9] These conditions, requiring rapid economic liberalization by developing country governments, were imposed after many developing countries reached the point where mismanagement of the economy had generated shortages in foreign currency reserves (Vreeland 2003). In about one-third of cases examined by Vreeland (2003), governments sought assistance when their economies were not in crisis but when political cover was needed to make economic reforms. The strings attached to the loans commonly include such measures as cuts in public expenditures, privatization of state-owned enterprises, maintaining a low rate of inflation and price stability, shrinking the size of the public bureaucracy, maintaining as close to a balanced budget as possible, increasing exports, and deregulating international trade and financial markets (Boyce 2004). Deregulation of international trade and finance entails such measures as lowering or eliminating tariffs on imported goods, dismantling quotas and domestic monopolies, deregulating capital markets, introducing currency convertibility, and opening industries and stock and bond markets to direct foreign ownership and investment (Meyer 1998).

Implementation of SAPs has led to many more failures than successes as measured by economic growth performance and adherence to human rights. Among the successful candidates, many would propose: Costa Rica, Ghana, India, Jordan, Morocco, Peru, Tunisia, Turkey, Uganda, and Vietnam. However, each case is contested. There may be some examples of equitable economic development in Central Europe such as Poland, but those cases are different. Central European countries, in general, have higher stocks of human capital because of their excellent and inclusive systems of education. Moreover, most had a history of experience with democratic institutions and civil liberties before the occupation by the Soviet Union. They offer clues about the conditions under which neoliberal economic reforms work, and we will examine those clues later, but, for now, we focus on the large group of countries

---

[9] The IMF has had conditionality associated with its loans as far back as 1952 (Sidell 1988).

commonly thought of as part of the "third world," where about three-fourths of the world's people live.

According to some observers, Ghana is a good example of a structural adjustment success story from this group. However, while Ghana may have experienced more economic growth than other poor, sub-Saharan African countries, it is not a good example of a country that has experienced equitable economic development as we have defined it. China is a good example of a country that has achieved equitable economic development without sweeping economic structural reforms mandated by the World Bank and the Fund. Bolivia is a good example of failure to achieve equitable economic development despite implementation of structural adjustment conditions over many years. Let us briefly consider the development policies and outcomes of each of these countries.

Ghana: economic growth without equity

Like many other countries in sub-Saharan Africa, Ghana suffered from serious post-colonial political instability, experiencing nine changes of government and four military coups in the twenty-six years between 1957 and 1983. In 1984, Ghana suffered a severe drought, which coincided with the expulsion of about a million Ghanaians from Nigeria. The drought and the refugees, together with a general feeling that the economy needed an extensive overhaul, forced the regime to negotiate its first structural adjustment agreement. Jerry Rawlings, who led the coup in 1981, participated in the negotiation of the first of many structural adjustment agreements with the IMF and World Bank in 1983. Rawlings held the Presidency until 2001, when there was a peaceful electoral transition of power (US Central Intelligence Agency 2005).

Structural adjustments of the economy did stimulate economic growth in Ghana. In 1990, the World Bank issued a comprehensive report on African development entitled *Sub-Saharan Africa: From Crisis to Sustainable Growth*. The Bank's report cited Ghana, then growing at a rate of 5 to 6 percent per year, as an important example of the benefits of structural adjustment policies. In part, the World Bank was responding to a report issued by the United Nations Economic Commission for Africa (1989), which was critical of structural adjustment programs. The UN report revealed that countries pursuing strong structural adjustment programs had significantly lower rates of economic growth in the 1980s than ones that did not.

During the mid-1980s, significant agricultural reform took place, and by 1988, cocoa production had increased by 20 percent. The rate of economic growth in Ghana declined somewhat, but was still good compared with most other sub-Saharan African countries (Muuka 1998; Parfitt 1995). Ghana opted for debt relief under the Heavily Indebted Poor Country (HIPC) program in 2002. Priorities now include tighter monetary and fiscal policies, accelerated privatization, and improvement of social services (US Central Intelligence Agency 2005). The economy grew at a rate of 5.2 percent during 2003. Inflation decreased from a high of 30 percent in April 2003 to 12.9 percent by August, and wages kept pace with inflation (US Department of State 2005).

Some argue that the adjustment program in Ghana has been more successful than elsewhere in sub-Saharan Africa, because Rawlings, throughout his tenure, first as military dictator and then as the demo-cratically elected Chief Executive, always behaved more like a dictator than a democrat (Kwame 1999). Critics also argue that economic growth has benefited the elite, but has not led to real improvements in the ability of the average Ghanaian citizen to enjoy their human rights to education or health care (Kwame 1999). Public Citizen, an interna-tional NGO, reported that, in 2002, about 35 percent of the Ghanaian population lacked access to safe water and 68 percent lacked sanitation services (Raja 2002).

Still, in addition to the economic growth, there were some undeniable human rights improvements. While the country was implementing structural adjustment, there was progress in government respect for the right of citizens to participate in the selection of their leaders. There was also advancement in government respect for the rights of citizens not to be tortured, disappeared, politically imprisoned, or murdered by police or soldiers. What's more, structural adjustment policies did not cause serious civil conflict.[10]

China: success without structural adjustment

China is the most successful development story over the past few decades if one uses the criteria of equitable economic development, or economic growth that benefits a broad swath of society (Stiglitz 2002). Its rate of annual economic growth over the past two decades has been in excess of 9 percent and the growth continues. Relative to other states

---

[10] Through most of the decade of the 1990s, there was sporadic violent ethnic conflict in northern Ghana. The conflicts were rooted, in part, over the inequitable distribution of landownership. There is little evidence that these conflicts were caused by structural adjustment policies. The government acted as mediator among warring ethnic groups, and the conflicts have subsided (European Centre for Conflict Prevention 2006).

having a similar level of GDP per capita, the Chinese government also provides a relatively high level of respect for the social and economic rights of its citizens. Some research has investigated how well governments, given their ability to do so, provide for the economic rights of their citizens. China ranked first among all nations of the world in 1980 and 1990, falling in 2000 to a still respectable sixteenth (Cingranelli and Richards forthcoming).[11]

According to *China Daily* (March 21, 2005), economic experts predict that the Chinese economy most likely will grow at an annual rate of 8 percent during the period of the eleventh Five-Year Plan (2006–2010). If it does, China will achieve its goal of quadrupling its GDP from 2000 to 2020. According to estimates released by the Chinese government, by the end of 2010, the country's GDP per capita will reach US\$1,700, and by the end of 2020 it will reach US\$3,200 per capita (*China Daily* 2005). The *China Daily* quotes a government spokesperson who noted that economic growth had enabled substantially increased spending for such things as health care, education, and housing, thus reiterating the close connection between growth and poverty reduction.

China has achieved this success without adhering to much of the policy advice of the World Bank and IMF, and, according to some observers, precisely *because* it has not engaged in the kind of structural adjustment programs advocated by the Bank and Fund (Stiglitz 2002). The usual structural adjustment formula is to shift power from the state to the market. The formula in China has been to introduce more private property rights and more freedom of transaction, but with substantial government involvement and regulation. Countries that have done well in the recent past have done so through their own efforts. Structural adjustment agreements have rarely played a critical role. The other clear success stories in terms of economic growth (not equitable economic growth) are Botswana, India, Mauritius, Taiwan, and Vietnam (Rodrik 2005). Aid, trade, and structural adjustment did not play a major role in any of these cases (Rodrik 2005).

Bolivia: failure of structural adjustment

Just as the World Bank claims success in Ghana, it acknowledges failure in Bolivia, another faithful implementer of structural adjustment reforms (Kaufmann 2005). Bolivia has been an independent republic since 1825, but it had been under virtually constant military rule until

---

[11] China's average rank over these three periods was highest among all nations of the world.

1982. Though technically a democracy since 1982, the country did not have its first peaceful transfer of power during the "democratic" period until 1985 (Banks, Muller, and Overstreet 2003). The fledgling democratic government agreed to a radical structural adjustment of its economy beginning in 1986 after the country had endured over half a century of political instability, autocratic rule, and poor economic performance including the worst hyperinflation episode for any country not at war (Kaufmann 2005).

Democracy is still in place, and, arguably, is getting stronger. Bolivia continues to implement the conditions of its structural adjustment agreements. Yet, according to the World Bank's own assessment, "economic growth has been disappointing, poverty alleviation has been scant, and social indicators have not improved significantly. Consequently, Bolivia, at an estimated per capita income of about US\$ 1,000, continues to be one of the poorest countries in the hemisphere" (Kaufmann 2005: 11; also see Kaufmann, Mastruzzi, and Zavaleta 2003). Others are even more explicit in their criticisms. They note that, in Bolivia, as in most of the less developed countries implementing structural adjustment, unemployment increased, real wages fell, income and land distribution became more unequal, poverty rose, food production per capita declined, external debt grew, and social expenditures were cut (Van Dijck 1998). In Bolivia, the hardships on those most adversely affected were great enough that the citizenry engaged in mass demonstrations against government economic policies. "Patience Runs out in Bolivia" was the heading of an article in *The Economist* (April 21, 2001) describing a recent spate of anti-government protests against the kinds of reforms stimulated by the IMF and World Bank. These protests, the article said, stemmed from "deep-seated discontent with reform." The protesters were farmers, coca-growers, public sector workers, and the unemployed. They demanded more public investment in depressed rural areas and an end to the United States-backed program of coca eradication. However, according to *The Economist*, the underlying message was more serious. It was "an expression of fatigue with 15 years of structural adjustment, privatisation and free-marketry." Continuous and militant demonstrations rocked the country and left over twenty-five people dead in the course of fifteen months in 2000–2001. The domestic unrest escalated.

There was a much-publicized struggle against privatization of water as part of a structural adjustment agreement and a 35 percent increase in water prices in the city of Cochabamba. The resulting protests in 2002 resulted in six deaths and the declaration of a state of emergency (Bendat 2006). At least fifty-nine people died in September and

October 2003 during anti-government protests sparked by plans to export Bolivian natural gas. The single bloodiest day was October 12, 2003, when twenty-six civilians were killed in El Alto, a poor industrial city overlooking the capital, La Paz. Many were shot when the army, using combat rifles, broke up crowds that were preventing fuel tankers from reaching the capital. At least fourteen civilians were shot and killed in La Paz on the following day, as the protests continued (Human Rights Watch 2003).

Some even thought that the increasingly violent protests over the government's economic policies would escalate to civil war (Tockman 2005). For four weeks in May and June 2005, indigenous activists, miners, laborers, students, and farmers staged almost daily demonstrations, shutting down much of the country, and cutting off all routes into La Paz. Miners set off dynamite blasts in the city's center, as the armed forces used tear gas to keep protesters away from the Government Palace. "'We want our oil and gas nationalized, so that our children can have them one day,' demanded Japth Mamani Yanolico, a young indigenous leader from the Omasuyos Province" (Tockman 2005).

Many protesters blamed the International Monetary Fund, which has pressured Bolivia since 1985 to adopt economic reforms that have disadvantaged the nation's poor. "This is a political crisis, because right now the government doesn't represent the interests of the citizens," said Sacha Llorenti, President of the leading Bolivian human rights organization. He went on to say that it was also "an economic crisis because the policies of structural adjustment and the processes of privatization have not resolved the situation of poverty, discrimination and social exclusion for Bolivians, and [there is] a social crisis because Bolivians now are in a much more vulnerable state in social terms than they were ten years ago" (Tockman 2005).

Lessons?

The pattern of events in Bolivia illustrates the basic argument of the book. Economic decisions pursuant to structural adjustment agreements led to greater hardships for the poorest people in Bolivian society. Those most adversely affected responded with demonstrations and protests. The government responded to these challenges to its authority by increasing its use of force against the protesters.[12] It is unwise to develop

---

[12] Structural adjustment may even be partly responsible for the low-intensity guerrilla warfare in the country since the mid-eighties. See Banks, Muller, and Overstreet (2003: 124) for a description of the guerrilla groups over this period.

generalizations from one case study, but the research findings we will present, based on a global, comparative systematic analysis, show that this pattern is common in other developing countries undergoing structural adjustment. The main purpose of this book is to demonstrate that this pattern of "increased hardship for the poor, leading to increased civil conflict, and more repression of human rights" exists, to some extent, in most developing countries that have been implementing structural adjustment conditions for a relatively long period.

China's economic success demonstrates that economic development can occur in developing countries without following the one-size-fits-all neoliberal structural adjustment formula. The case of China also shows how economic growth required increased respect for some human rights such as respect for private property and freedom of transaction. Finally, it illustrates that increased respect for at least some human rights such as economic and social rights depended upon economic growth. Some may feel that China's government policies do not provide a good example of the importance of respect for human rights as a facilitator of development. Without doubt, the Chinese government's record of respect for most human rights is well below the world average. That below average *level* of respect for human rights may well explain why China's *level* of economic development is worse than it could have been had its government pursued less repressive policies. On the other hand, China's *improvements* in respect for many human rights in recent decades may also explain why its rate of economic *growth* is so impressive today. Major improvements have been made in many areas if one thinks back to the horrific government human rights practices during the Cultural Revolution. Substantial improvements in respect for some human rights also have occurred since the transition from a pure communist to a socialist market economy.

There is probably not a single application of structural adjustment policies in the world that has not been criticized by at least one international or national nongovernmental organization. Libraries are full of case studies showing the negative effects of structural adjustment. NGO-sponsored web pages abound highlighting the horror stories. The examples of Ghana and Bolivia above illustrate that point pretty well. Was the rate of economic growth in Ghana better because its government was able to be more coercive? Alternatively, was it because Ghana has been able to avoid the kinds of violent domestic protests that have racked Bolivia? Whether Ghana's economy has even been a success may depend upon the particular definition of economic development one chooses.

A sharper definition of development success

The defenders and critics of structural adjustment use different standards of evaluation concerning the consequences of structural adjustment programs. The use of different standards of evaluation leads to different conclusions about which cases have been successes or failures. Defenders, for example, generally talk about economic development and the rate of economic growth. More recently, they have discussed equitable economic development, governance, property rights, and human rights. Critics focus more on poverty, inequality, sustainable economic development, human rights generally, and economic and social human rights in particular.

The language is so different that, at times, the participants in the debate appear to be using completely different standards of evaluation. Sometimes critics of structural adjustment use the terms poverty, inequality, and respect for social and economic human rights interchangeably. There are even differences of opinion about what rights are human rights. For example, the leadership of the Bank and IMF believe that the right to private property is a human right necessary for economic development. Critics rarely acknowledge the right to private property as a fundamental human right, yet they discuss the need to satisfy internationally recognized economic and social human rights. The Bank and Fund rarely use such language, preferring instead to focus on the goal of eliminating poverty.

"Equitable economic development," defined as the simultaneous achievement of economic growth and advancement in protections of economic and social rights of citizens, should be the goal of the IMF and the World Bank. Achieving one element without the other should be considered "development failure." If a poor country is able to achieve high rates of economic growth, while delivering substantial benefits to average citizens, it may begin a period of rapid, prolonged, self-sustained growth and development. Like others (Sen 1999; Kaufmann 2005), we argue that respect for some human rights will promote development. More precisely, *respect for some physical integrity and civil rights and liberties will lead to faster rates of economic growth and progress in achieving respect for economic and social rights to such things as health care, education, and housing.*

Citizens who benefit from their government's efforts to attain equitable economic development will tend to work harder and be more productive, since more growth is likely to produce greater benefits for them, such as increased access to education, housing, jobs, and health care. In this "virtuous circle," as citizens receive rewards for their efforts, they become healthier and more educated. With more education, their job-related skills advance. The benefits of an increasingly educated and productive workforce when coupled with wages that remain relatively low on a global standard make the country an increasingly attractive place for foreign investment. Rapid development may continue in this way until average wages in the previously poor country approach the global average.

In many ways, this story, though oversimplified, explains in broad detail the kind of equitable economic development that has occurred in China since about 1990. It describes the process that has occurred in some of the other East Asian economies, the so-called Asian Tigers: Singapore, South Korea, and Taiwan. Unfortunately, this story does not apply to most of the developing world, where very little actual economic development has occurred. It does not apply to most other places for many reasons including too much government corruption, civil war, and international war. It also does not apply because of the negative consequences of the structural adjustment policies pursued by the World Bank and International Monetary Fund.

Research methods

When we began this research project, we read many case studies describing the economic policies that had been conducted in various countries around the world. We were interested in what the authors had to say about the correlates and possible positive or negative consequences of structural adjustment, how, in particular, the implementation of structural adjustment conditions had coexisted or affected government human rights practices, and what role, in general, the World Bank and IMF had played in each country's economic development. In later chapters, we will refer to that literature in detail. For now, it is important to note that it is mostly critical of the effects of structural adjustment policies. After reading much of the literature describing structural adjustment and its consequences in particular countries, one comes to two conclusions. First, it is very difficult, if not impossible, to draw general conclusions from information about one or a few cases. Second, the defenders and critics of structural adjustment use different standards of evaluation concerning these processes and often talk past one another making appraisal of their consequences difficult.

The case studies we have read have been invaluable for developing hypotheses and illustrating them. Global, comparative research is best for testing those arguments. Those who are mainly concerned about the increased human rights violations as a matter of principle are outraged (Donnelly 2003). For them, any policy that leads, directly or indirectly, to more frequent and severe violations of human rights, should be stopped or substantially modified. They believe that the violation of any human rights for any reason is morally wrong. It never can be justified, even as a means to a higher goal. But, there is another, more practical reason to be concerned about what is happening. The pattern of hardship-conflict-repression is undermining prospects for economic development all over the developing world.

The findings we present were generated using an improved research design, a new data set describing the human rights practices of governments around the world, and state-of-the-art statistical techniques. There have been only two previous global, comparative studies of the human rights consequences of structural adjustment (Abouharb and Cingranelli 2006; Keith and Poe 2000). One way this study improves upon earlier research is that the time period examined in this work (1981–2003) is longer than the time period examined in any other study of the effects of structural adjustment on human rights. This is also the only study that examines the effects of structural adjustment policies on several types of internationally recognized human rights. Both previous studies noted above examined the effects of structural adjustment programs on government respect for "physical integrity" rights. We are able to examine a larger range of human rights practices in this work because of the availability of a recently assembled data set about the human rights practices of governments around the world (Cingranelli and Richards 2006).

We believe that our results are comprehensive. They examine the joint effects of structural adjustment, critical we believe to understanding the impact of these programs on loan-recipient states. Our results are robust to the arguments that countries entering into these programs are often facing economic difficulties, and that the Bank and Fund dealing with hard cases actually improved the situation in comparison to if they had never become involved. We explicitly examine and control for this possibility by correcting for issues of selection, a point we also explore in more detail below. All of our findings are robust to this critique. At every turn we give structural adjustment agreements the benefit of the doubt and in our examination of structural adjustment on democratic rights we find positive evidence. Still, by and large, we get negative results. Ours is not a polemic but a cold look at the best data available using the most sophisticated methods. Finally, we believe that the measures of human rights we use in this work are valid and accurate.

Examining both the World Bank and IMF

Most of the previous research by economists and political scientists on the effects of structural adjustment has focused on the IMF and its impacts, neglecting the role of the World Bank in promoting structural adjustment.[13] Yet, both are important actors. Over the period examined in this study, 1981–2003, the World Bank entered into 442 structural adjustment agreements, while the IMF made 431.[14] It is easy to underestimate the effects of structural adjustment if one only examines the human rights impacts of IMF agreements without including the impacts of World Bank agreements with the same countries.

For example, the Turkish government has been under twelve years of IMF structural adjustment conditions in the 1981–2003 period, but the period increases to sixteen years when structural adjustment agreements with the World Bank are included, originally underestimating the period the country has been under structural adjustment by 25 percent. If one just examined the number of years the Indonesian government has been under IMF conditionality we would also underestimate the number of years conditions had been in effect by about a third. The results change from seven years under IMF structural adjustment to eleven years when the impact of the World Bank is included. The book answers the question about the relationship between structural adjustment agreements and government respect for human rights. The empirical analyses and results presented emphasize the joint impact of World Bank and IMF structural adjustment programs on government respect for a variety of human rights.

Plan of the book

In Chapter 2, we more carefully define "equitable economic development" and extend the argument that respect for human rights promotes this type of development. The chapter concludes with a discussion about what human rights matter most for equitable economic development and why. Research by other scholars, including a World Bank economist, Daniel Kaufmann (2005), suggests that respect for some human rights may be necessary or crucial for development, while respect for others may facilitate or assist development. It is likely that future research will identify some set of human rights that, if respected, establish the ideal preconditions for equitable economic development.

---

[13] With the exception of Abouharb and Cingranelli (2006).
[14] The IMF data come from Vreeland (2003).

In Chapter 3, we provide more background on the histories, charters, and missions of the World Bank and International Monetary Fund. We then review different theoretical approaches concerning why governments repress the human rights of their citizens. These discussions frame our understanding of the link between structural adjustment and repression. Three main views have been put forward as explanations of the variations in government protections of their citizens' human rights. One approach emphasizes the role of threats to the regime as stimuli of repression. Another perspective explains repression as the result of state characteristics – mainly the level of democracy in a society or its degree of economic development or both. Yet another viewpoint stresses the growing importance of transnational noneconomic and economic forces. The first two causal forces have received considerable attention in previous research. The last has been the subject of many case studies, but little global, comparative research. We argue that structural adjustment, an important transnational economic force, has both direct and indirect effects on repression.

Then we explain why some neoliberal economic theorists believe that reducing the role of the state in the economy will stimulate economic growth. The neoliberal perspective links economic growth and development to improved human rights practices. Critics, on the other hand, argue that less state and more market usually only benefits the elite in society. It exploits the poor, women, and those in need. Chapter 3 reviews the large body of research showing that implementation of structural adjustment agreements has negative effects on economic growth and government respect for human rights.

In Chapter 4 we describe and explain other elements of the research design employed including how we chose the countries selected for the analysis, where we got information about the human rights practices and other characteristics of those countries, how we measured key concepts, and why we selected particular statistical techniques for the analyses. Also included is a detailed discussion about the empirical reasoning for the use of a two-stage approach that controls for issues of selection. Descriptions of the control variables used in the study are included in this chapter as well.

As noted above, this study also advances our understanding of the human rights consequences of structural adjustment by correcting for the effects of selection. It is possible that the worsened human rights practices observed and reported in previous studies resulted from the poor economic conditions that led to the imposition of the structural adjustment conditions rather than the implementation of structural adjustment conditions themselves. In other words, the human rights practices of loan-recipient governments might have gotten worse whether or not a structural adjustment agreement (SAA) had been implemented. In addition, as our results will show, some of the factors that increase the probability of entering into an SAA, such as having a large population and being relatively poor, are also associated with an increased probability of human rights violations. For these reasons, one must disentangle the effects of selection before estimating the human rights impacts of structural adjustment agreements. In order to control for the effects of selection, a two-stage analysis was undertaken. In the first stage of the analysis, the factors affecting World Bank and IMF decisions concerning which governments receive SAAs were identified. In the second stage, the impacts of implementing SAAs on governmental respect for human rights were examined, while controlling for the indirect effects of World Bank and IMF selection criteria concerning which types of countries were more likely to receive such loans.

In Chapter 5 we review the previous research on IMF and World Bank selection and present the selection model used in this analysis. We also present the results of an analysis of the characteristics that make it more or less likely that the government of a developing country will enter into a structural adjustment agreement with the World Bank or the International Monetary Fund. There are some interesting differences, but there is a lot of overlap in the factors considered by both institutions. We conclude, therefore, by estimating a model identifying the factors that make it likely that a government will enter into a structural adjustment agreement with one institution *or* the other. The results presented in this chapter are used later in controlling for the effects of selection in the findings chapters of our study, presented in Chapters 5 through 10. They also refine and update our earlier work on the subject of IMF and World Bank selection (Abouharb and Cingranelli 2004a; 2005).

Chapters 6 through 10 present the main findings of our study. Chapter 6 demonstrates the deleterious effects of structural adjustment on government respect for economic and social human rights. Chapter 7 shows that countries which enter into structural adjustment agreements are more likely to experience a rebellion while longer periods of structural adjustment conditionality increase the frequency governments have to endure anti-government demonstrations, riots, and rebellion. Chapter 8 extends our previous work showing that the implementation of structural adjustment conditions leads to worsened respect for physical integrity rights (Abouharb and Cingranelli 2006). Chapter 9 shows the negative effects of structural adjustment on government respect for worker rights. In contrast, Chapter 10 shows the generally positive effects of structural adjustment on procedural democracy.

The final chapter of the book summarizes the main findings and discusses their theoretical and policy implications. We argue that, theoretically, this work points to the importance of transnational forces in explaining the human rights practices of governments around the world. Our findings also suggest that the structural adjustment policies should be modified to recognize that respect for some human rights promotes equitable economic development. The revisions proposed would bring the World Bank and IMF closer to a human rights-based development strategy.

2 Respect for human rights promotes economic development

Introduction

There is a growing consensus that greater respect for certain human rights leads to economic development that benefits a broader section of society. In this chapter, we explore the logic behind this argument and discuss the relevant findings from previous research. Based on this logic and empirical findings, we conclude that the Bank and the Fund ought to be pursuing a human rights-based approach to economic development in less developed countries. In Chapter 11, we explicitly define what such an approach would look like. For now, let us simply define a human rights-based approach to economic development as one that explicitly seeks to improve the human rights practices of the governments of developing countries as a method to improve levels of economic development.

We begin by defining economic development. Economic development that includes economic growth accompanied by a relatively high level of respect for economic and social rights has been described as "equitable economic development" (Sen 1999). It is also sometimes called "high-quality economic growth," "pro-poor economic growth," or "equitable economic growth," the term we will use. This type of growth we believe is the appropriate measure to decide whether economic development is taking place within a society. This is also the standard that we believe should be used to evaluate the economic outcomes of structural adjustment programs. Since research shows that government respect for human rights makes it more likely that equitable economic growth will be achieved, then institutions charged with the responsibility of assisting economic development are also charged, by implication, with the responsibility of promoting better human rights practices.

Briefly, we review the evolution of international human rights law and the positions of the leaders of the IMF and the World Bank regarding the responsibilities of their institutions for improving human rights practices. The World Bank takes a stronger rhetorical position, but neither institution does much to ensure human rights advancement. In fact, as noted in Chapter 1 and elsewhere in this book, except for the promotion of procedural democracy, there is plenty of evidence that the main tool of economic development used by the international financial institutions – structural adjustment – has actually undermined respect for many human rights in developing countries. The rights that have been undermined include, among others, physical integrity rights – the rights not to be tortured, imprisoned for political reasons, disappeared, or murdered by one's government. These rights have been shown by other scholars including one of the World Bank's own economists, Daniel Kaufmann (2005), to promote economic growth.

The chapter concludes with some hypotheses about which human rights matter most for economic development and why. Respect for some human rights may be a necessary condition for economic development. Others may be important as facilitators of economic development. Moreover, there may be some set of human rights that, if respected, establishes the ideal conditions for economic development. Some research has been conducted on these points, but more research will be necessary to guide a human rights-based approach to economic development.

Defining economic development

Much of the confusion exists because there are so many definitions and measures of development. The debate centers on the appropriate breadth of the concept. From a policy perspective, the outcome of this debate is important, because what development "is" will help determine what goals agencies such as the World Bank and IMF should pursue. The United Nations Development Programme (UNDP) encourages the pursuit of "sustainable human development." There are five dimensions to this concept, all focusing on improving the lives of the poor: empowerment, cooperation, equity, sustainability, and security. Measuring any single dimension of the concept would be difficult. Attaching a single number to the umbrella concept to indicate the relative level of sustainable human development that has occurred or is occurring in country X versus country Y would be controversial and may not be very useful.

In contrast, the concepts of "level of economic development" and "rate of economic growth" are much too narrow to serve as indicators of economic development success. The value of these concepts is that they have well-understood meanings among economists who use these terms to measure the level or growth of productive national capabilities. The commonly used measures of these concepts are the gross domestic product (GDP) per capita, which measures the level of economic development or, over time, the rate of economic growth (or decline). We sometimes refer to the concepts of "economic development" and "economic growth" without qualifying adjectives, because the objectives of economic development and growth are worthy in the traditional senses of the meaning of these terms. The use of more narrowly defined concepts in some discussions should encourage future research leading to a better understanding of the relationship between the quality of human rights practices, the level of economic development, the rate of economic growth, and the achievement of equitable economic development.

Besides stimulating economic growth, so countries can achieve a higher level of economic development, critics say the World Bank and IMF should be doing more to reduce poverty and inequality, and increase government respect for both economic and social human rights in less developed countries. After all, countries at the same level of economic development, as indicated by their GDP per capita, may use their available wealth in very different ways (Sen 1999). In some cases, a small elite group consumes a large share of the available wealth, while the vast majority of citizens live in poverty. In acknowledgment of this criticism, the Bank and Fund, in recent years, have increasingly referred to their goal of "equitable economic development" or "high-quality economic development." They use these terms to refer to economic growth that benefits the least well off in society.

In most cases, if a society reduces its income inequality, it also reduces the share of its people living in poverty, but this is not true in all cases. Imagine a society at a very low level of economic development such as Haiti, Nepal, or Ethiopia. There is so little wealth to be distributed that, even with much less income inequality, there will still be high levels of poverty. Thus, the World Bank and IMF are justified in their focus on eliminating poverty and increasing rates of economic growth rather than simply reducing income inequality.

Eliminating poverty is an important instrumental objective of economic development. The reason for eliminating poverty is to ensure that everyone can enjoy their human rights to such things as education, health care, housing, and decent work. Producing a higher percentage of people earning more than the equivalent of 1 US dollar per day has a limited value unless there are also more people who benefit from these changes and can exercise their economic and social rights. The World Bank is already moving in the direction of evaluating its efforts in these terms. According to a World Bank publication titled, *Development and Human Rights: The Role of the World Bank*, the World Bank claims that its work contributes directly to many of the rights articulated in the Universal Declaration of Human Rights. Through its efforts, the report says, "the Bank has helped hundreds of millions of people attain crucial economic and social rights" (World Bank 1998: 2). In Chapter 6, we demonstrate that this statement is misleading. Other things being equal, governments of developing countries which implement structural adjustment conditions provide less protection of the economic and social human rights of their citizens.

The evolution of international human rights law

The codification of government responsibilities towards the promotion and protection of their citizens' rights began shortly after the end of World War II. The members of the United Nations approved the Universal Declaration of Human Rights (UDHR), the first major human rights agreement, in 1948 without a dissenting vote. Eighteen years later, the principles contained in the UDHR were codified into international law in the International Covenant on Civil and Political Rights (ICCPR) and the International Covenant on Economic, Social and Cultural Rights (ICESCR). Together, these three human rights documents make up the International Bill of Human Rights (IBHR). The creation and international acceptance of the IBHR began a new era in world history. In this new era, the governments of the world community, with very few exceptions, recognize both the existence of individual equal inalienable rights and the transcendence of these individual rights and freedoms over the laws of sovereign states.

The traditional view of human rights limits them to civil and political rights, the rights included in the International Covenant on Civil and Political Rights. Included among these are the right to life, liberty, and security; the right not to be discriminated against on the basis of race, color, sex, language, religion, social class, or political opinion; the right to vote, freedom of speech, and freedom of press; the right to be free from arbitrary invasion of privacy, family, or home; and legal rights such as the right to due process of law and the presumption of innocence until proven guilty. In the United States, Great Britain, and in most other economically developed countries of the West, most people think of these things when they hear or use the term "human rights."

Increasingly, however, this traditional view is being challenged, because it ignores economic and social rights. The UDHR, for example, recognizes the right to social security (Article 22), to work, to just and favorable conditions of work, to protection against unemployment, to equal pay for equal work, to an existence worthy of human dignity (Article 23), to rest and leisure, to reasonable limitation on working hours, to periodic holidays with pay (Article 24), to a standard of living adequate to maintain health and well-being, to food, clothing, housing and medical care, to necessary social services, to security in the event of unemployment, sickness, disability, widow-hood, old age, or other lack of livelihood in circumstances beyond his control (Article 25), to free elementary education, and to higher edu-cation on the basis of merit (Article 26). The ICESCR recognizes the right to work, to equal remuneration for work of equal value, to a decent standard of living, to reasonable working hours (Article 7), to social security (Article 9), to adequate food, clothing, and housing, to continuous improvement of living conditions (Article 11), to medical care (Article 12), and to education (Articles 13 and 14).

The 1986 UN Declaration on the Right to Development states that development is a human right. Article 1 states that "The right to development is an inalienable human right by virtue of which every human person and all peoples are entitled to participate in, contribute to, and enjoy economic, social, cultural and political development, in which all human rights and fundamental freedoms can be fully realized" (Office of the UN High Commissioner for Human Rights 2002). That proclamation was strengthened by the Declaration of the 1993 UN World Conference on Human Rights, which says "the right to devel-opment is an inalienable human right and an integral part of funda-mental human freedoms" (Office of the UN High Commissioner for Human Rights 2002). This view was confirmed at the UN global con-ferences on population and development (Cairo) and women (Beijing) and at the World Summit on Social Development (Copenhagen).

The meaning of the "right to development" is debatable, because it refers to so many different things, but the emphasis is upon the simul-taneous achievement of economic growth and realization of economic and social rights. According to the United Nations Independent Expert on the Right to Development, the right to development means that every individual has the right to:

improvement of a "vector" of human rights, composed of various elements including the right to food, the right to health, the right to education, the right to housing, and other economic, social and cultural rights, as well as all the civil and political rights together with the rates of growth of GDP and other financial, technical and institutional resources that enable any improvement in the well-being of the entire population and the realization of the rights to be sustained. (quoted in Brodnig 2005)

Presently, the focus of the World Bank and IMF is to promote growth through 1) neoliberal economic reforms that reinforce private property rights and an unregulated free market and 2) promotion of better governance, including the capacity to weed out corruption. Research conducted by the World Bank's Governance Project demonstrates that better governance stimulates economic growth (Kaufmann 2005; Kaufmann, Kraay, and Mastruzzi 2005). Governance refers to the traditions and institutions in a society that determine whether and to what extent government decisions are made to benefit the common good (Kaufmann 2005). Governance, as defined by the World Bank, has six dimensions. One of them is "voice and accountability," which is the Project's term for respect for civil and political human rights. Other dimensions include the extent of control of corruption and rule of law. The interest in voice and accountability as a dimension of governance indicates that the World Bank recognizes the value of improving respect for at least some human rights of citizens in developing countries.

Kaufmann's (2005) work highlighted the role of human rights protection as a precondition for economic development. He found that the rights to be protected from government torture, murder, disappearance, and political imprisonment and government infringement of civil liberties had not advanced significantly in developing countries in recent times. He argued that the lack of progress in first-generation human rights outcomes might have caused lack of progress in the attainment of economic and social rights. He contended that his findings, if corroborated through further research, had important implications for the World Bank, the IMF, and the bilateral donor aid community. In particular, his findings suggest that the promotion of better first-generation human rights practices such as physical integrity and civil and political rights by donors and creditors would enhance the effectiveness of development aid.

The politics of the World Bank and IMF

Whether the Bank and Fund have a responsibility to encourage the governments of developing countries to improve their human rights practices has been, and probably always will be, a matter of debate. Though the World Bank and IMF are United Nations organizations, and the United Nations adopted the Universal Declaration of Human Rights in 1948, the advancement of human rights is not explicitly part of the charter of either international financial institution. Until the 1990s, leaders of the Bank and Fund worried, sometimes publicly, that an emphasis on human rights when negotiating loans would allow politics to enter into decisions that should be purely economic. Indeed, the charters of the IFIs stipulate that they should not impinge on the sovereignty of their members by meddling in domestic political affairs. Neither institution wanted to encroach too much on the sovereignty of the governments they were trying to help. As an illustration of this position, during the 1960s, the United Nations General Assembly passed a series of resolutions urging the Bank not to provide loans to Portugal and South Africa because of their colonial and apartheid policies respectively. The Bank, preferring to maintain its apolitical character, ignored the resolutions and continued lending to both countries (Bleicher 1970).

Nevertheless, the World Bank and IMF have always been political organizations to some degree. One common definition of a political process is a set of activities in which authoritative decisions are made determining the allocation of scarce valued things (Easton 1965). The capital provided by the World Bank and IMF is scarce – especially for the least developed countries – and it is valued. "Politics" also has been defined as a process determining who got what, when, and how (Lasswell 1936). Which governments receive World Bank and IMF loans, when, and why are all decisions made by the Boards of Directors of these institutions.

World Bank and IMF representatives protest against any allegations that their lending policies are motivated by political considerations, but their internal decision-making process privileges the ideological perspectives of some governments over others, allows for logrolling and vote trading, and in all other respects provides fertile ground for what, in any other context, would be called "politics." The Bank and Fund use a weighted voting system for determining which loans or grants to approve and which to deny. The weights assigned are roughly in proportion to the shareholdings of the Bank and Fund's member governments. The World Bank is comprised of two legal entities: the International Bank for Reconstruction and Development (IBRD) which raises resources from the international capital market, and the International Development Association (IDA) which raises resources from donor countries and receives transfers from the IBRD. For the past twenty-five years, the United States, Japan, and Germany have accounted for more than half of all funds contributed (Banks, Muller, and Overstreet 2003), so it is reasonable to assume that the preferences of their country representatives have dominated the preferences of other members of the Bank and Fund's Board of Directors.

In addition, the code of practices governing the Bank and Fund's operations recommends that these institutions give preference to applicants that have a capitalist ideology, have not nationalized private industry without providing fair compensation to the owners, are not able to borrow on the private market, and are creditworthy (Van de Laar 1980). These criteria created an unabashed bias against making loans to communist countries (though some communist countries including Vietnam and the formerly communist Yugoslavia and Romania have received them). Through what can only be called a "political" process, the Boards must decide how to reconcile these criteria.

Recently the World Bank has issued selection criteria that it has generated with its Country Policy and Institutional Assessment (CPIA). Included in these publicly stated loan-allocation criteria are the quality of economic management, structural policies, social inclusion, and equity criteria, as well as public sector management and institutional criteria. However, until the late 1990s, the Bank did not have widely circulated, published criteria about the factors that affected whether countries became loan recipients. Even today, it is not clear that these criteria actually affect the selection process.

The World Bank now acknowledges its responsibilities for advancing human rights. As former World Bank President Wolfensohn said in his statement to the Bank's Development Committee, "There is, moreover, widespread recognition of the strong link between human rights and development ... The Bank is currently reviewing its role with a view to making a more explicit link between human rights and our work, while at the same time remaining fully in compliance with our Articles of Agreement" (World Bank 2005b). The new General Counsel to the Bank has been reviewing the Bank's Articles of Agreement to see how the Bank can intervene to support protections of those human rights that have been shown to produce either positive or negative outcomes in terms of economic and social development. Former World Bank President Wolfowitz expressed his commitment to this endeavor by emphasizing the role of respect for women's rights in development (World Bank 2005b).

Unfortunately, the IMF has been less willing to make similar commitments (Bradlow 1996; Clapham 2006; Tomasevski 1993). As recently as 2001, responding to criticism that the IMF was ignoring the human rights consequences of its activities, an IMF spokesperson declared that it was not obligated to promote human rights around the world. Grant B. Taplin, Assistant Director at the IMF's Geneva office, stated before the United Nations Subcommission for the Promotion and Protection of Human Rights that the Fund, in a strict sense, does not have a mandate to promote human rights. Taplin also stressed that the IMF is not "bound by various human rights declarations and conventions" (Capdevila 2001). Several members of the Subcommission expressed their disappointment. Yozo Yokota, of Japan, noted that human rights are "peremptory norms" that cannot be ignored in agreements between states or in the operations of international financial institutions (Capdevila 2001). Despite this resistance to explicit consideration of human rights when making loan decisions, our findings indicate that these institutions actually tend to enter into agreements with governments that have higher levels of respect for the physical integrity human rights of their citizens.

The "Washington Consensus" of 1990 emphasized institutions and governance as the essential elements of structural adjustment policies (e.g., Stiglitz 2002). Endorsed by the major shareholders of the institutions, this consensus guides the operations of the Bank and Fund. Over time, the interplay between officials of the World Bank and International Monetary Fund and the members of the Boards of Executive Directors from major shareholding countries – especially the United States – has created widespread agreement that the "Washington Consensus-Plus" represents the one and true way for less developed countries to achieve growth and development (Stiglitz 2002: 20).

Negotiating loan agreements with governments that respect human rights is consistent with US policy to deny capital to repressive regimes. Since the passage of the US International Financial Assistance Act in 1977, the representatives of the United States on the decision-making boards of the World Bank and IMF have been mandated to use their voices and votes to advance the cause of human rights in loan-recipient countries (Abouharb and Cingranelli 2004a). The size of US contributions to the Bank and Fund gives it a strong voice in loan negotiations (Banks, Muller, and Overstreet 2003). Thus, it is not surprising that the World Bank and IMF tend to enter into SAAs with countries that have relatively good human rights practices. We also argue that countries under structural adjustment the longest have become more democratic because promoting transparency and procedural democracy has been a long-standing foreign policy priority of the US government.

Are the Bank and Fund responsible for promoting better human rights practices?

In 1991, a new development bank was launched, the European Bank for Reconstruction and Development (EBRD), with a charter that calls upon the institution to promote multi-party democracy and human rights.

The IFIs are relics of the World War II era. At that time, the idea of an international institution interfering in the sovereign political affairs of a nation was unthinkable. Hence, the IMF and World Bank charters ban interference in domestic political affairs. There are many different views on whether international financial institutions should be explicitly concerned about the promotion of human rights (Decker, McInerney-Lankford, and Sage 2006) or whether the institutions should take a "do no harm" position – that is, not promote the abuse of human rights. At one end of the spectrum in the debate is the idea that full enjoyment of all human rights should be the goal of economic development. Economic growth is a necessary instrumental goal of economic development, but the ultimate objective is for societies to advance to the point where every human being reaches their full potential. According to some observers, no matter how wealthy a society is, it is not fully developed unless all members have certain human rights including: freedom of speech, freedom of religion, freedom from the threat of torture, and the ability to have access to education and health care (Alston and Bhuta 2005; Sen 1999). Arguments have been made that economic indicators, such as GDP per capita and the GINI coefficient, which measures income distribution, fail to capture what is really important to people: the freedoms associated with human rights (Sen 1999).

At the other end of the spectrum is the idea that economic growth will be most rapid if some human rights are restricted – especially the rights associated with democracy. This perspective is sometimes referred to as the "Asian Values Argument." While this view is rarely espoused by modern Western economists today, it was part of the conventional wisdom during the Cold War (Donnelly 2003: 196). However, there is no evidence that authoritarian regimes are more able to achieve equitable economic growth or even higher rates of economic growth (Donnelly 2003; Geddes 1999; Sen 1999). To the contrary, there is plenty of evidence that authoritarianism has negative impacts on economic growth and worsened levels of respect for some economic rights (Bueno de Mesquita et al. 2003; Sen 1999; Zweifel and Navia 2000). In fact, research results indicate that the economic performance of democratic countries is superior (see Chapter 6).

While there is little support for the idea that economic growth requires a sacrifice in democratic rights in developing countries, there is widespread tacit acceptance of the idea that rapid economic growth requires toleration of greater poverty, inequality, and violations of economic and social rights (Donnelly 2003: 197). One variation of this view is that savings from lower expenditures on social programs allow for greater investment in the productive capabilities of the state (Enke 1963: 181). Another variation, called "supply side" or "trickle down" economics, suggests that high levels of inequality actually contribute towards economic growth. At the risk of oversimplification, according to this view only the rich can save and invest, and investment is the key to economic growth. Thus, allowing the rich to grow richer, while the poor fall further behind, is the best way to stimulate rapid economic growth. This view implies that a strategy aimed at producing rapid economic growth and a high level of respect for economic and social rights is doomed to fail. Despite recent statements to the contrary by the Bank and the Fund, many believe that this perspective is dominant among the leaders of both institutions. They see this view as implicit in the common provisions of structural adjustment agreements that continue to be negotiated by the World Bank and IMF (Donnelly 2003; SAPRIN 2004).

Other things being equal, proponents of Keynesian or "demand-side" economics take the opposite position, believing that the best way to produce economic growth is to put resources into the hands of the poorest people. These people will not save or invest. Instead, they will spend any new money almost immediately on the things they need such as food, clothing, housing, and health care. These expenditures on goods and services will stimulate the economy, because more goods and services will be needed to meet the new demand. Business will hire new workers. Productive capacities will expand. This process will evolve into a self-sustaining cycle of economic growth. Thus, demand-side economic theorists see no reason why developing countries cannot pursue high rates of economic growth and a high level of respect for economic rights simultaneously. This was the strategy successfully pursued by the United States during the Great Depression of the 1930s. However, there are no structural adjustment agreements today that allow the governments of developing countries to pursue economic policies consistent with demand-side economic theory.

Beginning in the mid-1990s, the leaders of the World Bank issued a series of statements acknowledging that the advancement of at least some human rights was part of its mission. The Bank issued its clearest statement in commemoration of the fiftieth anniversary of the United Nations Universal Declaration of Human Rights (UDHR). The statement was titled *Development and Human Rights: The Role of the World Bank* (World Bank 1998). It describes the current view of the role of the World Bank in promoting respect for human rights around the world. First, it says that the World Bank must be concerned about the advancement of human rights around the world, because, as a creation of the United Nations, the World Bank must further the human rights goals of the parent organization. Second, the Bank acknowledges that it should be measuring its progress, not just by how much economic growth it helps produce, but also by the extent to which growth is accompanied by citizens' increased enjoyment of economic and social human rights. Economic growth, which does increase enjoyment of economic and social rights, should then include significant reductions in poverty and advances in standards of living for the masses. In other words, the growth should be equitable. Yet the implementation of structural adjustment conditions has reduced respect for at least some important economic and social rights around the world (see Chapter 6).

Finally, the Bank acknowledged that respect for some human rights might be the necessary precondition for growth to occur. Subsequent to the issuance of the 1998 report, then-President of the Bank James Wolfensohn started to redefine the operational procedures of the Bank to be consistent with the human rights statement. His new development paradigm was called the Comprehensive Development Framework.[1] In it, the Bank acknowledged that without the protection of human and property rights, and a comprehensive framework of laws, equitable development was not possible (World Bank 1998). The phrase "human and property rights" is intriguing. Besides property rights, what other human rights does the Bank believe are necessary for equitable economic development to occur?

Which human rights matter for economic development?

While the existing research does not actually use the operational definition of "equitable economic development" used in this research, there is work linking respect for human rights to faster economic growth (Kaufmann 2005). There is mounting evidence that national economies grow fastest when citizens can exercise their human rights. Respect for some human rights, such as the right to private property, is probably a necessary condition for equitable economic development. Respect for some other human rights, while not necessary, probably facilitates equitable economic development. While a final category may be unrelated to economic development. More research is required to determine what minimal set of freedoms is necessary before equitable economic development can occur, but it is clear that the freedoms are mutually reinforcing and one or two are not enough. The research program on this question is still at a nascent stage – but Table 2.1 hypothesizes that the human rights recognized in the IBHR are likely to be necessary conditions and facilitators. The list is not meant to be exhaustive, just

---

[1] A number of documents and other resources on the Comprehensive Development Framework are available on the World Bank website at www.worldbank.org.

Table 2.1. *Respect for human rights and equitable economic development*

Necessary or crucial conditions for equitable economic development	Useful facilitators of equitable economic development
	Physical integrity rights:
Right to private property including intellectual property (Sen 1999; World Bank 1998)	*Freedom from extrajudicial killing (Kaufmann 2005)
	*Protection against disappearance (Kaufmann 2005)
	*Protection against political imprisonment (Kaufmann 2005)
	*Protection against torture (Kaufmann 2005)
	Democratic rights:
Rights of women to participate fully in the labor force (Kaufmann 2005; Sen 1999; World Bank 1998)	*Right to participate in the selection of leaders (Sen 1999; World Bank 1998)
	*Freedom of opinion and expression (implies right to free speech and press) (Kaufmann 2005; Isham, Kaufmann, and Pritchett 1997; Sen 1999; World Bank 1998)
	*Freedom of association (Isham, Kaufmann, and Pritchett 1997; Sen 1999; World Bank 1998)
	*Freedom of assembly (Isham, Kaufmann, and Pritchett 1997; Sen 1999; World Bank 1998)
	*Worker rights:
Protection of children from exploitation in the workforce (Sen 1999; World Bank 1998)	Work
	Trade unions (implies freedom of association at the workplace and the right to collective bargaining)
	Other:
	Social security (Sen 1999)
	Legal remedy (World Bank 1998)
	Access to an independent judiciary (World Bank 1998)

Note: * = The effects of structural adjustment on respect for this human right are examined in this study.

illustrative of existing lines of research and promising possibilities for future research. The breakdown of rights into categories in Table 2.1 is based on logic, claims by the World Bank (1998), and previous research (Isham, Kaufmann, and Pritchett 1997; Kaufmann 2005; Sen 1999).

Based on this work, the necessary conditions for equitable economic growth probably consist of respect for private property including intellectual property, the rights of women to participate fully in the labor force, and protection of children from exploitation in the work-force.

Which human rights are necessary conditions for equitable economic development?

Most economists agree that property rights and the basic freedom of transaction are important ingredients in any recipe for promotion of economic growth. Classical models of general equilibrium have been used to demonstrate the merits of the free market in terms of economic efficiency (Sen 1999). Lack of governmental respect for the property rights of the poor in many developing countries may be a barrier to economic growth (DeSoto 2000). Many developing countries do not recognize the legal rights of the poor to the property they or their families have occupied over long periods. Estimates suggest that people who occupy land but do not have legal rights to it comprise more than half of poor people in developing countries (World Bank 1998: 18). Informal owners are unable to use their home as collateral to borrow money, to start a business, or even to pass their only significant asset on to their children. Under such circumstances, the potential for entre-preneurship, an important element in any nation's development strat-egy, is severely limited. Thus, it is not surprising that there are numerous studies at the macro-level (Eiras 2003) and micro-level (Sen 1999) that provide empirical support for the idea that free markets produce economic growth. The main reason for China's remarkable success since about 1990 was its abandonment of a planned economy and adoption of a socialist market model that increased respect for private property and allowed more freedom to participate in a market of goods and services.

There is one important caveat. While substantial respect for property rights and basic freedoms of transaction are necessary conditions for economic growth, they are not sufficient conditions, and they are cer-tainly not sufficient conditions for equitable economic development. A free market produces greater efficiency, but it also produces winners and losers. Without a mechanism to provide a safety net for the losers, reduced respect for economic and social rights is nearly certain.

Another potential precondition for equitable economic development is respect for the economic human rights of women. In many parts of the world, the freedom of women to seek employment outside the family is severely restricted. Where this freedom is restricted, about half of the human capital in a society is untapped for purposes of economic development. We use the term human capital to refer to people's skills and abilities as used in employment and which otherwise contribute to the economy. The destructive impact of limitations on the economic possibilities for women is compounded by the fact that there is a relatively high percentage of female-headed households in developing countries, especially among the lowest-income families (World Bank 1998). Thus, limiting the economic rights of women both lowers the potential for economic growth and increases the gaps in the level of enjoyment of many economic and social rights between men and women.

A third possible precondition for equitable economic development is respect for the rights of children in the workplace. Abuse of child labor refers to work for children that harms them or exploits them in some way (physically, mentally, morally, or by blocking their access to education). All forms of harm are morally shocking, but the last point, blocking access to education, is the most damaging aspect as a hindrance to economic development. If children do not attend school, human capital, which is a necessary ingredient for economic growth, is not developed. In Asia, especially South Asia, and in some other parts of the world, child labor is often combined with what is effectively slavery (Tucker 1997). Thus, allowing the abuse of child labor also lowers the potential for economic growth and increases the likelihood of violation of at least one social right, the right of access to education.

Abuse of child labor, like the lack of respect for property rights and women's economic rights, is a major problem in many developing countries. In 1998, the International Labour Organization (ILO) estimated that 246 million child workers aged five through seventeen were involved in child labor, of which 171 million were involved in work that by its nature was hazardous to their safety, physical or mental health, or moral development. "Of that number, some 8.4 million children were engaged in so-called 'unconditional' worst forms of child labor, which include forced and bonded labor, the use of children in armed conflict, trafficking in children and commercial sexual exploitation" (ILO 1998a: 7). The vast majority of child laborers work in less developed countries – 61% in Asia, 32% in Africa, and 7% in Latin America. In Asia, according to the ILO, 22% of the workforce is made up of children, while in Latin America children account for 17% of the workforce (ILO 1998a: 7).

Which human rights are facilitators of equitable economic development?

In Table 2.1 we list the human rights hypothesized to be facilitators of equitable economic development. We believe respect for these rights increases the probability that equitable economic development will occur, that development progress will be rapid, and that a high level of development will be achieved. However, they are not absolutely necessary for equitable economic development to take place. Research has shown that respect for human rights in the first two categories – physical integrity rights and democratic rights – has been associated with economic growth. These two categories of rights, plus respect for economic and social rights (which forms part of our definition of equitable economic development), and respect for worker rights are the categories of human rights closely examined in this book.

"Physical integrity rights" refer to the rights to be protected from being tortured, imprisoned for political reasons, killed without a fair trial, or disappeared. More respect for physical integrity rights may facilitate higher rates of economic growth, because, when government violates these rights, citizens become fearful and dissatisfied with the rules by which the regime in power makes authoritative decisions. In this way, abuse of physical integrity rights is likely to lead to a weakening of the legitimacy of the regime. Widespread fear, stress, and dissatisfaction among the citizenry would be likely to reduce productivity, and, therefore, negatively affect societal economic performance.[2]

One argument explaining why democratic rights might facilitate economic growth and higher levels of respect for social and economic rights is that politicians must maintain the support of their selectorates[3] in order to maintain their positions of power (Bueno de Mesquita *et al.* 2003). There is no need to assume that policy-makers want to do good things for their citizens. If they depend upon citizen support to stay in power, democratic procedures will push them in that direction.

Another linkage of democratic human rights to better economic policy-making emphasizes the importance of societal inputs into decision-making. Democratic institutional arrangements and political freedoms allow citizens to participate in policy-making, thus preventing their governments from making serious mistakes in economic development

---

[2] The positive relationship between job satisfaction and productivity is well established in the field of organizational behavior.

[3] A selectorate refers to the critical mass of population necessary for a leader to stay in political power.

strategies. For example, no democracy with a free press has ever experienced a serious famine (Sen 1999).

Still another line of reasoning emphasizes the importance of civil society in the economy. According to this view, democracies make better economic policies because, in democratic societies, interest groups can form to represent the interests of societal subgroups (Lindblom 1965). Representatives of citizens in the legislature have the benefit of hearing different proposals from different groups. After hearing from all sides interested enough to overcome the costs of organizing, representatives decide upon a particular public policy. This process of policy-making, whereby all interested parties exercise a voice in the process, is the principal reason for the "intelligence of democracy" (Lindblom 1965).

There is a large body of research demonstrating that countries having a high level of economic development also tend to have high levels of respect for physical integrity rights and democratic human rights (Poe and Tate 1994; Poe, Tate, and Keith 1999). The theory underlying most previous studies by political scientists is that economic development causes a higher level of respect for most human rights. In contrast, some economists argue that respect for procedural democratic rights (e.g., Kaufmann 2005; Sen 1999) and physical integrity rights (Kaufmann 2005) leads to higher rates of economic growth and higher levels of economic development.

Research seeking to untangle the causal relationship between respect for these types of human rights and economic development is in its early stages. The most comprehensive and methodologically sophisticated study on this topic explored the links among respect for human rights, the quality of governance, and the rate of economic growth (Kaufmann 2005). Three possible explanations for the strong positive correlation between average per capita incomes and respect for physical integrity and democratic rights were suggested (Kaufmann 2005). More respect for these human rights may exert a powerful causal effect on per capita incomes. Alternatively, higher incomes may lead to improvements in respect for physical integrity and democratic rights. As a final possibility, Kaufmann speculated that the relationship might be spurious. In other words, there might be another factor that makes countries richer and causes them to have more respect for physical integrity and democratic rights. His statistical tests indicated that more respect for physical integrity and democratic rights *caused* a higher level of respect for economic and social rights. An earlier study also found support for the hypothesis that more respect for democratic human rights led to higher levels of effectiveness of World Bank development projects around the world (Isham, Kaufmann, and Pritchett 1997).

The other human rights listed as facilitators of equitable economic development have received relatively less attention, but there are good reasons to believe that they too are important for understanding why equitable economic development occurs in some places but not others. Government respect for the rights of people to meaningful, decent-paying jobs and to the rights of workers to form trade unions if they wish to do so and to collectively bargain with their employers should lead to higher rates of economic growth. Since the vast majority of people in all societies are workers, respect for these rights will lead to higher levels of attainments of economic and social rights in society as well.

The World Bank's public position on the importance of protecting worker rights has been inconsistent. As an illustration, the Bank's 2006 *World Development* research report, titled *Equity and Development*, acknowledges the importance of worker rights to achieving equitable economic development. Specifically, the report says: "Collective organization of workers is one of the main channels for securing better and more equitable working conditions. Trade unions are the cornerstone of any effective system of industrial relations ... [they] can help provide a positive work environment by reducing labor turnover and by promoting worker training and higher productivity" and "Unions also can have an important non economic role. They have been a force for progressive political and social change in many countries (Poland, the Republic of Korea, and South Africa)" (World Bank 2005a: 190).

However, at roughly the same time, the Bank took the opposite position in important annual reports entitled *Doing Business*. These reports guide the formulation of policies and influence the operations of the institution (Sensor 2005). The World Bank assigns an overall "Ease of Doing Business" ranking to each country. Countries that do not have a minimum wage and do not restrict the number of hours an employee can work are ranked high. Indeed, rewarding lax or nonexistent labor standards contradicts ILO policy, which encourages countries to establish a minimum wage and regulate hours of work and to pass and enforce laws protecting freedom of association and collective bargaining (Durbin *et al.* 2006). In *Doing Business*, the report is clearly anti-worker rights since it rates governments in a way that penalizes countries for enforcing any sort of labor regulations (Sensor 2005).

Another example of a human right likely to be associated with equitable economic development is the right of access to a strong and independent judiciary. An independent judiciary is essential for the protection of all other human rights (World Bank 1998: 15). For this reason, future research may show that this human right is a necessary condition for equitable economic development. Similarly, it is difficult to imagine having any rights without having the right to due process of law and equal treatment before the law. Access to social security also may be instrumental in the promotion of economic growth, since a more secure workforce may participate more enthusiastically and productively in economic activities (Sen 1999: 39).

What would a human rights-based approach to economic development look like?

It is one thing to talk about general principles and quite another to recommend a specific operational approach to economic development that placed equal weight on economic growth and respect for human rights. Sérgio Pereira Leite, Assistant Director in the IMF's Office in Europe, contributed towards the effort to turn generalities into specifics when he described it this way:

One could define a rights-based approach to growth and poverty reduction as comprising six elements: (1) active protection of civil and political liberties; (2) pro-poor budgets and growth strategies; (3) policies geared toward ensuring that people receive adequate food, education, and health care; (4) broad participation in policy design; (5) environmental and social awareness; and (6) efforts to combat discrimination. (Leite 2001)

However, Leite (2001) says that human rights advocates should not expect the international financial institutions (IFIs) to impose human rights-related policy conditions on their member countries, because 1) the IFIs do not have the expertise required to make judgments about human rights practices; 2) constructive engagement is a more effective approach than imposing sanctions; 3) respect for economic and social rights is improving in countries under structural adjustment; and 4) nothing prevents developing country governments under structural adjustment from incorporating human rights into their "poverty reduction agreements." We consider each of the arguments in turn.

The Bank and the Fund do not have to make their own judgments about the quality of human rights practices by the governments that are the actual or potential recipients of loans. The IFIs can rely on the judgments of other credible organizations such as the United Nations Commission on Human Rights (UNCHR) that make those evaluations already. In fact, for several years now, the World Bank has utilized CIRI measures of the human rights practices of developing countries for its own decision-making purposes. In its annual *Governance Matters* report, the Bank publishes its assessment of the quality of governance in each developing county. One of the components of its measure is the quality of human rights practices of each country. Thus, the Bank already makes judgments about human rights practices, and there is some evidence that information about human rights practices already affects World Bank decisions. Statistical analyses have shown that the adoption of a UNCHR resolution condemning a country's human rights record has been followed by substantial reductions in the amounts of World Bank loans (Lebovic and Voeten 2006).

In addition, the research results presented in Chapter 10 of this volume demonstrate that long exposure to structural adjustment lending has improved democratic practices in less developed countries. If this outcome was intended, then it is evidence that the World Bank and IMF are capable of executing an effective human rights strategy of economic development. However, there is no evidence of any human rights successes beyond democracy promotion. Thus, democracy promotion may have been a priority of the international financial institutions, but the promotion of other human rights has not been a priority.

The argument that constructive engagement is better than confrontation as a way to change human rights practices of developing countries is an old and generally rejected one. It is the same argument that is raised against the incorporation of human rights conditions in legislation affecting many aspects of US foreign policy. Though there have been some good outcomes from "quiet diplomacy," there is no evidence that working quietly behind the scenes with government leaders is generally a more effective way to resolve abuses over time. Moreover, there are advantages in stating noble principles publicly. For these reasons, many European countries have followed the lead of the United States by explicitly including human rights provisions in legislation governing their foreign policy formulation (Donnelly 2003). Even the European Union requires a minimum level of respect for human rights and adoption of democratic institutions as a condition for admittance, as does the World Bank's sister institution, the European Bank for Reconstruction and Development (EBRD).

Except in the most trivial sense, it is not true that protections of economic and social rights are advancing in developing countries undergoing structural adjustment. Leite argues that data from countries with structural adjustment programs during 1985–1999 show that, on average, they "registered some improvement" in such things as overall primary school enrollment (0.8 percent per year) and infant mortality (2.8 percent per year). As we will demonstrate in Chapter 6, the average figures on outcomes such as these advanced for all developing countries during that period, but, other things being equal, countries implementing structural adjustment conditions for the longest time period had worse outcomes for life expectancy at age one, infant mortality, and adult literacy rate in 2003 than countries where they had not implemented such conditions.

Perhaps the most interesting argument in Leite's (2001) essay is that "nothing prevents" developing countries under structural adjustment "from incorporating human rights in their poverty reduction [structural adjustment] agreements." Whether they do so is determined mainly by each "government's commitment and leadership." Out of the more than 100 countries under structural adjustment agreements in 2000 or 2001, he lists only eight countries whose governments included such provisions in their agreements – Bolivia, Burkina Faso, Cambodia, Cameroon, Nicaragua, Tanzania, Uganda, and Vietnam. The inclusion of human rights provisions in structural adjustment agreements means nothing, of course, unless human rights objectives are specific and measurable, and that there are meaningful consequences if they are not achieved.

Leite (2001) explained that the Bank and the Fund were already working closely together to do everything they could to negotiate structural adjustment agreements that fulfilled all the reasonable requirements of a rights-based approach to growth and poverty reduction. The findings we present suggest that, except for the promotion of democratic institutions and political liberties, Bank and Fund efforts towards these ends have been weak and ineffective in most developing countries of the world. The question is: what can the Bank and Fund do that would be more effective? We will return to this question in Chapter 11.

3 Theoretical linkages between structural adjustment and repression

Introduction

What is the impact of the World Bank and International Monetary Fund on government respect for human rights and on equitable economic development? Many different groups have protested that the impacts have been negative. Recent anti-structural adjustment demonstrations have taken place at the 1999 Ministerial Meeting of the World Trade Organization (WTO) in Seattle, at the annual meetings of the IMF and World Bank (in Washington DC on alternate years), and at the annual summits of the Group of 8 (G8) industrialized countries. There were massive protests at the 2005 Summit of the Americas in Mar del Plata (near Buenos Aires), at the 2000 Annual Meeting of the IMF and World Bank in Prague, and at the 2001 G8 meeting in Turin, among others. Protesters have questioned the motives and criticized the impacts of these institutions on the economies and societies of liberalizing countries. The popular press has reported upon the activities of these institutions extensively, with much criticism of the austerity measures that have been associated with structural adjustment agreements and their harsh consequences in developing countries. With emotions raised and hyperbole flowing, we need to step back and ask if the criticism of these institutions is warranted. Has the academic community generated any answers when trying to assess the impact of these institutions?

Recent studies which have controlled for what have become known as "issues of selection" have concluded that IMF structural adjustment agreements have deleterious consequences on economic growth (Przeworski and Vreeland 2000; Vreeland 2003). There have been no similar studies of the economic effects of World Bank structural adjustment agreements that have controlled for the effects of selection, but since the World Bank and the IMF coordinate their structural adjustment efforts, one would expect to find the same negative economic outcomes.

The rest of the chapter briefly describes the theoretical perspectives adopted in previous research explaining variation in government respect for human rights practices, and how this study fits into those frameworks. Then, we discuss the origin and purpose of both the World Bank and the IMF. We show that both the World Bank and the IMF have acknowledged the primary goal of equitable economic development discussed in Chapter 2. We review the economic theories that form the foundation of structural adjustment policies and the critiques of the applications of those theories in the developing country context. We develop the linkage in neoliberal economic thought and critical perspectives between structural adjustment and human rights practices in developing countries. Finally, we review the current policy debate between the critics and defenders of structural adjustment policies.

Why governments violate the human rights of their citizens

Over roughly the past quarter of a century, scholars from different subfields of political science have tried to develop empirical models explaining why governments differ in their approach to and enforcement of human rights. There is a growing consensus concerning some relationships.[1] Three main views have been put forward as explanations of the variations in government protections of the human rights of their citizens. One approach emphasizes the role of threats to the regime as stimuli of repression. Another perspective explains repression as the result of state characteristics – mainly the level of democracy in a society or its degree of economic development or both. Yet another viewpoint stresses the growing importance of transnational noneconomic and economic forces. Typically, these three sets of factors are not presented as contending theories, but rather as complementary factors that must all be considered if one is to understand government tendencies to respect or violate the human rights of their citizens.

Threat

The main theoretical foundation for the global, comparative research conducted so far has been the Most-Starr rational actor decision-making model. This model was first presented by Most and Starr (1989) and was later expanded upon by Starr and his colleagues (Simon and Starr 1996; Starr 1994). The model suggests that if leaders believe their regime to be

---

[1] For a thorough review of this literature, see Poe (2004) and Landman (2005).

strong and secure, then they will not be inclined to violate the human rights of their citizens. They will become repressive if they believe that the strength of domestic threats or international threats or both combined is equal or greater than the strength of the regime they wish to protect. They may use repression of human rights as one of the strategies to redress an undesirable imbalance in the strength/threat ratio (Poe 2004).

One important variant of the threat–repression linkage emphasizes that the main source of domestic conflict within developing countries is the hardships experienced by some segments of their populations. Hardships may be the basis for social movements that threaten elites, who respond with increased repression (Arat 1991; Blomberg and Hess 2002; Fearon and Laitin 2003; Gurr 2000; Lindstrom and Moore 1995). Thus, to the extent that structural adjustment policies cause increased hardships for the poor, those policies also, indirectly, cause greater repression of human rights.

Testing the theory is complicated, because the regime has multiple strategies or tools available to reach a more desirable ratio of strength-to-threat. Still, research has shown that domestic threats, especially violent domestic threats, are associated with subsequent increases in the level of repression of civil and political rights (Davenport 1995; 1996; Gurr 1986; Poe 2004; Poe and Tate 1994; Poe, Tate, and Keith 1999). The findings have not been quite as strong and consistent, but many studies also have shown that involvement in international war is associated with increased repression (Poe 2004; Poe and Tate 1994; Poe, Tate, and Keith 1999). The Most and Starr theory has not yet been explicitly tested, however, because no one has measured the ratio of strength to threat and connected that ratio to repression of various types.

State characteristics: authoritarianism, poverty, and constitutional provisions

Previous studies examining variations in the human rights practices of governments have concentrated almost exclusively on state-level characteristics such as wealth, constitutional provisions, or level of democracy (e.g., Davenport 1996; Davenport and Armstrong 2004; Mitchell and McCormick 1988; Poe and Tate 1994; Poe, Tate, and Keith 1999). All of the most respected empirical work on this topic also examines the importance of the level of a state's democratic institutional and economic development on its propensity to violate the human rights of its citizens. However, there is less theoretical development or consensus about how these factors affect government behavior. The expectation in all of the existing research is that more democratic institutions and a higher level of economic development will cause a government to have better human rights practices. At the most basic, intuitive level, democracy produces better human rights practices, because democratic institutions empower the masses. The masses want more respect for their human rights, so they use their power to produce those policy outcomes.

This line of thinking suggests a positive linear relationship between the degree of democratic institutional development and the degree of respect for various human rights. However, a few scholars think that the relationship is "U-shaped." That is, repression is lowest in both the least and the most democratic societies, and greatest in transitional societies. This idea is sometimes referred to as the "more-murder-in-the-middle" hypothesis (Fein 1995) and has garnered some empirical support (Regan and Henderson 2002). Still another hypothesis that has received some support is the idea that there is a threshold effect of democracy on government respect for human rights. According to this argument, democratic institutional development has little or no effect on government behavior until a certain level of institutional development is reached. After that, the consequences for improved human rights practices are dramatic (Davenport and Armstrong 2004).

The literature in political science assumes that economic development causes democratic development (Lipset 1959; Przeworski et al. 2000) and greater respect for the human rights of citizens (Keith 1999; Hathaway 2002; Mitchell and McCormick 1988; Poe and Tate 1994; Poe, Tate, and Keith 1999; Zanger 2000). The literature in economics considers the possibility that the causal direction is reversed: better human rights practices stimulate economic growth (Isham, Kaufmann, and Pritchett 1997; Kaufmann 2005; Sen 1999). As is the case for democracy, there is much empirical support for the positive relationship between economic development and government respect for human rights, but little consensus about why it exists. One possibility is that protecting all human rights requires resources on the part of the state to create a well-functioning bureaucracy, to have well-trained police, soldiers, and judges, and to compensate public officials sufficiently so that they will not be subject to corruption. Another view suggests that protecting some human rights – the so-called "positive rights" to such things as decent work, access to health care, and education – requires government to promote legislation and enforce these rights through bureaucratic and legal mechanisms. Both explanations suggest that it is easier for governments to promote positive rights when they have additional resources. Another, advanced by Lipset (1959), is that a well-functioning democracy depends upon an informed and educated electorate. It is facilitated by urbanization where more face-to-face interactions among citizens and between citizens and leaders are possible. It is also facilitated by a good system of mass communications, so citizens, even the illiterate, no matter where they live can be informed of government debates and decisions. All of these things come with more economic development.

Besides level of economic development and democracy, the other set of state-level characteristics that help explain variations in government protections of human rights are institutional design characteristics (Davenport 1996; Keith 2002a; 2002b; 2004). The existence and extensiveness of a constitution, bill of rights, the degree of independence of the judiciary, and a difficult procedure for declaring a state of emergency are all associated with better human rights practices. In contrast, there is less consensus about the effects of federalism on human rights practices (Alexander 2006b; Blasi and Cingranelli 1996). In federal systems (e.g., the US, Brazil, and India), subnational governments have significant power and autonomy, whereas in unitary systems (e.g., France) this is not the case.

Transnational forces

While these explanations focus on the importance of state characteristics, or, in the case of interstate war, on the relationships between states, there has been more attention in recent years, especially in the field of international political economy, on the role of transnational actors, trade regimes, human rights regimes, and, in the case of this study, the international finance regime. A "regime" as defined by Young (1992) is a set of rights and rules, decision-making procedures or programs that gives rise to social practices, assigns roles to the participants in these practices, and governs their interactions. Regimes structure the opportunities of actors interested in a given activity and they contain the expectation of compliance by their members (Young 1980: 333–342). Similarly, a "regime" is defined by Krasner (1983: 4) as a set of explicit or implicit "principles, norms, rules, and decision making procedures around which actor expectations converge in a given issue-area."

Realists believe that regimes simply reflect the distribution of power in the international system. Powerful states create regimes to serve their security and economic interests. Regimes have no independent power over states, particularly over great powers. As such, regimes are simply intervening variables between the real independent variable (power) and the observed outcome (cooperation). According to this view, the post-World War II international organizations such as the World Bank and IMF are simply instruments of American grand strategy (Strange 1988).

Neoliberals view regimes as independent actors in the international system. International regimes can increase the probability of cooperation by monitoring the behavior of members and reporting on compliance (Keohane and Martin 1995). The structural adjustment regime defines what constitutes a defection and prescribes punishments. Regimes also generate the expectation of cooperation among members (Keohane and Martin 1995). The program exploring why governments follow or defy the norms and rules established by different international regimes suggests that several characteristics of the norms and rules determine whether they will be followed by particular target governments (Chenoweth and Teets 2004; Hathaway 2002; Keith 1999; Legro 1997; Ratner 2004; Shannon 2000). The more states that share the norms and accept the expectations associated with them, the more they will be followed by targets. In the case of structural adjustment norms, this might be indicated by the number of states signing SAAs each year. In the case of human rights norms, it would be indicated by the number of states that have signed and ratified various human rights instruments. The "durability" of the system of norms refers to "how long the rules have been in effect and how they weather challenges to their prohibitions" (Legro 1997: 34). The longer a norm has been in existence without significant challenge, the stronger its effect on targets will be. The human rights regime has been in existence longer than the structural adjustment regime, but both have faced significant challenges. Perhaps the most important difference among international regimes is their relative ability to enforce compliance with their norms and rules. Because of the resources they allocate the IFIs are strong on this dimension.

Human rights scholars have focused most of their attention on the international human rights regime that exists to ensure government compliance with human rights norms as codified in conventions and treaties, to develop new norms, and to encourage acceptance of those norms by states that have not joined the regime. Partly as a result of the activities of this regime, human rights norms are generally accepted by states. As of May 2001, the six most important human rights agreements had an average of 157 parties (Donnelly 2003: 127). For the international human rights regime, the mechanisms for ensuring compliance have indeed grown stronger over time, but they still remain relatively weak (Donnelly 2003).

Despite the weak enforcement mechanisms, research indicates that international human rights regimes do change the behavior of their members. Numerous studies have shown that states that join international human rights regimes improve their human rights practices

(Hathaway 2002; Keith 1999; Landman 2005). Other studies have emphasized the roles of international nongovernmental organizations as part of the human rights regime (Welch 1995). Their activities speed the diffusion of international human rights norms (Burgerman 1998; Keck and Sikkink 1998). Human rights regimes have been one source of transnational influence on government behavior towards their citizens; another source has been the impact of international financial institutions.

Northern governments and private international banks assigned the IMF with the responsibility for establishing the system of rules and decision-making procedures that determine which developing countries receive capital and under what conditions. The IMF is essentially the head of an international creditor cartel and, when it declares that a government's economic reform program is "off track," governments and banks usually withhold most financing from the government (Alexander 2006b).

This international financial regime is much stronger than the international human rights regimes because it has the ability to enforce its rules. The international trade and finance regime requires that the governments of developing countries that are seeking capital adopt neo-liberal economic practices as a precondition for obtaining financing or admittance to the World Trade Organization. Both the financing and trade regimes also seek to promulgate other norms as is illustrated by the World Bank's recent focus on encouraging better practices such as good governance.

The Bank and the Fund do this through their technical assistance programs, through rating the performance of governments according to the criteria in the Country Policy and Institutional Assessment, and, more particularly, through the withdrawal of financing for governments that do not comply with their financing agreements. Through what may be called "mission creep," the roles of various international regimes can overlap. In effect, human rights-related decisions made by the World Bank, the International Monetary Fund, the North Atlantic Treaty Organization, the European Union, the World Trade Organization, or multinational corporations become part of the larger international human rights regime as it operates on the government of any developing country (Meyer 1996; 1998; Richards, Gelleny, and Sacko 2001). The results of this study show that the amount of contact a developing country has with the international finance regime has an independent effect on its respect for human rights. This finding, along with others noted above, suggests that existing theories of repression should be revised to take greater account of the effects of such transnational causal forces on the human rights practices of governments around the world.

The results of this study also suggest that existing theories of repression should be revised to take greater account of transnational causal forces. Previous studies examining variations in the human rights practices of governments have concentrated almost exclusively on state-level characteristics such as wealth, constitutional provisions, or level of democracy (e.g., Davenport 1996; Davenport and Armstrong 2004; Mitchell and McCormick 1988; Poe and Tate 1994; Poe, Tate, and Keith 1999). The dominant theoretical framework underlying this research argues that, other things being equal, "repression will increase as regimes are faced with a domestic threat in the form of civil war or when a country is involved in international war" (Poe 2004; Poe, Tate, and Keith 1999: 293; see also Davenport 1995; Gurr 1986). Other international factors besides involvement in international war – such as the degree of integration into the global economy, sensitivity to international norms, and involvement with international financial institutions – have received much less attention.[2] This work provides an important theoretical improvement delineating the effects of IFIs as additional independent factors affecting the level of government respect for the human rights of their citizens. The theoretical framework emphasizes that multiple international organizations exert simultaneous effects on government human rights practices. In this work we refer to these simultaneous effects as the "joint effects."

Foundation of the World Bank and International Monetary Fund

The International Bank for Reconstruction and Development, otherwise known as the World Bank, and the International Monetary Fund (IMF), were established towards the end of World War II in 1944 at the Bretton Woods Conference in New Hampshire. The establishment of the International Monetary Fund came about in part because of the perception that the international community had been unable to respond adequately to the economic instability that racked Germany throughout the late 1920s and early 1930s. This insecurity spread to other countries in Europe and the United States much like the negative effects of the 1997–1998 Asian financial crisis spread to Russia and

---

[2] Some scholars have focused on transnational forces affecting human rights practices. For example, increased integration into the international economy has been associated with both worse (Meyer 1996; 1998) and better (Blanton and Blanton 2007; Milner 2000; Richards, Gelleny, and Sacko 2001) protection of physical integrity rights by governments. Other studies have discussed the impacts of international nongovernmental organizations (Welch 1995) and even the diffusion of international norms (Keck and Sikkink 1998; Landman 2005) on the human rights practices of governments.

parts of South America (Alexander 2001). The IMF was designed to promote international monetary stability through policies that provided short-term support for the balance of payments systems (Boughton 2001; Rapley 1996). Short-term financial difficulties in the balance of payments system were managed through IMF financing of member states. A government can borrow up to its "access limit," or a specific multiple of its IMF quota. The IMF performs three functions: financing, surveillance, and technical assistance.[3]

While policy conditionality has been associated with the IMF since its inception, the passage of time has seen the development of specific credit facilities. According to the IMF website,[4]

Low-income countries may borrow at a concessional interest rate through the Poverty Reduction and Growth Facility (PRGF)[5] and the Exogenous Shocks Facility (ESF). Nonconcessional loans are provided mainly through Stand-By Arrangements (SBA), and occasionally using the Extended Fund Facility (EFF), the Supplemental Reserve Facility (SRF), and the Compensatory Financing Facility (CFF). The IMF also provides emergency assistance to support recovery from natural disasters and conflicts, in some cases at concessional interest rates.

Governments borrowing from each of the facilities face differing levels of conditions, repayment schedules, and eligibility status. Agreements, in general, have ranged in length from about one to three years.

In comparison, the World Bank was established to promote the economic reconstruction of post-World War II Europe and, later, the economic development of developing countries. From its inception until the late 1970s the Bank had mostly engaged in project lending, the promotion of building infrastructure like dams and power plants. In 1980, the Bank shifted from project to structural adjustment lending (Mosley, Harrigan, and Toye 1995). The IFI SAAs promoted export-led trade and investment (Harrigan and Mosley 1991; Mosley, Harrigan, and Toye 1995; Meilink 2003; Przeworski and Vreeland 2000). The policy conditions attached to these agreements were intended to promote economic growth by focusing on macro-economic (monetary and fiscal) factors as well as structural factors. Structural

---

[3] Originally, the IMF performed these functions for all member countries. However, during the past few decades, the IMF has lost its multilateral character insofar as it no longer provides financing for industrialized countries. However, it does provide "surveillance," or oversight, of all member country economies through "Article IV" consultations.

[4] www.imf.org/external/np/exr/facts/howlend.htm.

[5] Formerly called the "Enhanced Structural Adjustment Facility" (ESAF), which was established in 1987.

reforms included policies of deregulation, privatization, and reducing the size and scope of government within a broader framework of increased exports and greater private investment.

The World Bank's and IMF's imperative of high-quality economic growth

The imperative to promote economic development through economic growth is one of the founding principles of both the World Bank and the International Monetary Fund. The IMF Articles of Agreement (Article I, paragraph ii) state that the purposes of the International Monetary Fund are:

To facilitate the expansion and balanced growth of international trade, and to contribute thereby to the promotion and maintenance of high levels of employment and real income and to the development of the productive resources of all members as primary objectives of economic policy. (IMF 2004)

Very similar language is found in the Articles of Agreement establishing the World Bank or, as it is formally known, the International Bank for Reconstruction and Development (IBRD). The IBRD Articles of Agreement (Article I, paragraph iii) state that the purposes of the International Bank for Reconstruction and Development are:

To promote the long-range balanced growth of international trade and the maintenance of equilibrium in balances of payments by encouraging interna-tional investment for the development of the productive resources of members, thereby assisting in raising productivity, the standard of living and conditions of labor in their territories. (World Bank 1989)

Indeed, the World Bank and IMF have taken to presenting common approaches to the structural adjustment agreements "often under the banner of growth orientated adjustment" (Meilink 2003: 17). Since 1989 in the case of the World Bank and since 1999 in the case of the IMF, the Managing Director of the IMF and the President of the World Bank have stated publicly that the goal of their respective institutions is to promote the kind of economic development that benefits most people in societies – especially the poor. It was the first time that an IMF Managing Director had embraced poverty reduction as a goal when Michel Camdessus stated that:

Our primary goal is growth ... It is toward that growth that our programs and their conditionality are aimed. It is with a view toward growth that we carry out our special responsibility of helping to correct balance of payments disequilibria and, more generally, to eliminate obstructive macroeconomic imbalances. When

I refer to growth, I mean high-quality growth, not ... growth for the privileged few, leaving the poor with nothing but empty promises. (Camdessus 1990: 235)

We refer to this goal as equitable economic development (Sen 1999). Another former Managing Director of the IMF, Horst Köhler, stated that "the IMF should strive to promote non-inflationary economic growth that benefits all people of the world" (Köhler 2000). James Wolfensohn, a former President of the World Bank Group, has stated in several different venues his desire to see the eradication of poverty. In his closing remarks at the Shanghai Conference on "Scaling Up Poverty Reduction" in 2004, he noted that "[A]ll of us has to work politically to ensure that poverty and the alleviation of poverty is central on the global agenda" (World Bank 2004). Recent joint statements by leaders of the IMF and World Bank underlie the common goals of these institutions. A joint statement made by James Wolfensohn and Agustín Carstens, former Deputy Managing Director of the IMF, at a meeting with Church leaders in Switzerland stated that:

Central to the common ground is the fight against global poverty – particularly the extreme poverty that remains all too prevalent in much of the world. We all agree that poverty reduction at the pace that is needed requires policies to improve both economic growth and equity. We all emphasize the importance of keeping the focus of the global agenda, national leaders, and international organizations on the objective of poverty reduction. (World Bank 2004)

Over time these institutions have come together in their policies towards structural adjustment; from this perspective it is useful to view each theory as part of a larger comprehensive framework of economic policy reforms (Abouharb and Cingranelli 2004a; 2006; Khan, Montie, and Haque 1990; Meilink 2003).

Economic theory of structural adjustment

The theoretical underpinning for structural adjustment agreements stems from work examining demand and supply side imbalances within an economy (Chenery and Strout 1966; Domar 1946; Harrod 1939; Polak 1957). Two related economic theories, the Polak model (Polak 1957) and the Revised Minimum Standard model, form the theoretical "building blocks" for the separate approaches taken by the IMF and World Bank (Meilink 2003; Tarp 1993).

The Polak economic model is the foundation for many IMF policies. It emphasizes the importance of managing credit expansion to improve the balance of payments situation (Polak 1957). Credit expansion increases imports and inflation within a country. These increased imports have the effect of lowering levels of foreign currency reserves because there has been no commensurate increase in the level of exports bringing foreign exchange into the economy. This situation generates inequality in the balance of payments. The key to lowering inflation, and improving the balance of payments situation, is to constrain credit expansion (Khan, Montie, and Haque 1990).

Two related arguments are also brought forward. The first is that the IMF wants to prevent crowding out of private sector investment. Private sector investment is impeded when a government uses an excessive level of its available credit to manage its deficits (Meilink 2003: 12). Governments must, according to the IMF, cut back on expenditures or raise taxes in order to reduce deficits and free up credit for use by the private sector (Meilink 2003: 13). A second policy, which governments are generally mandated to undertake by the IMF, is real devaluations of the exchange rate, which make exporting firms more competitive by lowering the price foreigners pay for their (tradeable) goods. These devaluations increase the price of imports (non-tradeables) (thus, reducing demand) and improve the balance of payments (Meilink 2003; Rapley 1996; Vreeland 2003). The expected consequence of devaluation of the exchange rate is an expansion of export-orientated economic growth.

The theoretical underpinning for the approach taken by the World Bank may be found initially in the Harrod-Domar Growth model (Harrod 1939; Domar 1946) with subsequent improvements made by Chenery and Strout (1966) in their two-gap model of economic growth. The Revised Minimum Standard model presently used by the World Bank and IMF in their structural adjustment agreements is an extension of the two-gap model (Tarp 1993; Lensink 1996). The key concept behind the Growth model is the idea that economic growth is a function of accumulated capital. The promotion of savings is central to the promotion of economic growth. Greater savings permit greater investment, which generates economic growth.

The framework presented by the Growth model permitted decision-makers in government to set targets for economic growth. The role for institutions like the World Bank came about in situations when a government's level of savings was insufficient to achieve a desired rate of economic growth. This "savings gap," as it was known, could be filled by the World Bank through its financing of recipient states. Later work refined the approach taken by the World Bank to a "two-gap model" of economic growth (Chenery and Strout 1966). The refined approach noted that economic growth was conditional on not only sufficient savings within an economy, but also the presence of enough capital goods, fundamental to economic growth, but not available within the state. Capital goods could be imported, but foreign exchange was needed for their payment. Shortages of foreign exchange were a limit to economic growth because they prevented the purchase of foreign capital goods necessary for economic development. This second gap was known as the "foreign exchange gap" or "trade gap." The role of the World Bank was to provide loans that filled these gaps and to promote policies that also increased exports and inward investment as a tool to close the foreign exchange and savings gaps.

The policies implied by these approaches are similar. Both institutions promote exports to increase receipts of foreign exchange and equalize balance of payments. They also seek to limit the size of government and promote balanced budgets. Both these measures are intended to increase private investment and involvement in the economy. The private sector is assumed to undertake tasks more efficiently than the state because of the profit incentive. The intended consequence of these policies is to promote economic growth and the generation of wealth in the liberalizing state.

There are many variants of privatization. Indeed, some policy experts only use the term "privatization" to apply to the divestment of an asset. That is, the transfer of asset ownership from the public to the private sector. While some critics of the IFIs may condone privatization of productive assets, such as factories, under some circumstances, many more oppose the privatization of basic services, such as education, health care, and water. At present, divestment of basic services is a rarity. Instead, financiers promote public–private partnerships (PPPs). Public–private partnerships may not only include private enterprises and governments, but also nonprofit organizations, such as nongovernmental organizations (NGOs). Indeed, the IMF, World Bank, and World Trade Organization consider NGOs as part of the private sector since, along with private enterprises, NGOs dismantle public service provision (Alexander 2005). This text refers to the varieties of private sector ownership and service provision as "privatization."

Generations of structural adjustment[6]

Structural adjustment loans provide quick-disbursing financing to those governments of developing countries that are willing to implement economy-wide "policy conditions," or economic reforms, identified in their IMF and World Bank loan documents. The idea of structural

---

[6] This discussion of the history of structural adjustment benefited from research conducted by Nancy Alexander (2001) and her communications with the authors.

adjustment extends back to 1981 when the administration in the US, the Thatcher administration in the UK, and their allies urged the IFIs to insist on the imposition of more conditions when the IFIs made loans and grants. Since 1981 the IFIs have financed structural adjustment agreements (SAAs) requiring neoliberal economic reforms in developing and transition countries.

In 1990, policy-makers from international agencies, think tanks, and the Latin America and Caribbean region identified ten economic reforms – now called the "Washington Consensus" – implemented in the region after the debt crisis of the 1980s. These featured the policy conditions for SAAs, including: fiscal discipline, financial liberalization, unified and competitive exchange rates, tax reform, trade and investment liberalization, deregulation, privatization, macroeconomic stability, and protection of property rights. Although with different emphases from year to year, these basic thrusts of adjustment have persisted from 1980 to the present.

As a condition for financing, the IMF and World Bank require that recipient governments carry out "policy conditions" attached to loans. Since government compliance with some conditions was low, the IMF and World Bank began to require that governments accomplish "prior conditions" or "prior actions" before actually obtaining financing. Until recently, the World Bank's policy relating to adjustment[7] stipulated that adjustment lending should not exceed 25 percent of overall lending (30 percent for low-income countries). This ceiling of adjustment lending was established because the institution's Articles of Agreement[8] stipulate that the Bank, except in "special circumstances," should only make loans for projects or reconstruction purposes. In 1999, when the volume of adjustment lending exceeded the volume of project investments, the exception became the rule and the Bank's policy was changed (without a corresponding change in the Articles of Agreement). Often, governments prefer SAPs over project investments because SAPs provide faster cash injections and require less accountability.

The World Bank was stung by the rising tide of criticism of SAPs (e.g., Cornia, Jolly, and Stewart 1987). Finally, in 1989, then-President of the World Bank Lewis Preston declared that, henceforth, poverty reduction would constitute the aim of the institution. This marked the beginning of the second generation of structural adjustment. The "second" generation of SAAs required some level of protection to the poor who bore the brunt of adjustment. That is, steps were taken to mitigate the impact of

---

[7] Operational Policy 8.60.   [8] Article III, Section 4(vii).

adjustment measures. This move was in response to a wave of critiques of SAPs during the 1980s. The IMF issued several publications intended to demonstrate how IMF-financed SAPs protect public expenditures for social services. However, these studies tend to use 1990 as the base period since SAPs had ravaged social expenditures during the 1980–1989 time frame and, by 1989, such spending was at its nadir.

By the late 1990s, the IFIs needed to explain the failure of the Washington Consensus to promote robust economic growth and reduce poverty. The 1980s were known as the "lost decade" for development in Africa and Latin America.

The reevaluation of adjustment by the IFIs was also intensified by the East Asian crisis of 1997–1998 in which capital hemorrhaged out of the region throwing millions of people into poverty. Many blamed the IMF for promoting "fast-track capitalism." Ultimately, the IMF and World Bank attributed the failures of structural adjustment programs to the fact that the programs neglected the role of social, political, and economic institutions in establishing the preconditions for growth (Burki and Perry 2001).[9] As a result of this analysis, the Bank launched the third generation of adjustment focusing on institution-building, labor-market flexibility, enhanced financial supervision and prudential regulation, transparency, and good governance (Alexander 2001).

After the US election of 2000, a new Republican White House sought to put its stamp on the IFIs. With regard to the World Bank Group, the US lobbied the Board of Executive Directors to adopt a new Private Sector Development (PSD) Strategy as the overarching purpose of the institution. The PSD Strategy also launched the fourth generation of adjustment focused on the investment climate in recipient countries. This generation of adjustment has redoubled the institutions' financing for increasing the flexibility of labor policies in order to attract investors in search of cheap labor (Alexander 2001).

Theoretical critiques of structural adjustment

A number of critiques have been made about the theoretical foundations and policy implications of structural adjustment. These critiques fall along four broad themes. The first argues that the similarity between how industrialized and developing economies work has been overstated. The

---

[9] See, for instance, "Opening Remarks to IMF Conference on Second Generation Reforms" by Michel Camdessus, Managing Director of the International Monetary Fund, Washington, DC, November 8, 1999, www.imf.org/external/np/speeches/1999/110899.htm.

second concerns the applicability of economically based rational-choice approaches to the actions of people living in developing countries. The third concerns the impact of greater inequality on the prospects for economic development. The fourth argues that in contrast to the beliefs of neoliberal economists all markets do not arise spontaneously: some need government assistance to be promoted and maintained.

Industrialized and developing economies do not work the same An important critique of the neoliberal approach to economic liberalization is the assumption that the economies of the industrialized societies and those of developing countries are fundamentally similar. A number of arguments have been made as to why this similarity may be overstated. Developing economies suffer from more serious obstacles that retard the functioning of a flourishing free market (Killick 1989). Restrictions take on a variety of forms (Stewart 1985). For example, developing economies exhibit greater market fragmentation. Thus, the market mechanism where price paid for labor is a function of demand and supply often does not work properly. Instead, the salaries companies pay for highly skilled workers are relatively unaffected by changes in the size and composition of the labor market. More people entering into the workforce has little impact on the supply of these jobs and the wages paid because very few people have the skills necessary to become employed in these professions. Thus, even if the World Bank and IMF wanted to promote high-skill high-wage employment, the human capital necessary is in very short supply in many developing economies for these countries to respond in the short to medium term. In many countries, the informal economy employs more people than the formal economy.

For a population to respond to proposals of industrialization as a means to increase levels of economic development the labor force needs to have sufficient levels of education. The generation of higher levels of education requires that the government provide educational opportunities to all regardless of income level. Yet, one of the consequences of structural adjustment agreements has been the imposition of user-fees for access to education, causing enrollment in schools to plummet and levels of human capital to decline as well (SAPRIN 2004). This outcome usually worsens an already bad situation, because, in many developing countries, familial and communal structures may discourage individual investments in education. At present, World Bank-financed operations do not require imposition of user-fees for primary education. However, the World Bank promotes public support for private education that does require user-fees. In order to make education more "efficient," the World Bank also encourages the hiring of unqualified contract workers at a fraction of the wages paid to qualified teachers. The World Bank's policy conditions have increased fees for secondary and tertiary education. The IMF and the World Bank also finance SAPs that impose a wage ceiling that constrains the hiring of sufficient numbers of teachers (SAPRIN 2004).

Economic-based rational-choice approaches may not explain all decisions   There is considerable debate about how often people in less developed countries actually engage in the rational-choice manner that neoliberal economic approaches claim: maximizing their income when opportunity permits (Bates 1993; Killick 1989; Meier 1993). People may often prefer to satisfice rather than maximize (Rapley 1996: 100), since the risks associated with higher levels of income also vary. While the structural adjustment process may generate more opportunities to earn higher incomes, people may choose not to take advantage of them if the risks associated are perceived to be too high (Bates 2001).

A related argument is that people in developing countries may focus less on the individual and more on the collective (Scott 1976). If choices about undertaking economic activity are less individualistic in developing countries than in the industrialized West, then opportunities to increase income, if they also increase levels of familial and communal instability, may be avoided or taken under extreme care. For example, large numbers of children provide familial security in agrarian-based economies (Bates 2001). When (usually) sons are sent further afield to earn higher levels of income in urban areas for their families it should not be surprising if only one or two leave at any particular point in time (Bates 2001). While many of the policy initiatives that have been proposed by the World Bank and IMF have promoted free markets, increasing opportunities in some cases for higher incomes, in many they have reduced assistance for families and communities in other ways by retrenching the state from the provision of education and health care which had previously lowered the risks faced by families and communities in agrarian-based economies. Rural education and health care are increasingly financed through donor- and creditor-financed Social Funds and Community Driven Development (CDD) programs. A dominant model involves the transfer of resources to communities for contracting out the delivery of these services (often in parallel with and undercutting public provision of services). There are mixed reviews of these programs, with some evaluations highlighting that the elites tend to monopolize the resources. Agricultural dislocation has happened primarily as a result of promoting export growth at the expense of production for domestic consumption; the privatization of land for plantation agriculture, including with GM crops; and the reduction or elimination of credit or subsidies for farmers leading to indebtedness and loss of land. Hence the mass rural–urban migration (Alexander 2005).

Whatever benefit these agrarian-based societies may have garnered through the wealth-generation mechanisms promoted by neoliberal economic freedom may be offset by the increased levels of economic insecurity that families and communities face when the state reduces its involvement in society. A related source of economic insecurity, which makes the promotion of economic development more difficult, concerns the consequences of promoting a free-market approach that leads to increased levels of economic inequality within societies (Alexander 2005).

Higher levels of economic inequality make economic development difficult Free-market economics generate winners and losers. Recent work has linked free trade with increased economic inequality (Friedman 2000; Rapley 2004). Criticisms of the consequences of increased inequality have been made on moral grounds (Donnelly 2003). However, increased inequality also makes little economic sense since it limits the ability of people to fulfill their potential. For example, if people are less able to afford to educate their children, as is often the case when dealing with the consequences of structural adjustment (Nwosu 1992), then the possibility of the next generation fulfilling their potential is being lost. To compound matters, increased levels of economic development which come about through higher levels of education are then also being squandered.

Markets do not arise spontaneously A number of critiques have been made that point to the need for government to promote the existence of markets. The neoliberal approach is based upon the argument that markets arise spontaneously because of the imperative to exchange goods and services for the purposes of both survival and wealth generation. Groups variously described as neo-institutionalists have pointed to the need for the state to actively regulate the economy (Chaudhury 1994) and be able for example to enforce laws, otherwise extralegal methods of enforcement are sought as was seen in post-Soviet Russia with the rise of the Russian mafia (Stiglitz 2002).

The state is critical to the functioning of a free market especially in situations where other nongovernmental or quasi-governmental institutions such as business and trade organizations do not exist or are in embryonic form only. Yet, structural adjustment calls for less state, not more, retrenchment not intervention in the marketplace. While

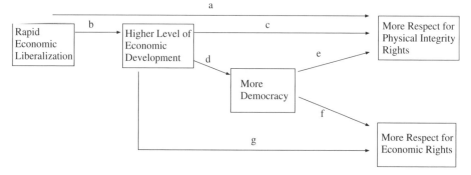

Figure 3.1 Structural adjustment and human rights: the neoliberal perspective

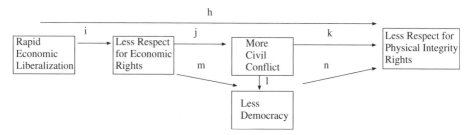

Figure 3.2 Structural adjustment and human rights: the critical perspective

this may be appropriate in industrialized economies where a variety of long-standing institutions and agreed-upon regulatory frameworks exist to maintain oversight of the economy, in developing economies these institutions and frameworks are much more limited and less well developed. Government engagement remains absolutely necessary (Platteau 1994).

The link between the consequences of structural adjustment agreements and government respect for its citizens' human rights are explored below. The expectations differ markedly depending on whether one is a proponent or critic of the structural adjustment process.

Theory: the effects of structural adjustment on human rights

Direct effects

Figures 3.1 and 3.2 depict the main causal arguments of the conventional neoliberal and more critical views of the direct and indirect effects of structural adjustment on the human rights practices of governments. The direct effects may be theorized as positive (linkage "a") or negative (linkage "h"). The "positive" argument (linkage "a") is that a relatively limited government as required by SAAs is fundamental to all human freedoms. Limited government reduces barriers to the functioning of the free market, allowing human beings to pursue their own interests in their own ways and allowing them to pursue opportunities that are likely to be lost if human freedom is restricted (Friedman 1962; Hayek 1984). Consistent with this line of thought, Cranston (1964) has argued that respect for most human rights, including physical integrity rights (such as the right not to be tortured), only requires forbearance on the part of the state.

However, as linkage "h" of Figure 3.2 indicates, structural adjustment programs also may have the direct effect of worsening government human rights practices, because a substantial involvement of government in the economy is essential for the protection of all human rights (Donnelly 2003). The historical record demonstrates, for example, that a reduced role of the state in capitalist economies has led to less protection of some human rights such as worker rights. From a principal–agent theoretical perspective, reducing the size of government also reduces the ability of principals (government leaders) to constrain the discretion of agents (police and soldiers). More administrative discretion is likely to lead to greater abuse of physical integrity rights (Policzer 2004). Also, in practice, the acceptance of structural adjustment conditions by less developed countries causes the adoption of new policies and practices. These new policies are designed to produce substantial behavioral changes in the affected populations. Evidence from literature about human learning suggests that people have a natural tendency to resist making substantial changes in their previous behavior (Davidson 2002). One of the tools government may use to overcome such resistance is coercion.

As depicted by linkage "i" in Figure 3.2, and as discussed in earlier chapters, some aspects of structural adjustment programs may have a direct effect on worsened respect for economic rights. In Chapter 9 we discuss the provisions in structural adjustment agreements that have been shown to have reduced respect for worker rights in developing countries. As noted in Chapter 1, other scholars and NGOs have argued that structural adjustment policies have damaged women's economic and social rights.

Neoliberal theory: indirect effects of adjustment on human rights

Figure 3.1 also depicts the expected indirect effects of structural adjustment on the human rights practices of loan-recipient governments from a neoliberal economic theory perspective. As noted, neoliberal economic theory suggests that structural adjustment will promote economic development (linkage "b" in Figure 3.1).[10] Many previous studies (e.g., Poe, Tate, and Keith 1999; Poe et al. 2004) have shown that wealthier states have provided greater levels of respect for a wide variety of human rights including physical integrity rights (linkage "c"). Thus, if the imposition of an SAA increases the level of wealth in a less developed country, then the indirect effect of SAA implementation should be an improvement in the human rights practices of governments.

Despite findings showing that structural adjustment has not led to faster economic growth, the empirical debate over linkage "b" will continue. There will be more studies of the economic effects of structural development. Defenders of structural adjustment policies often claim that the main problem is that there has been a failure to implement them (Dollar and Svensson 2000; Van de Walle 2001). For example, Dollar and Svensson (2000), after reviewing internal and private World Bank records, estimated that about one-third of loan recipients did not fully implement the adjustment criteria demanded by the World Bank. We provide a more complete discussion of this argument in Chapter 4. For now, the important point to keep in mind is that the defenders of structural adjustment programs believe that these policies should not be blamed for disappointing rates of economic growth.

Thus, it is important to understand the remainder of the neoliberal argument. As is indicated by linkages "d" and "e" in Figure 3.1, previous research has shown that wealthier states are more likely to be democratic (e.g., Boix 2003; Boix and Stokes 2003; Lipset 1959; Przeworski et al. 2000), and relatively high levels of democracy are associated with a higher level of respect for most human rights including physical integrity rights (Davenport and Armstrong 2004; Mitchell and McCormick 1988; Poe et al. 2004; Poe, Tate, and Keith 1999). Therefore, if the imposition of a structural adjustment agreement promotes higher levels of democratic development through increased wealth, then an indirect consequence of SAA implementation should be an improvement in human rights practices.

Neoliberal defenders of the effects of SAAs on government respect for economic human rights have argued that higher levels of economic development caused by the implementation of an SAA will lead to improvements in government respect for economic rights (linkage "g") through what is now commonly referred to as the "trickle down" effect. That is, wealth will accumulate faster under a structural adjustment

---

[10] For a review of literature developing this argument, see Rapley (1996).

program, and, once accumulated, will trickle down to help the less fortunate in society. A number of studies have shown that the level of economic development has a strong, positive impact on basic human needs fulfillment (Milner 2000; Milner, Poe, and Leblang 1999; Poe et al. 2004; Moon and Dixon 1985; Park 1987; Rosh 1986; Spalding 1986). Moreover, as indicated by linkage "f", previous research has shown that democratic governments have been shown to make greater efforts to provide for the economic human rights of their citizens (Milner, Poe, and Leblang 1999; Moon and Dixon 1985; Poe et al. 2004).

Unfortunately, all of the indirect neoliberal arguments linking SAAs to better human rights practices depend upon supporting evidence for linkage "b" in Figure 3.1. Without linkage "b" all of the other indirect causal chains from rapid economic liberalization to better human rights practices by governments are broken. At an earlier point in time, one might have argued that it was too soon to conclude that there was no evidence that the implementation of SAAs led to the accumulation of more wealth by loan recipients, but SAAs were initiated by the World Bank in 1980, and the IMF has had conditionality associated with its loans as far back as 1952 (Sidell 1988). In an attempt to carry out their fiduciary responsibility, there have always been conditions. However, the neoliberal conditions were applied beginning in 1980. If SAAs have had a stimulative effect on economic development, it should be observable by now.

Critical theory: indirect effects of adjustment on human rights

The indirect effects posited by the critical perspective are summarized in Figure 3.2. There is a large body of research showing that implementation of an SAA has negative effects on government respect for economic human rights (linkage "i"). Rapid economic liberalization, according to many observers, forces loan-recipient states to reduce or even stop making efforts to help their citizens enjoy internationally recognized rights to health care, education, food, decent work, and shelter, because structural adjustment conditions almost always require reductions on government spending for social programs (Chipeta 1993; Fields 2003; Handa and King 1997; Sowa 1993; Meyer 1998; World Bank 1992; Zack-Williams 2000). Some studies have emphasized the disproportionate negative economic human rights consequences for women (Buchmann 1996; Commonwealth Secretariat 1989; Elson 1990; Sadasivam 1997), public sector employees, and low-wage workers (Daddieh 1995). The poor and those in the public sector have seen their wages fall in real terms (Daddieh 1995; Munck 1994), while at the same time they have faced increased living costs due to the removal of price controls and subsidies for essential commodities (Zack-Williams 2000). The implementation of SAAs also has worsened the relative position of the poorest by increasing income inequality (Daddieh 1995; Friedman 2000; Handa and King 1997). Moreover, efforts by developing countries to make their economies more business friendly have resulted in the adoption of policies hostile to worker rights.

Less attention has been given to the relationships explicitly linking the implementation of SAAs to subsequent government respect for physical integrity rights.[11] As shown in Figure 3.2, there are three indirect causal paths that should be considered (linkages "j–k," "j–l–n," and "m–n"). All lead to less respect for physical integrity rights, and all depend upon empirical support for linkage "i," which is plentiful. One line of thinking is that, by causing loan recipients to reduce their respect for the economic and social human rights of their most vulnerable citizens, externally "imposed" rapid economic liberalization of the type required by an SAA promotes civil conflict (linkage "j"), which, in turn, leads loan-recipient governments to become more repressive (linkage "k"). Acceptance of SAA conditions requires that decision-makers in loan-recipient countries enact unpopular policies. These policies cause hardships, especially among the poorest citizens, who are most dependent upon social programs (Vreeland 2002).

Citizens, often led by organized labor, protest against reductions in social welfare programs and public employment, commonly required in structural adjustment agreements (Pion-Berlin 1983; 1984; 1989; 1997; 2001). Sometimes the protests become violent (Auyero 2001; Fields 2003). The adjustment process also has intensified regional and ethnic conflicts as groups compete for a "dwindling share of the national cake" (Zack-Williams 2000: 64). Increased repression (linkage "k") by the recipient government is one tool by which it can deal with violent protest (Davenport 1995; Fields 2003).

However, it is important to distinguish incremental economic liberalization that results from a societal choice without undue external interference and pressure from the kind of rapid economic liberalization required by SAA conditionality. Economic liberalization that is not required by the conditions found within an SAA may not affect or may actually reduce civil conflict in societies. For example, Hegre, Gissinger, and Gleditsch (2003) examine the impact of economic liberalization and find no discernible impact on the probability of civil conflict.

---

[11] There is a large body of literature from a dependency theory perspective arguing that rapid economic liberalization can worsen government human rights practices. For an excellent review of this literature, see Richards, Gelleny, and Sacko (2001).

Other critics of structural adjustment would like the Bank and IMF to give greater attention to the impacts of SAAs on issues such as democratic development (Pion-Berlin 1984; Stiglitz 2002). Increased civil conflict caused by the implementation of SAAs presents serious challenges to democratic systems (linkage "l"). Also, as indicated by linkage "m," requiring democracies to enact unpopular policies, the Bank and Fund may be undermining democratic systems (Fields 2003; Haggard 1995). The positive relationship between a state's level of democracy and its respect for all types of human rights (linkage "n"), as noted above, is well established in the literature. Any policy that undermines democracy, undermines government respect for human rights.

Many scholars have examined the link between structural adjustment policies and economic growth using all of the approaches described above, and the weight of the evidence so far is that structural adjustment is not effective (Harrigan and Mosley 1991; Przeworski and Vreeland 2000; Rapley 1996; Van de Walle 2001; Vreeland 2003). This was the finding of two studies that corrected for the effects of selection (Przeworski and Vreeland 2000; Vreeland 2003). According to critics, the Fund and Bank use a conception of development that is too focused on economic growth, have misdiagnosed the obstacles to development in less developed countries, have failed to appreciate the value of government interventions into the private economy, and have insisted that structural adjustment reforms be implemented too quickly (Stiglitz 2002). It is possible that developing countries like China have been more successful, in terms of both aggregate economic growth and poverty reduction, because they have avoided SAAs financed by the IMF and World Bank. Unlike Russia, which has received a number of SAAs, China has avoided a rapid increase in economic inequality (Stiglitz 2002).

The policy debate: structural adjustment critics and defenders

The debate in the policy community about the propriety and consequences of structural adjustment was briefly described in Chapter 1. Kenneth Rogoff, economic counselor and Director of the research department at the International Monetary Fund, has defended its role in the economies of developing countries (Rogoff 2003). He identified and rebutted four common criticisms that have been directed at both the IMF and the World Bank structural adjustment programs. The first is that these institutions impose harsh fiscal austerity measures. The second is that they encourage financiers to invest recklessly, knowing the Fund will bail them out. The third is that the advice the IMF gives to countries in economic difficulty only makes matters worse. The fourth is that the Fund has irresponsibly pushed countries to liberalize their capital markets exposing themselves to volatile flows of capital. The first, third, and fourth arguments are relevant to our discussion about the consequences of these programs on the economic, social, and physical integrity rights of citizens in liberalizing countries.

The austerity myth

The first criticism concerns what is called the austerity myth (Rogoff 2003: 40). He notes that "developing countries don't seek IMF financial assistance when the sun is shining; they come when they have already run into deep financial difficulties" (Rogoff 2003: 40). Previous research has demonstrated that governments seek loans from these institutions under a variety of conditions: mostly when they are in economic difficulty, but also when they are not (Abouharb 2005; Vreeland 2003). Furthermore, in about 28 percent of cases governments in economic difficulty choose not to enter into a structural adjustment agreement because the conditions attached to a potential loan are too tough for the government negotiating the agreement (Vreeland 2003). Rogoff (2003: 40) continues that structural adjustment loans allow a government to "tighten their belt less than it would have to otherwise." Indeed, his argument is that these governments would have had to make these cuts anyway because of their budget constraints (Rogoff 2003: 41).

Considerable evidence exists that these programs require governments to cut back on their spending more than other governments also in economic difficulty, but not under structural adjustment conditions, because of the World Bank and IMF's attachment to a neoliberal policy perspective (Abouharb and Cingranelli 2006; Mosley, Harrigan, and Toye 1995; Stiglitz 2002; Vreeland 2003). These criticisms hold even if we account for the fact that the countries which go under structural adjustment programs represent a non-random sample of all countries which could enter into structural adjustment agreements (Abouharb and Cingranelli 2004a; 2005; 2006; Joyce 1992; Przeworski and Vreeland 2000; Vreeland 2002; 2003).

For example, countries in economic difficulty and authoritarian governments are more likely to enter into structural adjustment agreements (Abouharb and Cingranelli 2004a; 2006; Przeworski and Vreeland 2000; Vreeland 2003). Governments in economic difficulty tend to spend less on public services, while research indicates that autocratic governments have less concern for the economic welfare of their citizens

(Bueno de Mesquita *et al.* 2003; Navia and Zweifel 2003; Zweifel and Navia 2000). Even when such factors are accounted for, the consequences of these structural adjustment policies are negative for broad swathes of the public in developing countries under these programs (Abouharb and Cingranelli 2006; Przeworski and Vreeland 2000; Vreeland 2002; 2003).

Making matters worse: bad advice

The third, and related, criticism is that these institutions worsen matters through the advice they give to countries already in economic difficulty. Rogoff (2003: 42–43) discusses the limited options that less developed countries have in their policy choices about promoting economic growth during times of difficulty. There is considerable debate over the prudence of fiscal expansion, through increased government spending based upon the idea of deficit financing, where the government borrows to promote continued economic growth, rather than working within existing budget constraints (Rapley 1996; Stiglitz 2002; Vreeland 2003). Rogoff avoids discussion of criticisms that the IMF has, in many cases, micromanaged the policy choices made by less developed countries (Stiglitz 2002). For those countries in economic difficulty, the concept of advice seems disingenuous when the Bank and Fund can threaten to withdraw financial assistance if these countries do not heed such guidance (Mosley, Harrigan, and Toye 1995; Stiglitz 2002). Moreover, the advice given by these institutions stems from a neoliberal economic perspective that influences what factors are considered important in the promotion of a sustainable economic policy and also what options are given to governments, during the period when they implement these structural adjustment conditions (Stiglitz 2002).

Forced capital account liberalization

The fourth criticism is that the IMF has pushed governments to open their economies to destabilizing capital flows (Rogoff 2003: 40). Indeed, Rogoff (2003: 45) argues that liberalized capital markets are the long-term goal of many countries as a means to enable continued inward investment. Yet, it is the demand of the IMF that developing countries *rapidly* liberalize their capital accounts (the mechanism which permits flows of capital both into and out of countries) that has drawn much criticism (Stiglitz 2002). While industrialized countries long protected their domestic capital markets only beginning to slowly liberalize their economies in the 1970s, the IMF has pressured developing countries to liberalize their economies much more quickly, removing controls on the flow of what is called "hot money." This hot money or speculative capital flows to countries where profits can be made quickly, sometimes literally overnight, and where this capital can be withdrawn at a moment's notice. From the neoliberal perspective, capital account liberalization is meant to encourage inward investment. However, these hot-flows of money are, by definition, not invested into industrial plants and other types of infrastructure projects (Stiglitz 2002: 66). Indeed, China is the largest recipient of foreign investment, but has long had a policy which limited the openness of its capital markets (Stiglitz 2002: 66). Capital account liberalization also is meant to promote economic stability by increasing the range of funding sources which governments can draw upon in times of economic difficulty. Governments would be able to summon funds from outside sources to make up for domestic shortfalls.

However, research indicates that investment money does not flow into countries in economic difficulty, rather money is withdrawn and sent out to more secure locations (Green 1972; Quinn and Woolley 2001; Stiglitz 2002). In fact, rather than improving the situation, these agreements have worsened the economic situation within countries under these programs. They have both lowered levels of economic growth and generated higher levels of income inequality within states by shifting wealth from the poor to sections of the elite (Przeworski and Vreeland 2000; Stiglitz 2002; Vreeland 2002; 2003), making subsequent improvement in economic development more difficult.

Conclusions

The theory that structural adjustment policies promote export-led economic growth and generate higher levels of economic development based upon limited government and free markets has been critiqued on theoretical grounds. The similarities between the workings of industrialized and developing economies have been overstated. The applicability of economically based rational-choice approaches to the actions of people living in developing economies has been overstated. Greater inequality, a consequence of unfettered free-market competition, has detrimental consequences on the prospects of future economic development. Finally, all markets do not arise spontaneously. Government assistance is needed if they are to be promoted and maintained.[12]

---

[12] For instance, during the 1980s and 1990s, 40 percent to 50 percent of budget cuts in sub-Saharan Africa were achieved through sacrificing infrastructure investment. The World Bank expected that the private sector would enter the liberalized infrastructure

Neoliberal approaches to structural adjustment have also been critiqued on empirical grounds, which indicate that these programs have had a negative impact on economic growth and development. The neoliberal perspective would indicate that the theory of structural adjustment should have both direct and indirect effects improving levels of human rights through limited government and increased levels of wealth generation. The evidence about the negative macroeconomic consequences of structural adjustment in most of the countries under these programs leads us to suspect that the weight of the evidence thus far supports the more critical perspective.

market. However, that never happened to a meaningful extent – leaving Africa as well as Latin America with decrepit infrastructure (Alexander 2001).

Part II

Estimating the human rights effects
of structural adjustment

4   Methods

Introduction

Based on the critiques of structural adjustment programs described in Chapter 3, the weight of most case study findings, and the findings of the highest-quality large-n comparative studies, our main hypothesis was that, other things being equal, the more years a developing country had been under structural adjustment the worse its government's respect for most human rights. In addition, consistent with the critical perspective presented in the previous chapter, we expected to find that greater exposure to structural adjustment conditions would be associated with more civil conflict, especially violent civil conflict.

In this chapter we examine a number of issues that recur throughout the rest of the book. We describe the importance of studying both the World Bank and IMF if one is interested in estimating the impact of structural adjustment. We explain the importance of controlling for the effects of selection. We also discuss how we measured structural adjustment receipt and implementation: two of the key variables used. Part of the chapter discusses the use of the CIRI data set which provides the source of many of the dependent variables used in the analyses (Cingranelli and Richards 2006). Finally, some of the control variables common to several of the chapters are described.

Why study both the World Bank and International Monetary Fund?

Both institutions promote structural adjustment policies, yet the great majority of existing research has concentrated on one institution. If we are trying to understand the consequences of structural adjustment, examining one institution to the exclusion of the other will most likely underestimate the consequences of these programs, since most countries enter into and implement structural adjustment agreements (SAAs) with both the World Bank and International Monetary Fund. Both are important actors. Over the period examined in this study, the World Bank entered into 442 structural adjustment agreements, while the IMF made 431. Studying both institutions is the first refinement we make in our research design when assessing the impact of structural adjustment. The second concerns the importance of controlling for issues of selection when trying to estimate the consequences of these policies. We build upon previous research that has discussed the selection criteria of the World Bank and IMF and the need to address these concerns when estimating the impact of these agreements on the human rights practices of loan-recipient countries (Abouharb and Cingranelli 2004a; 2005; 2006).

Previous research: assessing the impact of structural adjustment on economic growth and development

Previous research has utilized a variety of approaches to assess the macroeconomic consequences of these programs. What has become important in the debate about whether these programs have been beneficial or detrimental is how one actually assesses the consequences of any public policy. This is where the application of a social science framework is critical to understanding the consequences of any policy choice that is made. As our understanding and application of social science frameworks to the topic of public policy outcomes become more sophisticated it is important to examine the validity of previous research given our new knowledge of best practice in these situations. The approaches taken by previous research examining the consequences of structural adjustment fall into four broad categories: planned target method; before and after; with and without, and controlling for issues of selection.

Planned target method

This method was an early approach used by the World Bank and IMF to assess the effectiveness of their programs. The "planned target" method compares what was expected to happen during the period and what actually happened (Mosley, Harrigan, and Toye 1995: 189). This method, however, suffers from a number of limitations. Some have argued that World Bank targets are "optimistic guesses ... and cannot predict exogenous events bearing on the economic outcomes" (Mosley, Harrigan, and Toye 1995: 189). Thus, if a country under-performs economically this may be erroneously attributed to a fault in the design of the program or in its implementation. In fact an under-performing economy may have nothing to do with the design of the program or its implementation. It may be that the indicators examined do not reflect the effects of the program but instead some exogenous factor (Mosley, Harrigan, and Toye 1995: 189).

Before and after approach

This approach compares the situation in a loan-recipient state before and after it enters into an agreement. Any change in outcomes of interest is attributed to the loan agreement. Previous research examining the consequences of structural adjustment agreements has taken this approach (Chipeta 1993; Commonwealth Secretariat 1989; Handa and King 1997; Kane 1993; Pastor 1987a; 1987b; Sadasivam 1997; Sowa 1993; Vuorela 1991). The findings across these approaches have been uniformly negative, indicating that the consequences of structural adjustment have had a variety of negative economic effects lowering economic growth, lowering government spending in areas of health and education, lowering personal income, increasing income inequality, reducing protections for workers, and having detrimental economic and social effects on women.

While this approach is intuitive it cannot control for the counter-factual: what would have happened if the country had not gone under a program? A number of authors have noted that a key problem with this approach is that other factors outside of the program that also affect, for example, economic growth, may change over the period under exam-ination (Mosley, Harrigan, and Toye 1995; Vreeland 2003). Thus, if the situation has improved or worsened in comparison to the time before the countries implemented these programs then one may conclude (incor-rectly) that the change in situation is simply due to the imposition of structural adjustment agreements (Mosley, Harrigan, and Toye 1995: 190). However, this is an inappropriate conclusion because there may well be a myriad of other factors that effect this change (Harrigan and Mosley 1991: 65). Each of these critiques calls for an approach that includes a counterfactual: a counter example of what would have hap-pened had a country not undertaken a structural adjustment agreement from these institutions.

With and without approach

A third approach which is also intuitive is to use a counterfactual method which explicitly attempts to assess what would have happened in these countries had they not entered into structural adjustment agreements. A number of different procedures have been undertaken utilizing counterfactual econometric simulations and most similar system designs which paired similar countries that did and did not enter into these agreements and then compared the levels of economic growth across them (Dorosh, Essama-Nssah, and Samba-Manadou 1996; Frausum and Sahn 1996; Gylfason 1987; Harrigan and Mosley 1991; Mosley, Harrigan, and Toye 1995; Sahn 1996). The findings of this approach have varied from indicating that structural adjustment programs have had no effects, to marginal macroeconomic effects. In many cases, the findings are sensitive to small changes in the samples of cases used.

The most similar systems design has attracted concern (King, Keohane, and Verba 1994; Przeworski and Tuene 1970) because of the difficulty in being able to control for all factors that may have a subsequent impact on, in this case, economic growth. Nevertheless, the idea of controlling for other factors associated with economic growth as an attempt to tease out the impact of structural adjustment agreements by comparing cases where similar countries did and did not enter into them does control for the impacts of the world economy. The limitation to this approach is that there may be systematic differences between countries that enter into these programs and others that do not. Many of the factors that make countries good candidates for structural adjustment such as economic difficulty are also likely to have an effect on the subsequent success of any agreement. For example, it is possible that a country's economic growth would have declined regardless of a structural adjustment agreement because it was already in economic difficulty. Indeed, a structural adjustment package may actually have made that drop in growth smaller than it would have otherwise been. The problem of course is that without controlling for the factors that affect whether countries enter into these agreements it is difficult to conclude whether the consequences witnessed were a function of structural adjustment or would have taken place anyway.

Controlling for issues of selection

A number of studies have approached discerning the (mostly) economic effects of structural adjustment by controlling for issues of selection (Abouharb and Cingranelli 2004a; 2004b; 2005; 2006; Conway 1994; Khan, Montie, and Haque 1990; Przeworski and Vreeland 2000; Vreeland 2003). The concept of selection refers to the idea that there are a variety of factors which make countries candidates for structural adjustment agreements, such as being in economic difficulty, especially issues like shortfalls in foreign currency reserves, which are also important factors in affecting the macroeconomic conditions conducive to economic growth. These reserves are necessary for the continued purchase of key goods and services that may be important for the maintenance of economic growth and development. The findings of this research have described the consequences of these programs on economic growth as negative.

Estimating the selection-corrected human rights effects of structural adjustment requires the use of a two-stage econometric model. As explained by Achen (1986), Heckman (1988), Przeworski and Vreeland (2000), and Vreeland (2002; 2003), issues of endogeneity, selection, and randomization must be accounted for when assessing the impact of any public policy. One needs to disentangle the impacts of the policy from any prior attributes that may also have an impact (Collier 1991). In the context of the present research, one must be able to distinguish whether the negative effects on the human rights practices of governments found by previous research (Franklin 1997; Keith and Poe 2000; McLaren 1998) were the result of the economic difficulties that made the loan-recipient country a good candidate for a structural adjustment agreement in the first place or were the consequence of the SAA itself.[1] Single-stage models cannot provide an answer to that question.

Methods used and not used in this study

There are a variety of two-stage models that allow the researcher to correct for issues of selection. Nevertheless not all of these models are appropriate given the nature of the relationships in question or the structure of the data under examination. The nature of the relationship between receipt of a structural adjustment agreement and government respect for the different human rights is described in the econometric literature as "fully observed." In our case this means that whether and to what extent a government respects the human rights of its citizens[2] will take place regardless of whether or not the country enters into a structural adjustment agreement. We can all think of countries that did not enter structural adjustment agreements where human rights violations take place. All these cases highlight the nature of a fully observed relationship.

---

[1] See also Blanton (2000; 2005) who uses two-stage econometric models when examining other human rights issues.

[2] All two-stage relationships discussed here also apply to domestic instability relationships explored in Chapter 7.

In comparison, an example of a partially observed relationship would be one where the dependent variable in the second stage is conditional upon the occurrence of the dependent variable in the first stage. For example, countries must first enter into a war before they can subsequently win or lose them. Scholars in the international relations literature have explored these questions (e.g., Clark and Reed 2003). Government respect for human rights is not conditional on entering into a structural adjustment agreement. The methodological consequences of a fully observed rather than partially observed relationship mean that Heckman-style selection models where the dependent variable in the second stage is conditional on the existence of the dependent variable in the first stage (for example, as mentioned above, winning a war is conditional upon entering into one) are not present in the relationships we are examining. For these reasons we do not use a Heckman approach. Our theoretical arguments suggest that the processes of accepting a structural adjustment program and the subsequent impacts on government respect for human rights are linked, but in a fully observed manner. The limitation is that given the structure of our data, explored in more detail below, to our knowledge there were no existing fully observed two-stage models that could accommodate the need to link these processes while also allowing us to accurately estimate the relationships under examination. For this reason we undertook a two-step approach. We first estimated the initiation of a structural adjustment program and linked the second-stage equations predicting government respect for human rights by generating predicted probabilities from the equation predicting structural adjustment receipt and adding them into the second-stage equations as our "selection effects" variable. The structure of the dependent variables means that some estimation processes were more appropriate than others and are explored in more detail below.

Negotiation of a structural adjustment agreement is a dichotomous dependent variable, meaning that logit or probit is the most appropriate method. The measure of government respect for physical integrity rights is an index which sums respect for freedom from political imprisonment, torture, extrajudicial killing, and disappearance into a nine-point scale from 0 to 8, while the institutionalized democracy measure is the 0–10 POLITY democracy variable. The relatively large number of categories led us to decide upon ordinary least squares regression. Likewise the measure of respect for economic rights is the physical quality of life index and is on a 0–100 ratio scale; again we chose ordinary least squares regression as the most appropriate estimator for this dependent variable. The other human rights variables – government respect for worker rights, freedom of speech, assembly and association, and free and fair elections – are on a three-point ordinal scale. The ordered nature of these variables means ordered logit is the most appropriate method of estimation for these dependent variables. Finally, the event count structure of the domestic instability measures – riots, demonstrations, rebellion[3] – make an event count model the most appropriate. We chose to use the negative binomial regression model because it accounts for the possibility that the occurrence of domestic instability has a subsequent impact on future instability, which has been found in the literature.

Depending on the structure of the dependent variable, we have two approaches to control for the issues of temporal dependence. Where the dependent variable is dichotomous we follow the approach taken by Beck, Katz, and Tucker (1998) to account for issues of temporal dependence through the use of cubic splines. This approach is used in each of the models used throughout the book where the dependent variable is dichotomous: each model examining when governments enter into structural adjustment agreements with either the World Bank or IMF, or both institutions, and the impact of structural adjustment on the incidence of civil conflict. Where the dependent variable is not dichotomous we generate a one-year lagged dependent variable to account for issues of temporal dependence. In addition to controlling for issues of selection and using a variety of econometric models, another advantage of the approach taken is the breadth and temporal coverage of the sample used.

The countries included in this study

We examined 131 developing economies in the 1981–2003 period. We excluded 23 wealthy OECD countries, since they were not candidates for structural adjustment agreements. We also excluded 25 countries that achieved international recognition as independent countries after our period of study began (e.g., the former member states of the Soviet Union) and some that ceased to exist sometime between 1981 and 2003 (e.g., Czechoslovakia and North Yemen). Since we are interested in measuring the impact of spending greater time under structural adjustment conditionality it is important to only include developing countries that have been in existence for the entire period of the study. This choice is based on our assessment of the fairest way to assess the

---

[3] The exception concerns the model which estimates the impact of entering into a structural adjustment agreement on the probability of a rebellion.

implementation of structural adjustment and is explained below. Over the period of our study, some countries, like China, had little exposure to structural adjustment conditionality. Others have been operating their economies under structural adjustment conditions for nearly the whole period of the study. To illustrate this point, we placed each of the 131 developing economies included in our study into one of four quartile groups based on the number of years since 1981 that each had operated under a structural adjustment agreement negotiated with the IMF, the World Bank, or both.

Tables 4.1 and 4.2 list the four groupings of countries. Thirty of the countries in the first group have had no experience with structural adjustment or just one year of experience between 1981 and 2004. One country in this group had one year of exposure (Paraguay). Another three had two years (Cyprus, Myanmar, and South Africa). More than a third of the developing countries with the least exposure to structural adjustment during this period were in the Middle East. Though most Middle Eastern countries have large populations of poor people, they have been rich enough to avoid accumulating large debts and, as oil exporters, have maintained substantial flows of international trade. Island states of the Pacific with small populations were also over-represented among those states with little structural adjustment experience. As we will show in Chapter 5, governments with little debt, substantial involvement in international trade, and small populations are least likely to enter into structural adjustment agreements with the Bank and Fund.

Countries in the second column of Table 4.1 had between three and eleven years of experience under structural adjustment between 1981 and 2004. China is in this second group, because it had seven years of structural adjustment experience. Russia is also in this group, though, technically, it could have been excluded, because it did not exist in its present geographic form throughout the entire period. We include it anyway as the successor country to the former Soviet Union. Countries listed in the first column of Table 4.2 had between twelve and sixteen years of experience with structural adjustment during the period of our study. Serbia and Montenegro is also included in this group as the successor to the former Yugoslavia. Countries in the fourth group had seventeen years of experience or more operating under structural adjustment conditionality between 1981 and 2004. Many types of developing countries are in this last group. They are not just the "basket-cases" where one might expect high levels of civil conflict and low levels of respect for human rights.

Table 4.1. *Countries included in this study grouped by number of years under structural adjustment between 1981–2004, the low and medium-low quartiles*

0–2 years	Years under	3–11 years	Years under
Afghanistan	0	Algeria	11
Angola	0	Barbados	5
Antigua & Barbuda	0	Belize	3
Bahamas	0	Burundi	9
Bahrain	0	Cambodia	10
Bhutan	0	Cape Verde	5
Botswana	0	Chile	9
Cuba	0	China	7
Cyprus	2	Colombia	11
Fiji	0	Comoros	4
Iran	0	Democratic Republic of the Congo	11
Iraq	0	Djibouti	8
Israel	0	Dominica	10
Kuwait	0	Dominican Republic	8
Lebanon	0	Ethiopia	11
Libya	0	Grenada	5
Maldives	0	India	9
Malta	0	Indonesia	10
Myanmar	2	Liberia	7
Oman	0	Malaysia	3
Paraguay	1	Nepal	11
Qatar	0	Nigeria	10
St. Lucia	0	North Korea	4
St. Vincent & Grenadines	0	Russia	10
Saudi Arabia	0	Rwanda	11
Seychelles	0	Samoa	4
Singapore	0	Sao Tome and Principe	8
South Africa	2	Solomon Islands	4
Suriname	0	Sudan	7
Swaziland	0	Thailand	10
Syria	0	Trinidad and Tobago	5
United Arab Emirates	0	Venezuela	8
Vanuatu	0	Vietnam	11

Describing structural adjustment receipt and implementation

Entering into a World Bank or IMF structural adjustment agreement is a dependent variable. It is a dichotomous measure that indicates whether a country received a World Bank or IMF structural adjustment agreement or not in a particular year. It is coded "1" for the years an agreement was

Table 4.2. *Countries included in this study grouped by number of years under structural adjustment between 1981–2004, the medium-high and high quartiles*

12–16 years	Years under	17–24 years	Years under
Albania	12	Argentina	21
Bangladesh	14	Bolivia	21
Benin	13	Central African Republic	20
Brazil	14	Costa Rica	18
Bulgaria	13	Ecuador	19
Burkina Faso	13	Gabon	19
Cameroon	14	Gambia	17
Chad	16	Ghana	19
Congo	14	Guinea	20
Egypt	12	Guyana	18
El Salvador	15	Honduras	17
Equatorial Guinea	12	Hungary	17
Guatemala	14	Ivory Coast	22
Guinea-Bissau	14	Jamaica	19
Haiti	16	Kenya	23
Jordan	14	Madagascar	21
Laos	16	Malawi	23
Lesotho	13	Mali	22
Mauritius	12	Mauritania	22
Mongolia	13	Mexico	17
Nicaragua	15	Morocco	18
Papua New Guinea	12	Mozambique	17
Peru	16	Niger	18
Poland	13	Pakistan	21
Serbia and Montenegro	13	Panama	22
Somalia	13	Philippines	22
South Korea	12	Romania	17
Sri Lanka	15	Senegal	24
Tunisia	14	Sierra Leone	18
Turkey	13	Tanzania	23
Zimbabwe	14	Togo	20
		Uganda	22
		Uruguay	22
		Zambia	19

made and "0" for all other years. The authors gathered the information necessary for constructing this measure from correspondence with officials at the World Bank and, for the IMF data, Jim Vreeland (2003).

The measure of implementation of a World Bank and IMF structural adjustment agreement, an independent variable in the second stage of all the other models used in the book, was generated by the authors. We combined information that we had collected about when governments enter into World Bank structural adjustment agreements together with Jim Vreeland's (2003) data examining when governments enter into IMF structural adjustment agreements. We updated Vreeland's data to 2004 by reading the IMF Annual Report which publishes information about which countries entered into IMF structural adjustment agreements in a particular year. Each year a country entered into a structural adjustment agreement with either institution is coded "1" – and "0" otherwise.

Our measure of number of years under structural adjustment was coded in two stages. Our reading of studies about the impact of structural adjustment conditionality suggests that these programs often do not have an effect on the economies of loan-recipient countries until about eighteen months after loan receipt. The average length of these programs was three years; we coded years two, three, and four after a country received a loan from the World Bank or IMF as being under conditionality. Years two, three, and four were coded "1" – and "0" otherwise. We generated the number of years under structural adjustment, which provides a running count of the time countries have been under these programs, by summing each additional year in a new column of data. Table 4.3 provides an illustration of how we generated both the receipt and implementation measures of structural adjustment used throughout the book.

Table 4.3 describes the years Benin entered into World Bank and IMF structural adjustment agreements. The columns labeled "World Bank structural adjustment receipt" and "IMF structural adjustment receipt" indicate the years Benin entered into an SAA with each institution. The next column, "Joint structural adjustment receipt," collates these two indicators into one column and is coded "1" each time a country entered into an SAA with either institution. The column "Joint implementation" reflects our coding rules: years two, three, and four after structural adjustment receipt are coded "1" to indicate when a country, in this case Benin, was under structural adjustment conditions from either institution. Finally, our running count of the numbers of years under structural adjustment is generated in the last column. In this example Benin had been under structural adjustment conditionality between 1990 and 1999 and then again between 2002 and 2004. Thus the number of years under in 2004 is a steady count that increases each year joint implementation took place. Since Benin had implemented between 1990 and 1999, resuming again in 2002, the count stopped at ten in 1999 until 2002. Then it increased to thirteen by 2004.

As an additional example Table 4.4 describes the years Dominica entered into World Bank and IMF structural adjustment agreements. The columns are labeled as before. In this example Dominica entered

Table 4.3. *Illustrative case: World Bank and IMF structural adjustment receipt and implementation, Benin 1981–2004*

Year	World Bank structural adjustment receipt	IMF structural adjustment receipt	Joint structural adjustment receipt	Joint implementation	Joint number of years under structural adjustment conditionality
1981	0	0	0	0	0
1982	0	0	0	0	0
1983	0	0	0	0	0
1984	0	0	0	0	0
1985	0	0	0	0	0
1986	0	0	0	0	0
1987	0	0	0	0	0
1988	0	0	0	0	0
1989	1	1	1	0	0
1990	0	0	0	1	1
1991	1	0	1	1	2
1992	0	0	0	1	3
1993	0	1	1	1	4
1994	0	0	0	1	5
1995	1	0	1	1	6
1996	0	1	1	1	7
1997	0	0	0	1	8
1998	0	0	0	1	9
1999	0	0	0	1	10
2000	0	0	0	0	10
2001	1	0	1	0	10
2002	0	0	0	1	11
2003	0	0	0	1	12
2004	0	0	0	1	13

into its first structural adjustment agreement in our sample with the IMF in 1981, entering into its second in 1984, and third in 1986. We code conditionality beginning the year after receipt and lasting for three years, indicated by the joint implementation column. After receipt and implementation of its third IMF agreement, Dominica had been implementing structural adjustment agreements for eight years as of 1990. For the period 1990–2002 Dominica does not receive any additional structural adjustment agreements, and the number of years the country has been implementing remains at eight for that entire period. In 2002 Dominica entered into a fourth structural adjustment agreement, this time with the World Bank. The number of years under conditionality increases in 2003 to nine years and 2004 to ten.

Table 4.4. *Illustrative case: World Bank and IMF structural adjustment receipt and implementation, Dominica 1981–2004*

Year	World Bank structural adjustment receipt	IMF structural adjustment receipt	Joint structural adjustment receipt	Joint implementation	Joint number of years under structural adjustment conditionality
1981	0	1	1	0	0
1982	0	0	0	1	1
1983	0	0	0	1	2
1984	0	1	1	1	3
1985	0	0	0	1	4
1986	0	1	1	1	5
1987	0	0	0	1	6
1988	0	0	0	1	7
1989	0	0	0	1	8
1990	0	0	0	0	8
1991	0	0	0	0	8
1992	0	0	0	0	8
1993	0	0	0	0	8
1994	0	0	0	0	8
1995	0	0	0	0	8
1996	0	0	0	0	8
1997	0	0	0	0	8
1998	0	0	0	0	8
1999	0	0	0	0	8
2000	0	0	0	0	8
2001	0	0	0	0	8
2002	1	0	1	0	8
2003	0	0	0	1	9
2004	0	0	0	1	10

Our coding then is slightly different to that of Vreeland's about when countries are actually under conditionality since his measures of conditionality begin with the years countries enter into structural adjustment agreements. Nevertheless we are convinced that this slight difference has little substantive impact on the findings, which have proven to be extraordinarily robust to removal or addition of different control variables in other work (Abouharb and Cingranelli 2004a; 2005; 2006). Indeed, other work that we have undertaken separately on the impact of the World Bank (Abouharb and Cingranelli 2006) and IMF (Abouharb and Cingranelli 2004b) – examining just the periods governments had been under structural adjustment conditionality, rather than the cumulative effect of these programs on government respect for physical integrity rights – mirrors that presented later in the book. In each case governments under structural adjustment conditionality had worsened levels of respect for the physical integrity rights of their citizens.

We are interested in the cumulative effect of structural adjustment. Proponents of structural adjustment argue that these programs enact the necessary reforms to generate high-quality economic growth or what we have described as equitable economic growth. If this is true then those countries that have restructured their economies the most should have fared the best. Their economies will have removed more of the barriers to economic growth than those that restructured little. From this perspective the approach we take is a conservative one that provides a best-case scenario for defenders of these programs, especially since many of the neoliberal defenders of structural adjustment argue that the first few years a country undertakes these programs will necessitate difficult choices which mean things will be tough for a while. However, after this period of adjustment the economy will benefit and economic growth will be generated. The expectation is that the greater the periods of time these countries have been liberalizing their economies the more beneficial will be the outcome of structural adjustment.

Do the governments that receive structural adjustment loans really implement them?

Our determination of whether a government implemented a structural adjustment loan was automatic. If a government received a loan, we assumed that implementation began the following calendar year. Since the average length of these programs was three years, we coded years two, three, and four after a country received a loan from the World Bank as being years when structural adjustment agreements were being implemented. As described above, this measurement procedure is similar to the one followed by Przeworski and Vreeland (2000) and by Vreeland (2003) and by others who have conducted global, comparative research concerning the effectiveness of structural adjustment policies.

However, this measurement strategy ignores the argument that many developing countries have not implemented the conditions associated with their structural adjustment agreements (Dollar and Svensson 2000; Eiras 2003; Van de Walle 2001). Research sponsored by the Heritage Foundation showed that the countries that received the most funds from the World Bank and IMF still had not fully liberalized their economies (Eiras 2003). The study also shows that countries with more liberal economies had higher per capita incomes (Eiras 2003). There are good reasons to doubt these claims. Countries with the highest per capita incomes such as the United States or Finland are not the most liberalized. They retain a substantial role for the state in their economies. Also, the Heritage Foundation's own data seem to show that countries must get beyond a certain threshold level of liberalization before they receive any benefits from it as measured by income per capita. Most developing economies have not reached that threshold. Thus, it may be that the world's developing economies are caught in a trap. They may be liberalizing, and the poor may be paying the costs, but their societies, on average, may not be reaping the benefits of increased aggregate wealth, because they have not liberalized enough.

An ideal test of the main hypothesis of this study would measure the degree to which the provisions of structural adjustment agreements were implemented for each country year of the study. That would require that the investigator know the provisions of each structural adjustment for each country for each year. It would also require that the investigator know which of those provisions were implemented and to what extent for each year. This might be possible for single-country studies or even a study of a few countries, but it would require tremendous resources to collect such information for all developing countries annually for a long time period.

In his study of structural adjustment in Africa, Van de Walle (2001) illustrated the difficulty of assessing the degree of implementation even for a region. He identified several different common provisions in structural adjustment agreements, which he divided into two main categories – stabilization and adjustment. Ten economic policies were classified as being part of each main category. He then evaluated the degree to which each of the ten policies had been implemented, on average, for all countries in Africa between 1979–1999 (Van de Walle 2001: 90). He did not attempt to do this for each country in the region for each year of his study. Except for civil service reform, where he rated the degree of implementation as "poor," he concluded that every policy had been implemented to some extent even in Africa, where the average quality of governance is poor.

The question then becomes "how much implementation is required before we agree that the agreement was implemented?" Killick (1996) has conducted the most thorough and comprehensive studies of implementation of structural adjustment programs. He defined a structural adjustment program as incomplete if a country had implemented less than 81 percent of its program conditions. He surveyed 305 IMF agreements in less developed countries, and found that 53 percent had not been completed during the loan period. Though both Van de Walle and Killick criticize developing countries for not fully implementing the provisions of their structural adjustment agreements, both provide ample evidence that the governments of most less developed countries implement many, if not most, of the provisions of their agreements. Many specific examples are included throughout this book of specific provisions, their implementation, and public reactions. Essentially, we assume that the longer a country has been under structural adjustment, the more structural adjustment provisions have been implemented.

Measuring the human rights practices of governments

This research would not have been possible without the availability of a new data set measuring government respect for a broad array of human rights in every country in the world annually from 1981 to the present. Now covering 24 years, 13 separate human rights practices, and 195 countries, the CIRI Human Rights Data Set is the largest human rights data set in the world. It contains standards-based measures of the human rights practices of governments around the world. Standards-based human rights measures are produced by having trained coders use a carefully constructed measurement scheme (a set of a priori-determined standards which provide a yardstick against which to compare human rights behaviors) to assign score values to countries, based on the coders' reading of certain source materials (Cingranelli and Richards 2006).

The CIRI Human Rights Data Set includes measures of many human rights recognized in the 1948 Universal Declaration of Human Rights. Activists, scholars, and policy-makers need a human rights profile for countries around the world that better reflects the range of human rights recognized in the Universal Declaration. Existing annual reports by Amnesty International and Human Rights Watch strongly emphasize physical integrity rights (the rights not to be tortured, imprisoned for political reasons, disappeared, or extrajudicially killed). Their selectivity means that their reports are not fair to countries that are weak in their protection of these rights but stronger in their efforts to protect economic, social, and cultural rights (e.g., China). The CIRI data set already is much more comprehensive than any other data set on government human rights practices. It already presents a fuller picture of each country's strengths and weaknesses than any other human rights data set now available.

The sources of information used to develop this data set were the annual *US State Department Country Reports on Human Rights Practices* and Amnesty International annual reports. Human rights measurements prior to 1981 are not included in the CIRI data set because of criticisms of bias in the reporting by the US State Department in the 1970s. But there is widespread agreement that the reports since 1980 are objective and accurate (Innes 1992; Poe, Carey, and Vazquez 2001). The measures code the human rights practices of governments rather than their human rights laws.

It is useful to think of human rights policies and practices as early phases of a process leading to satisfactory human rights conditions. Human rights policies are statements of intent by governments to change or maintain the degree to which citizens can exercise various types of human rights. Citizens can exercise their human rights if they can use them without fear of reprisal by government officials or with confidence that, if they are interfered with by private actors, government officials will provide an effective remedy. Put simply, human rights policies are what governments say they are going to do to protect the human rights of their citizens. Such policies are contained in national statutes, executive orders, administrative rulings, and judicial decisions. The defining characteristic of human rights policies is that they direct agencies of the state to protect the human rights of citizens. Governments around the world vary in the number of economic and other human rights protected through government policies and the strength of protections promised for various rights.

Human rights practices refer to the efforts of government officials directly affecting the degree to which citizens can exercise various types of human rights. Practices refer to what efforts governments actually make, not what they promised to do. Human rights policies affect practices. A strong policy protecting a human right may be a necessary, but not a sufficient, condition for a strong government effort or, in other words, good human rights practices. India, for example, has a strong government policy against the use of bonded child labor, but actual government follow-through in implementing the policy is weak at best (Tucker 1997). Both strong government policies protecting economic and social human rights and significant government efforts to execute the policies are necessary conditions for achieving good human rights conditions. So it is not surprising that bonded child labor remains a significant problem in India today.

By "human rights conditions" we refer to the degree to which citizens actually can exercise various types of human rights. If human rights policies are easiest to change, human rights conditions are the hardest, because many things affect human rights conditions besides what governments say and do. Nongovernmental actors such as terrorists or revolutionaries may violate human rights, and, thereby, worsen human rights conditions in a country, contrary to government policies and practices. What we know from research in other areas of public policy is that social and economic outcomes result from many things besides the public policies and practices designed to change them. One way to think about the whole field of implementation theory and research is that it is designed to help us understand why policies fail. The most important explanations are the use of an inadequate theory of what factors cause outcomes of interest, lack of commitment by policy-makers and implementing officials, and a lack of adequate resources (Mazmanian and Sabatier 1989). We are interested in what governments do to promote and protect human rights, rather than what they promise to do, thus the CIRI data set (Cingranelli and Richards 2006) codes actual deeds rather than government intentions about the conditions of human rights in their countries.

Variables used in the analyses

Tables 4.5, 4.6, 4.7, and 4.8 describe the variables used in Chapters 5 through 10.

Table 4.5. *Operationalization of World Bank and IMF selection (first stage) equation variables*

	Indicator	Source
Dependent variable		
Entering into a World Bank or IMF SAA	Dichotomous "1" if SAA received, "0" if not	Correspondence with World Bank and Vreeland (2003)
Independent variables Economic		
Debt as a proportion of GNP	Total debt service as a percentage of GNP	World Bank: World Development Indicators CD-Rom (WDI)
GDP per capita change	Percentage change in GDP per capita current US$ Purchasing power parity (PPP)	World Bank: WDI
Foreign currency reserves	Average government foreign reserves to reflect monthly imports	World Bank: WDI

Table 4.5. (*cont.*)

	Indicator	Source
Exchange rate value	Average annual official exchange rate local currency unit per US$	World Bank: WDI
GDP per capita	GDP per capita current US$ (PPP)	World Bank: WDI
International trade	Trade as a percentage of GDP	World Bank: WDI
Political		
Alliance with the United States	Correlates of war (COW) alliance measure	COW alliance data set
Democracy	Democracy-autocracy measure	POLITY IV data set
Population size	Logged midyear country population	US census: international database
Cold War	Dichotomous, "0" before 1991, "1" if 1991 or later	Banks, Muller, and Overstreet (2003)
Conflict proneness		
Interstate conflict	0–3 ordinal scale of interstate conflict	Strand, Wilhelmsen, and Gleditsch (2005)
Rebellion	0–3 ordinal scale of civil conflict	Strand, Wilhelmsen, and Gleditsch (2005)
Human rights		
Respect for human rights	Mokken scale: Killing, disappearances, torture, imprisonment	Cingranelli and Richards (CIRI) (2004)
Respect for worker rights	0=not protected by govt. 1=somewhat protected by govt. 2=protected by govt.	CIRI (2004)
Temporal dependence		
Cubic splines		Beck, Katz, and Tucker (1998) BTSCS method

Table 4.6. *Operationalization of economic and social rights and worker rights practices (second stage) equation variables*

	Indicator	Source
Dependent variables		
Respect for worker rights	0=not protected by govt. 1=somewhat protected by govt. 2=protected by govt.	CIRI (2004)

Table 4.6. (*cont.*)

	Indicator	Source
Physical quality of life index	Ranges 0 low PQLI to 100 high PQLI: composite index ranges of infant mortality rate, life expectancy at age one, and the adult literacy rate	Callaway (2001). Updated with UN population data and World Bank: WDI
Independent variables		
Implementation of structural adjustment agreement (SAA)	Running count of years a country has been implementing SAAs	Correspondence with World Bank and Vreeland (2003), updated
Control variables Economic		
GDP per capita	GDP per capita current US$ (PPP)	World Bank: World Development Indicators CD-Rom (WDI)
Increase GDP per capita	Percentage increase in GDP per capita current US$ (PPP)	World Bank: WDI
Political		
Democracy	Democracy-autocracy measure	POLITY IV data set
Military regime	Type of regime: civilian or military	Banks (2002)
Population size	Logged midyear country population	US census: international database
Population change	Percentage change in yearly population (constructed)	US census: international database
UK dependent/ colonial experience	The decision rule of the most recent possessor is used to identify the relationships under examination	Issues COW colonial history data set
Conflict proneness		
Interstate conflict	0=no interstate conflict, 1=1,000 battle deaths or more	Strand, Wilhelmsen, and Gleditsch (2002)
Rebellion	Ordinal level of civil conflict	Strand, Wilhelmsen, and Gleditsch (2002)
Temporal dependence		
Cubic splines		Beck, Katz, and Tucker (1998) BTSCS method

Table 4.7. *Operationalization of physical integrity rights practices (second stage) equation variables*

	Indicator	Source
Dependent variables		
Disappearances	0=occasional or frequent, 1=none	Cingranelli and Richards (CIRI) (2004)
Killings	0=occasional or frequent, 1=none	CIRI (2004)
Torture	0=occasional or frequent, 1=none	CIRI (2004)
Political imprisonment	0=occasional or frequent, 1=none	CIRI (2004)
Independent variables		
Implementation of structural adjustment agreement (SAA)	Running count of years a country has been implementing SAAs	Correspondence with World Bank and Vreeland (2003), updated
Implementation of structural adjustment agreement	Dichotomous, "1" for the 3 years following SAA receipt and "0" otherwise (constructed)	Correspondence with World Bank
Entering into World Bank structural adjustment agreement	Dichotomous	Correspondence with World Bank
Control variables		
Economic		
GDP per capita	GDP per capita current US$ (PPP)	World Bank: World Development Indicators CD-Rom (WDI)
Increase GDP per capita	Percentage increase in GDP per capita current US$ (PPP)	World Bank: WDI
Political		
Democracy	Democracy-autocracy measure	POLITY IV data set
Military regime	Type of regime: civilian or military	Banks (2002)
Population size	Logged midyear country population	US census: international database
Population change	Percentage change in yearly population (constructed)	US census: international database

Table 4.7. *(cont.)*

	Indicator	Source
UK dependent/colonial experience	The decision rule of the most recent possessor is used to identify the relationships under examination	Issues COW colonial history data set
Conflict proneness		
Interstate conflict	0=no interstate conflict, 1=1,000 battle deaths or more	Strand, Wilhelmsen, and Gleditsch (2002)
Rebellion	Ordinal level of civil conflict	Strand, Wilhelmsen, and Gleditsch (2002)
Temporal dependence		
Cubic splines		Beck, Katz, and Tucker (1998) BTSCS method

Table 4.8. *Operationalization of rebellion incidence and prevalence of civil conflict equation variables*

	Indicator	Source
Dependent variables		
Rebellion incidence	Incidence of a rebellion with at least 25 annual battle deaths	Constructed, Strand, Wilhelmsen, and Gleditsch (2002)
Rebellion prevalence	Running count of years: consecutive rebellion 25 annual battle deaths	Banks (2005)
Demonstration prevalence	Running count of years: consecutive anti-govt. demonstrations	Banks (2005)
Riots prevalence	Running count of years: riots	Banks (2005)
Independent variables		
Implementation of structural adjustment agreement (SAA)	Running count of years a country has been implementing SAAs	Correspondence with World Bank and Vreeland (2003), updated
Physical quality of life index	Ranges 0 low PQLI to 100 high PQLI: composite index ranges of infant mortality rate, life expectancy at age one, and the adult literacy rate	Callaway (2001). Updated with UN population data and World Bank: WDI
GDP per capita	GDP per capita current US$ (PPP)	World Bank: WDI
Population density	Population size divided by country size in square miles	constructed, US census: international database and EUGene
Mixed regime POLITY score	Dichotomous measure coded "1" if democracy-autocracy POLITY score between 8–12, and "0" otherwise	POLITY IV data set

Table 4.8 (*cont.*)

	Indicator	Source
Ethnic heterogeneity	Ranges 0–177, extreme homogeneity to extreme heterogeneity	Vanhanen (1999)
	Index of racial division, national language division, and religious division in country	
Regime durability	Running count of number of years without a change in POLITY score of 3 during three-year period or regime transition	Constructed measure POLITY IV data set
Log of primary commodity exports	Interpolated annual measure of primary commodity resources as a proportion of GNP	Fearon (2005)
Log of mountainous states	Log of percentage that states are mountainous	Fearon and Laitin (2003)
World Bank and IMF selection effects	Predicted probabilities from selection equation used to control for World Bank and IMF selection effects	Constructed
Temporal dependence		
Cubic splines	BTSCS method	Beck, Katz, and Tucker (1998)

5 Determinants of structural adjustment lending

Introduction

In 1982 the Republican administration of Ronald Reagan voiced concern over the state of emergency decreed by the Chilean military government of Augusto Pinochet and the increased levels of human rights abuses that were taking place. The administration threatened to direct its representative to the IMF to vote against the award of structural adjustment packages unless the Pinochet regime lifted its state of emergency and improved its record of respect for human rights. Three years later the Reagan administration also abstained in its support for World Bank and IMF loans to Chile for several months until the regime lifted its state of siege (Coad 1985; Omang 1985). Apparently the administration was concerned over the levels of human rights abuses taking place; most attention had been paid to the opposition press censorship (Coad 1985).[1]

This example provides an intriguing contrast to the founding charter of both the World Bank and International Monetary Fund, which excludes political considerations in the loan-agreement process of these institutions. When decisions are being made about the allocation, amount, and conditions under which resources are apportioned, the idea that only economic factors affect the evaluation of member countries' representatives to these decision-making boards, is, at best, wishful thinking: politics inevitably becomes involved. In our historical assessment of how these institutions came to make their decisions over the 1981–2003 period, we built upon the existing literature that identified significant factors affecting the decisions of these institutions to enter into structural adjustment agreements with developing countries.

We have argued in previous chapters that if one is interested in understanding the impact of structural adjustment then the consequences

---

[1] To be sure, subsequent investigation found that despite the removal of the state of siege the human rights situation did not improve over the rest of 1985 (Millard Jr. 1986).

of both World Bank and IMF agreements need to be examined. Both institutions are heavily involved in promoting structural adjustment agreements as a device to generate high-quality economic growth and development, and both play a critical role in determining the amount of capital developing countries will receive from external sources. Thus, it is not surprising that there has been much controversy over the lending practices of these international financial institutions. Most of the controversy has been centered upon the fairness and efficacy of the structural adjustment conditions imposed by both institutions on loan-recipient countries and the effects of these loans on economic development. In recent years, scholars have also focused attention on country characteristics used by the Bank and Fund to determine which governments will receive loans and which will not. In order to assess the impact of these agreements on the level of government respect for the physical integrity, economic and social, and democratic rights of citizens in loan-recipient countries it is important to account for the selection criteria of these institutions.

Many of the factors which make countries good candidates for structural adjustment agreements have in previous research been connected to differing levels of human rights respect (e.g. Poe, Tate, and Keith 1999). By accounting for these selection criteria we can better understand whether consequences previously linked to structural adjustment were due to the loan conditions themselves or the preexisting situation found in that country.

In this chapter, the factors that increased or decreased the probability of a country entering into World Bank or IMF structural adjustment agreements (SAAs) in the period from 1981 to 2003 are identified; 131 developing countries were included in the analysis. The results have both theoretical and practical importance.

We identify four different theoretical perspectives that could be used to describe or explain the selection criteria of the World Bank and IMF: classical economic theory (Van de Laar 1980); the theory of two-level games in international affairs (Putnam 1988); the related "credible commitments" argument (Leeds 1999; Martin 2000); and dependency theory (Pion-Berlin 1983; 1984). These theoretical perspectives and the results of previous empirical research suggest the importance of economic, political, and human rights factors in the criteria used by the World Bank and IMF in their decisions to award loans. The results provide support for expectations generated by classical economic theory, very limited support for arguments concerning credible commitments and dependency theory, and none for those associated with the theory of two-level games.

The results of our study indicate that states associated with a higher probability of entering into a structural adjustment agreement with either the World Bank or IMF during this period were: greater debt; low levels of international trade; higher levels of government respect for physical integrity rights; and larger populations. These states were more likely to enter into these agreements when larger numbers of developing economies were under these agreements in a particular year. Some previous research on the selection criteria of the IMF had found that it preferred to give loans to more authoritarian states; we found marginal evidence, using a different sample, that the IMF favors more democratic regimes. Understanding the selection criteria of the financing agreements of the World Bank and IMF is also of crucial practical importance to any estimation of the effects of structural adjustment. Simply comparing recipient to non-recipient as some previous research has done (e.g., Harrigan and Mosley 1991) will not advance our knowledge of loan impacts because a non-random process generated which countries became recipients and which countries did not (Achen 1986; Heckman 1988; Przeworski and Vreeland 2000; Vreeland 2002; 2003). This means that in order to isolate the impact of structural adjustment, work needs to "disentangle" (Collier 1991) the selection criteria of World Bank and IMF from the actual impact of the loan itself. Disentangling this process allows research to answer the question: All other things being equal, was it the loans or the preexisting situation that account for the impact attributed to World Bank and IMF structural adjustment agreements?

The chapter follows in four sections. The first describes the four theoretical arguments, the second reviews some of the previous findings and generates a number of hypotheses, the third describes our research design, and the fourth discusses our findings and conclusions.

Theoretical arguments

We assume that developing countries would like to receive money from both the World Bank and IMF, because these institutions make loans at rates of interest and with other repayment terms that are far superior to what can be found on the open market (Van de Laar 1980). The situation in recent years has been different, since a variety of countries are seeking to renegotiate their debt and withdraw from relationships with the IMF (Kapur and Webb 2006). Loan-recipient governments are often also seeking the "seal of approval" from the Fund as a means to attract private investment to their countries. The leaders of developing countries know that the US government, the governments of other wealthy countries, and private banks will be less willing to provide grants and loans if the IMF does not give them the "green light" (Pion-Berlin 1984; Przeworski and Vreeland 2000).

The decision-making process of the World Bank and IMF

Which governments receive World Bank and IMF loans is decided by each institution's Board of Executive Directors. Both institutions use a weighted voting system for determining which loans are approved and which are denied. The weights assigned are roughly in proportion to the share of the Bank and Fund's resources contributed by each of the member governments. The United States government has been the largest shareholder in both institutions for the past twenty-five years – holding 16.8% of the shares in the IMF and the IBRD and paying 13% of the contributions to IDA. In the World Bank and IMF, the G8 countries hold 44% and 47% of the shares, respectively (World Bank 2006b). Hence, it is reasonable to assume that the preferences of the US Executive Directors have dominated the preferences of other members of the Bank and Fund's Board of Directors. At present, the IMF in particular has come under fire due to the underrepresentation of economies, such as China's and India's, which are more powerful than some of those in Europe.

World Bank and IMF representatives protest against any allegations that their lending policies are motivated by political considerations (e.g., Farnsworth 1984), but the internal decision-making process of the World Bank and IMF privileged the ideological perspectives of some governments over others, allowed for logrolling and vote trading, and in all other respects provides fertile ground for what, in any other context, would be called "politics" (see Broz and Hawes 2006a; 2006b; Dreher and Sturm 2006; Dreher and Jensen 2007; Oatley and Yackee 2004; Stone 2004; Thacker 1999).

Chapter 3 discussed how both the Bank and Fund are mandated and have stated their support for the promotion of macroeconomic stability, high-quality economic growth, and poverty reduction. The founding principles and subsequent public policy statements made by representatives of these two international financial institutions provide some guidance about which economic factors – including worker rights, and in the case of the World Bank respect for physical integrity rights – figure highly in their decisions about with whom to lend. To be sure, elsewhere in the chapter we also highlight a number of noneconomic selection criteria which affect whether or not countries enter into structural adjustment agreements with the World Bank or International Monetary Fund.

The selection criteria of the World Bank The World Bank was founded to promote reconstruction in postwar Europe and later took on the challenge of financing developing economies. In 1960, the Bank's soft-loan window, the International Development Association (IDA), was founded to provide concessional finance for low-income countries. It is financed in three-year cycles ("replenishment") through donor contributions and transfers of resources from the IBRD. In 2001, during negotiations of the thirteenth replenishment of IDA, the US aggressively marketed and sold the idea that many IDA-eligible countries should receive grants rather than loans (Citizens Network for Essential Services 2001–2002).

With the advent of structural adjustment agreements, the IBRD and IDA focused on promoting export-led economic growth in the developing world. During the Cold War, there was an unabashed bias against making loans to communist countries (though some communist countries including the formerly communist Yugoslavia and Romania did receive them). They also indicated that poor countries, those in economic difficulty, and with little international trade would be more likely to enter into structural adjustment agreements (World Bank 1992).

There have also been statements by the World Bank about its commitment to the promotion of physical integrity rights with the fiftieth anniversary of the Universal Declaration of Human Rights (World Bank 1998). In comparison, the Bank's promotion of worker rights has been inconsistent with policy statements promoting both higher (Nelson 2000; Sensor 2003) and lower level of respect for worker rights (Klak 1996; World Bank 2006a).

As stated in Chapter 2, recently the Bank has issued selection criteria that it has generated with its Country Policy and Institutional Assessment (CPIA) Criteria for Loan and Grant Allocation. Included in these criteria are economic management, structural policies, social inclusion, equity, and public sector management and institutional criteria. However, until the late 1990s, the Bank did not have widely circulated, published criteria about the factors that affected whether countries became loan recipients.

The selection criteria of the International Monetary Fund The IMF was founded to promote and maintain international economic stability, and with the advent of structural adjustment there has also been an emphasis on export-led economic growth. The founding principles of the IMF provide guidance about which factors we should expect are important in the loan-selection criteria of the Fund. They indicate that countries in economic difficulty, those with balance of payments difficulties, often indicated by shortages in foreign currency reserves, and little international trade would be more likely to enter into structural adjustment agreements (Vreeland 2003). The IMF has been much less effusive in support for physical integrity and worker rights, with some indications that its preference for flexible labor markets translates into policies that reduce levels of protection for worker rights (Lloyd and Weissman 2001: 6).

Structural adjustment conditions While there are some differences of emphasis in the stated selection criteria of these international financial institutions, all structural adjustment loan recipients are required to comply with certain conditions, mainly demonstrating their adherence to neoliberal ideology. These conditions are also political in the sense that they have been the subjects of contentious debate among scholars, policy-makers, and social activists in the United States and abroad. The purpose of these structural adjustment conditions is to encourage recipient governments to put on what Thomas Friedman (2000: 105) calls "the Golden Straightjacket":

To fit into the Golden Straightjacket a country must either adopt, or be seen as moving toward, the following golden rules: making the private sector the primary engine of its economic growth, maintaining a low rate of inflation and price stability, shrinking the size of its state bureaucracy, maintaining as close to a balanced budget as possible, if not a surplus, eliminating and lowering tariffs on imported goods, removing restrictions on foreign investment, getting rid of quotas and domestic monopolies, increasing exports, privatizing state-owned industries and utilities, deregulating capital markets, making its currency convertible, opening its industries, stock and bond markets to direct foreign ownership and investment, deregulating its economy to promote as much domestic competition as possible, [and] eliminating government corruption, subsidies and kickbacks as much as possible.[2]

While exact measures insisted upon between the World Bank, IMF, and recipient countries differ on a case-by-case basis, common steps often

---

[2] The perspective found in the *World Bank Structural Adjustment Policy Operational Manual* (World Bank 1992) is less elaborate. It notes that: "Success with stabilization usually requires a sustainable mixture of cuts in government spending, reductions in public enterprise losses, tightening of domestic credit, and increases in tax revenues. Central bank losses that result from the provision of credit subsidies to particular sectors, often through the exchange rate or banking system, are frequently an important source of inflationary pressure that need to be eliminated immediately."

cited by critics of the World Bank and IMF (Bello, Cunningham, and Rau 1994; Palast 2003) include reductions of social spending for such things as education, health services, income subsidies, housing, and reductions in public employment.

There is considerable debate about both the reasons why governments enter into structural adjustment agreements and the selection criteria used by the Bank and Fund. We situate these discussions within broader theoretical frameworks about the conditions under which governments and international financial institutions agree and implement loan packages. Framing these discussions in broader theoretical frameworks generates knowledge about both the applicability of these theories and the selection criteria used by these international financial institutions. A number of theoretical frameworks exist that provide insight into why governments seek international financial assistance and when these institutions are more or less likely to grant such assistance. These include classical economic theory, the theory of two-level games, credible commitments, and dependency theory.

Classical economic theory

Proponents of structural adjustment   Both proponents of structural adjustment as well as many of its critics use classical economic theory to form their arguments about the appropriateness of these policies. Classical economic theory is the basis of the mainstream argument used by the World Bank, IMF, and economically developed countries to justify support for economic stabilization and structural adjustment conditions agreed upon with loan-recipient countries. The intention of these conditions is to encourage the economic growth of loan recipients (Harrigan and Mosley 1991; Przeworski and Vreeland 2000), which the Bank and Fund's Board of Directors believe is the linchpin of economic development. Structural adjustment programs reduce the size and role of government in the economy and free monies to be used in a presumably more productive way by the private sector. A minimalist state produces and encourages the economic growth that will lead to a better society (Rapley 1996: 58).

Limited government empowers individuals by giving them more personal freedom, making it more likely that individuals will realize their potential. The ability to realize one's potential, according to this line of reasoning, leads to individual responsibility and self-reliance. Both classical and neoclassical economic theory advocate limited government with individuals acting in their own self-interest, maximizing any opportunities and possible gains. Reduction in the size of the state reduces the opportunity for corruption and releases talented people into the private sector (Rapley 1996: 59). Neoclassical thought also promotes strategies of export-led growth through free trade. Essentially, expanding levels of trade is a synonym for growth (Rapley 1996: 59). This suggests that when a country is characterized by economic underdevelopment, economic slowdown, or high levels of indebtedness, there is a likelihood that it will receive IDA grants and either an IMF loan or an IMF Policy Support Instrument (PSI). The PSI provides oversight of a government's policies without any financial assistance. Though economists associated with the IMF and World Bank use classical economic theory to justify structural adjustment policy, others use the same theory to criticize structural adjustment programs.

Critiques of the World Bank and International Monetary Fund   These criticisms take many forms including the arguments that the Bank and Fund use a conception of development that is too focused on economic growth without appropriate attention to the pattern of growth; have misdiagnosed the obstacles to development in the less developed countries; have failed to appreciate the value of government interventions in the economy; and have insisted that structural adjustment reforms be implemented too quickly and without the proper sequencing (Stiglitz 2002).

Some argue that the Fund and Bank have been too focused on Gross Domestic Product (GDP) per capita and growth in GDP per capita as the only indicators of economic development. They suggest this focus is too narrow since economic growth does not necessarily translate into development if the profits from such growth are not spent on health care, education, and infrastructure, improving the situation for most people rather than just a small ruling elite (Knack and Keefer 1997; Stiglitz 1999). Indeed, Nobel Laureate Joseph Stiglitz, formerly Chief Economist at the World Bank, has even argued that the developing countries which are likely to develop the fastest are those that avoid loans from the IMF and World Bank. He notes that China, a country that has received no help from the IMF or the World Bank, is probably the most successful of the low-income countries, both in terms of aggregate economic growth and in terms of poverty reduction.[3] Moreover, unlike Russia, China has avoided a rapid increase in economic inequality (Stiglitz 2002).

---

[3] Our data set indicates that China has been under structural adjustment agreements for a relatively short period of time, which is detailed in Chapter 3.

Some critics also argue that the real obstacles to economic growth in less developed countries have little to do with the size of government or its role in the economy. Among the real obstacles not addressed by SAAs, they contend, are the need for land reform, elasticities in foreign demand for primary products produced in the developing world, and low internal rates of saving in the private sector (Pion-Berlin 1984). The critics argue that there are no short-term solutions to these problems. Long-term solutions include land reform to raise agricultural output and government investment in infrastructure and capital-creating industries and also improving the terms of trade (Moyo 2001; Pion-Berlin 1984). In the formerly communist countries, the absence of a well-developed system of private property is also a major obstacle (Stiglitz 2002).

Critics also contend that the structural adjustment policies of the Bank and Fund impose a "shock therapy" approach on poorly per-forming economies, especially in the formerly communist world (Stiglitz 2002). In many cases, they argue, an incremental and adaptive longer-term approach would be more effective (Murrell 1992; Stiglitz 2002). In many formerly communist countries major problems have been created because privatization preceded the development of regulatory and cor-porate governance institutions and even banks (Schleifer and Vishny 1997; Stiglitz and Squire 1998).

Both critics and proponents of structural adjustment who work within the classical economic framework highlight the importance of economic factors driving the decisions of which countries enter into structural adjustment agreements with either the World Bank or International Monetary Fund. While classical economic theory provides one rationale for the types of factors the World Bank and IMF would take into account in determining whether to extend an SAA loan to a govern-ment, other theories, which focus on the ability of countries to negotiate at the international level, may also provide some purchase in under-standing the selection criteria of the Bank and Fund.

The theory of two-level games

Two contrasting theories appear in the literature concerning the impact of domestic politics on the abilities of states to cooperate. Putnam's (1988) and Milner's (1997) work on the impacts of both domestic and international politics in international affairs suggests that, unless the Bank and Fund adopt a kind of "affirmative action policy" towards democracies, they will be at a disadvantage in their attempts to negotiate these agreements. Critics of the IMF have also noted its preference for working with authoritarian regimes (Przeworski and Vreeland 2000).

Putnam's (1988) theory of two-level games and a similar argument put forward by Milner (1997) both provide an explanation for the finding in the literature that the IMF prefers lending to authoritarian regimes (Pion-Berlin 1984; Przeworski and Vreeland 2000; Stiglitz 2002). Putnam (1988) suggests that negotiations between an international agency like the World Bank or IMF and the leaders of a nation state can be thought of as a two-level negotiation game. Level-one negotiation occurs between the leaders of the Bank or Fund and the leaders of the potential loan-recipient country. Level two is played between the country leaders and their citizens. A formal model of this game would be exceedingly complex, since the negotiations at both levels are interdependent.[4]

At level one, the leaders of the Bank and Fund behave as autonomous, unitary actors in the model. They are hierarchically organized and they express clear preferences. At the risk of oversimplification, the preferences of the Bank and Fund are that decision-makers in recipient countries (i.e., the Finance Minister and Cabinet) will agree to a set of economic reforms, that these reforms are implemented faithfully, that the economy of the recipient country improves, and that the loans are paid back in a timely fashion (Williamson 1990). The mix of factors that changes the size of win-sets can be both "sweet and sour" according to Putnam. That is that domestic opposition may improve one's negotiating ability (Schelling 1960) and so improve the terms of any agreement, but domestic opposition also makes it harder to reach any agreement. Domestic opposition might arise as a result of the efforts of domestic interest groups and opposition political parties, electoral cycles, and even institutional arrangements requiring legislative approval of loan agreements.

The prospective inability to have an agreement ratified at the domestic level will reverberate at the international level curtailing the possibility of signing an agreement in the first place (Putnam 1988). From this perspective the greater the autonomy of country leaders at level one from influence by their level-two constituents, the greater the likelihood of achieving international agreement. At level one, the leaders of authoritarian states can negotiate with greater authority and

---

[4] See Milner (1997) for some examples of formal models of these relationships. Vreeland (2001) also uses a number of formal models to generate expectations about countries with which the IMF prefers to sign agreements. His expectations suggest that the IMF prefers to deal with regimes that have fewer veto players.

independence from domestic forces at level two. A bias against democracies in the selection processes of the Bank and Fund is, thus, a predicted outcome of the model. It is the natural result of the rational preferences of both sides of the negotiations at level one. Democratic leaders prefer not to lose the support of their constituents, and Bank and Fund leaders prefer not to give loans/grants with conditions that may not be met by the loan recipient. However, there is a contrasting theoretical argument suggesting that democracies have an advantage when negotiating international agreements, because their governments can make more credible agreements (Leeds 1999; Martin 2000).

Credible commitments and international agreements

Another contrasting theory concentrates on the ability of democracies to make credible commitments that inform other players in the international system of their intent with respect to an international agreement. Both Leeds (1999) and Martin (2000) argue that the properties of democratic accountability and institutionalized cooperation afford democracies the ability to send clear and credible signals concerning their ability to cooperate. These signals increase the probability of cooperation. Martin (2000) makes a strong argument concerning the ability of democracies to implement agreements signed at the international level making the necessary changes in domestic law and government policy. The informational properties of democratic regimes – in comparison to nondemocratic regimes – increase the level of certainty that players in the international system have about the probability that any signed agreement will be implemented in these states. Thus, democratic leaders will only commit at the international level to policies for which they believe they can garner the support of their legislatures. While Martin's (2000) argument is limited to advanced industrialized democracies, research by Dollar and Svensson (2000) suggests that Martin's contentions may be generalizable to democracies in developing countries as well. They provide evidence that democracies are much more likely to implement the World Bank structural adjustment conditions their governments accept.[5] Of course, many of the policy changes that governments undertake with structural adjustment agreements are made mainly with the executive branch. However, democratic

---

[5] Dollar and Svensson are only interested in the types of countries that implement already agreed-upon loans, so their work remains limited in informing us about the selection criteria of the World Bank; however, it does suggest that democracies are more likely to implement loan agreements than autocratic regimes.

leaders will face reelection, part of which will depend on how the public views their handling of the economy. Martin's (2000) theoretical argument and the Dollar and Svensson (2000) findings lead us to expect that democracies generally are more likely to receive structural adjustment packages, all other things being equal.

While the two theories of two-level games and credible commitments differ in their expectations about the abilities of democracies to negotiate successfully, one expectation that does appear common to both is that any domestic factor or international behavior that makes it less likely that the SAA conditions are implemented faithfully would discourage the leaders of the Bank and Fund from concluding an agreement. Examples of domestic instability might include being involved in civil or interstate conflict, which makes it more difficult for governments to implement agreements already signed, since they are diverted from regular government activities when in conflict. There is also some possibility that a government which entered into an agreement might be defeated in a war and replaced with a new regime that might choose not to fulfill the conditions of any existing loan/grant package.

Dependency theory

The most controversial perspective comes from dependency theorists who argue that governments of less developed (peripheral) countries often are forced to depend upon the IMF and the World Bank for external capital (Moyo 2001; Palast 2003).[6] They contend that the relationship between countries on the periphery of the world economic system and the international financial institutions is far more coercive than the leaders of the Bank and the Fund are willing to acknowledge. Furthermore, because of the weighted voting systems these institutions employ, lending policies are strongly influenced by the preferences of US leaders and other major shareholders such as Japan and Germany (Parenti 1989). Indeed, malevolent intent by leaders of the Bank, the Fund, and the major contributors underlies much of this perspective. Core countries use the structure of the international financial system to maintain a core–periphery relationship, since the periphery provides cheap areas of production and helps maintain the profits of companies in the core.

Structural adjustment conditions, especially conditions that increase unemployment and reduce wages, serve to maximize profits for

---

[6] For an excellent review of this literature, see Richards, Gelleny, and Sacko (2001).

multinational corporations operating in recipient countries. However, these policies tend to produce threats to the regime, because they require that decision-makers enact unpopular policies. These policies cause hardships, especially among the poorest citizens, who are most dependent upon social programs. These hardships, in turn, often provoke protests that may turn violent (Auyero 2001), and tend to elicit government repression (Davenport 1995), increasing the level of human rights abuse. Members of the lower class are not only the most direct victims of the new policies, but are also the most common victims of physical integrity rights abuse (Richards 1999).

From the perspective of dependency theory, therefore, the IFIs turn a blind eye to government violations of physical integrity rights in peripheral states that do the bidding of the core countries (Parenti 1989). Repression, which indicates the willingness of governments to put through unpopular economic measures, is likely to be rewarded with bilateral foreign aid from core states and with loans from the World Bank and International Monetary Fund. Structural adjustment programs ensure that the core receives cheap goods and that multinational corporations based in core states receive large profits. Some argue that this arrangement allows elites in loan-recipient countries to receive extra rents at the expense of their own populations (Berkeley 2001).

Dependency theorists see the World Bank and IMF as institutions designed to maintain the dependency of less developed countries on core states like the United States (Palast 2003). Thus, they would expect the Bank and Fund to give more loans to states that were authoritarian (but not communist), that showed little respect for the rights of workers (Meyer 1998; Pion-Berlin 1989; 1991; 1997; 2001), and violated the physical integrity rights of their citizens. Finally, dependency theorists argue that these institutions promote loan agreements which benefit corporations in the industrialized countries, while also burdening developing countries with debt, and through a variety of loan instruments perpetuate this debt burden through flawed development programs (Palast 2003).

Previous research: determinants of structural adjustment agreement

The stated selection criteria of the Bank and Fund together with the findings of previous research on the World Bank and IMF lead us to believe that the countries which enter into these agreements are a non-random group of all potential loan recipients. If, for example, authoritarian countries or those in economic difficulty were more likely to receive these loans, based upon previous research these countries were also more likely to abuse the rights of their citizens. Thus, it is important to distinguish the factors which make countries good candidates for these agreements from the impact of these SAAs on the human rights practices of recipient governments.

The theories described above suggest four categories of selection criteria that determine the probability of entering into a World Bank or IMF structural adjustment agreement. The first concerns economic issues. The second concerns political issues. The third concerns issues of human rights, and the fourth concerns issues of domestic and international conflict. Since both the World Bank and IMF insist upon the imposition of conditions for structural adjustment loan recipients and since both use a similar weighted voting system for deciding upon loan applications, the previous discussions lead us to expect that the selection criteria of both institutions would be similar.

Economic determinants

A number of different studies have examined how the economic slowdown of the 1970s and early 1980s and its impacts increasing debt, deteriorating economic growth, and worsening balance of payments problems in developing countries generated a need for major economic adjustments (Commonwealth Secretariat 1989: 19–22; Harrigan and Mosley 1991; Mehra 1991). A variety of country case studies in Africa, South and East Asia, Latin America, and the Caribbean note a litany of economic misery – including declining exports, increasing imports, inflation, state control of the economy, government spending outstripping government revenues, declines in the inflow of concessionary capital, deteriorating terms of trade, overvalued currencies, corruption, political instability, poor economic growth, high debt, and severe financial imbalances – in countries prior to the receipt of structural adjustment programs (Adepoju 1993; Çağatay 1994; Chipeta 1993: 105–107; Dennis 1992; Dorosh, Essama-Nssah, and Samba-Manadou 1996: 147; Eliott 1993: 40–42; Frausum and Sahn 1996: 311; Handa and King 1997; Kane 1993; Kanji and Jazdowska 1995: 134–136; Klak 1996; Konadu-Agyemang 2001; Krueger and Ruttan 1989; Krueger, Michalopoulos, and Ruttan 1989; Lele 1991; Mwanawina 1993: 69–71; Ndongko 1993: 119–121; Pion-Berlin 1989; Riphenburg 1997: 33–34; Sahn 1996: 3; Sahn and Haddad 1991; Sowa 1993: 8–9; Stryker and Tuluy 1989; Subramanian 1996: 62; Sukhamte 1989; Tanski 1994; Vuorela 1991).

Some research has modeled the economic characteristics of IMF program countries in comparison to non-recipients (Joyce 1992). His work assessed a range of economic factors that changed the probability of loan receipt. Low foreign exchange reserves and other economic factors played some role in the probability of entering into a structural adjustment agreement. Joyce (1992: 242) notes that purely economic models exclude institutional and social factors that affect a government's decision about whether to accept Fund assistance.[7]

Many of the previous large-n comparative studies which account for issues of selection have been conducted by scholars operating within the classical-economics or critical-economics schools. Thus, the emphasis has been on economic characteristics of potential loan recipients that make them more or less likely that they will enter into an SAA with the International Monetary Fund. According to IMF policies, a balance of payments deficit or a foreign reserves crisis was the prerequisite for signing an IMF agreement (Przeworski and Vreeland 2000). Even so, previous research results have been divided on whether a balance of payments deficit was sufficient to explain whether a government will receive an IMF loan or not (Bird 1996; Goldstein and Montiel 1986; Knight and Santaella 1997; Przeworski and Vreeland 2000). Przeworski and Vreeland (2000) also conclude that a large balance of payments deficit was not sufficient to explain agreements.

Some work that has examined the loan-selection criteria of the World Bank has also found that economic factors play a role in affecting with which countries it enters into agreements. Poor countries and those with foreign currency shortages were more likely to enter into structural adjustment agreements (Abouharb and Cingranelli 2004a; 2005). Moreover, a number of these articles have also pointed to the role of politics affecting the decisions of governments to seek assistance and in the decisions of the IFIs to provide it.

---

[7] Some work has examined the size of loans countries have been able to negotiate with the World Bank (Frey and Schneider 1986), but this does not inform us about the institution's selection criteria. Loans were bigger if the loan recipient showed a high degree of economic need (per capita income was low, the rate of inflation was high, external debt was high, and past economic growth was poor). They received bigger loans from the World Bank if they were politically stable and had a good "capitalist climate." They also found that former colonies of the United Kingdom, France, and the United States received larger loans. Finally they indicated that dependence was important because larger loans were made to countries that had relatively large imports from the United Kingdom, France, and the United States – three major shareholders and contributors to the Bank. The authors suggested that the larger loans were approved by the donor countries so that the loan recipients could pay for those imports (Frey and Schneider 1986: 242).

Political determinants

Economic factors were part of the explanation, but the literature suggests that they do not provide a complete picture. Previous research has found that about a third of governments which entered into structural adjustment agreements with either the World Bank or IMF did not have balance of payments difficulties (Abouharb 2005; Vreeland 2003). Is there an explanation of why governments would accept World Bank or IMF conditions when they are not in economic difficulty? Governments of low-income countries have few other sources of financing other than these institutions (and their regional counterparts: the African Development Bank, the Asian Development Bank, the Inter-American Development Bank, and the European Bank for Reconstruction and Development) for external capital necessary for economic development. However, many believe that some governments entered into IMF or World Bank agreements because they want conditions to be imposed (Bjork 1995; Dixit 1996; Drazen 2002; Przeworski and Vreeland 2000; Putnam 1988; Remmer 1986; Stein 1992; Vaubel 1986; Vreeland 1999; 2003). Government leaders may know that some areas of their economy need restructuring to be more efficient and competitive. Yet reform, while possibly necessary and in the long-term interests of most people in a particular country, may pose significant electoral hazards for leaders. These leaders need to blame the IMF or World Bank for imposing reform. In short, politics matters and may be a key consideration in the determinants of loan receipt. A more controversial version of this argument suggests that not only do political considerations on the part of domestic governments matter, but also that governments seeking loans may restrict the rights of some of their citizens in order to make themselves more attractive to international financial institutions (Pion-Berlin 1984).

Some previous comparative studies have examined the role of politics in the selection criteria of the World Bank and IMF in determining which countries received structural adjustment loans (Abouharb and Cingranelli 2004a; Przeworski and Vreeland 2000; Vreeland 2003). The existing research has generated a variety of findings about the extent to which democracies were disadvantaged in negotiating structural adjustment agreements with the World Bank and International Monetary Fund. Some cross-national work has examined the effect of regime type on the probability of a government signing IMF agreements and found that "the IMF is more likely to sign with dictatorships" (Przeworski and Vreeland 2000: 394). There is also some case study evidence suggesting that the IMF has shown a preference for military dictatorships by financially rewarding military governments which overthrew democratically elected administrations (Meyer 1998: 186; Pion-Berlin 1984; 2001). In contrast, using a different temporal sample, other work has found that the IMF was more likely to enter into agreements with democracies over the period 1981–1993 (Abouharb and Cingranelli 2004a).

There is some reason to believe that the World Bank in comparison to the IMF may not have paid much attention to regime type. Nelson (2000) notes that the World Bank was restricted from becoming involved in political matters. From this perspective the World Bank did not discriminate between democratic and nondemocratic regimes and so we would not expect to find a bias with respect to either kind of regime. Existing cross-national studies about the impact of regime types on the probability of entering into a structural adjustment agreement with the World Bank have not found democracies to be less likely to receive these loans over the period 1981–1993 and 1981–2000, providing support for Nelson's contention (Abouharb and Cingranelli 2004a; 2005; 2006).

Population size   The size of a country's population is another important political determinant of adjustment lending. More populous countries are likely to command greater attention and possibly have greater influence over Bank and Fund policies. More populous countries tend to have more influence in the international system, even if they are still developing. Indonesia is a good example. The previous research has found that populous countries were more likely to enter into structural adjustment agreements with both the World Bank and International Monetary Fund (Abouharb and Cingranelli 2004a; 2005).

The end of the Cold War   The end of the Cold War also had a significant impact on changing the calculation of decision-makers. The West provided considerable assistance promoting economic development in former communist countries, which had in practice been ineligible for World Bank and IMF loans during the Cold War (Van de Laar 1980). Supporting development in these newly independent countries was intended to cement both democratic and pro-Western attitudes (Tarnoff and Nowels 2001). With limited resources being devoted to the formerly communist states, other areas of the developing world may have faced greater competition to receive funds from these international financial institutions.

Human rights determinants

There is some work suggesting that the human rights situation in potential recipient countries, including respect for both worker rights and physical integrity rights, is an important determinant of World Bank and IMF loan receipts.

Physical integrity rights   Competing arguments exist about how government respect for the physical integrity rights of their citizens affects the probability of structural adjustment loan receipts from the World Bank and International Monetary Fund. Some have argued that governments will repress in order to show international financial institutions that they are tough enough to put through the necessary but unpopular economic reforms required, thereby improving their chances of obtaining sorely needed financial assistance (Keith and Poe 2000; Pion-Berlin 1984). Empirical studies, however, have provided little evidence for this argument (Keith and Poe 2000; Abouharb and Cingranelli 2004a; 2005; 2006).

Others have argued that the involvement of international actors can have a moderating effect on civil conflicts (Grove 2001), which should indirectly improve government respect for physical integrity rights. There also is a specific reason to expect that both the World Bank and IMF are more likely to lend to governments that respect the human rights of their citizens. The US International Financial Assistance Act 1977 requires US government representatives on the decision-making boards of the World Bank and IMF to use their voices and votes to advance the cause of human rights in loan-recipient countries (Abouharb and Cingranelli 2004a). Physical integrity rights are the rights that most nongovernmental organizations focus upon, so we think it is reasonable to argue that these are the types of rights people consider most when discussing human rights. The size of US contributions to the Bank and Fund gives it a strong voice in loan negotiations. Thus, one would expect both the World Bank and IMF to make SAAs with countries that have greater levels of respect for the physical integrity rights of their citizens.

Worker rights   Some work has argued that the rights afforded to workers are important factors in the decisions made by the World Bank and IMF concerning with which countries they will enter into structural adjustment agreements. Arguments in both directions have been made. Some suggest that the IMF prefers to work with governments that are more business friendly and willing to repress labor in order to carry out necessary reforms.

Discussing the actions of a military government in Argentina led by General Ongania, Pion-Berlin (1984: 116) contends that the Ongania administration engaged in 'preemptive coercion' including the banning of unions, freezing of union accounts, and the use of force to break up strikes to convince the IMF that Argentina was worthy of a loan. He contends that Argentina was quickly rewarded by the IMF for these policies. Governments may also show their resolve through labor-wage repression (Dymski and Pastor 1990). Moreover, wage repression was found to increase the probability of loans from the IMF (Dymski and Pastor 1990).

In yet another case, Pion-Berlin (1984) describes the IMF's unwillingness to give loans to the democratically elected government of Isabel Peron. When that government was toppled in a military coup in 1976, he writes that "the international credit came pouring in" including a substantial IMF loan (Pion-Berlin 1984: 118). Each time Argentina was successful in attracting IMF loans, repression of labor, especially organized labor, which rebelled against the new policies, increased dramatically. Referring to the Frondizi administration in 1958, Pion-Berlin (1984: 115) writes that "the government thought that its use of force to end a railroad strike in November would enhance its chances of gaining IMF credit. Apparently it was right."

More debate concerns those who have written about the World Bank. Some suggest that, unlike the IMF, the Bank may prefer to work with governments willing to respect worker rights. Nelson (2000) contends that the Bank has in fact had a long-standing commitment to maintaining labor standards, because Bank officials believe that respect for three core labor standards – against child labor, forced labor, and discrimination in hiring and treatment at work – actually promotes economic growth (Sensor 2003). In contrast, the "Doing Business" rating system of the Bank supports the view that structural adjustment conditions may provide direct or indirect incentives to limit worker rights in order to make countries more competitive internationally. The establishment of export processing zones (EPZs) is encouraged by the World Bank (Klak 1996: 358). In an effort to make these zones as competitive as possible, developing countries attempt to keep wages low (Klak 1996: 358). Thus, labor loses out in order to make countries as attractive as possible to international investors.

Previous research investigating these competing claims on a large-n comparative basis has found evidence that the Bank is more likely to enter into agreements with countries that have higher levels of respect for worker rights (Abouharb and Cingranelli 2004a; 2005). In comparison, previous large-n comparative research has found little support for the contention that the IMF prefers to work with governments that repress the rights of their workers (Abouharb and Cingranelli 2004a).

International and civil conflict

There is some discussion in the literature that when structural adjustment conditionality is imposed the effect on the recipients of IMF and World Bank loans often leads to increases in domestic unrest (Bello, Cunningham, and Rau 1994; Pion-Berlin 1984; Przeworski and Vreeland 2000). However, much less research has assessed how the likelihood of conflict domestically or internationally affects the probability of getting a loan from either international financial institution or a grant from the Bank. If the Bank and Fund do operate along classical economic lines, it would view both domestic and international conflict as factors reducing the probability of a prospective agreement being implemented and existing loans/grants being repaid in a timely manner. Countries in conflict are a poor investment. If there is domestic unrest, a new government may be installed. Previous agreements made by former governments, including those made with the World Bank and IMF, may not be honored. Argentina is a good example where large-scale riots led to a revolving door of presidents, most recently during the 2001–2002 period, generating considerable uncertainty about the likelihood of IMF loan repayment. Similarly, if a potential recipient is involved in a war with another state, the governments of the warring parties may be conquered and replaced. The previous research on this topic has generated mixed results. International and civil conflict have reduced the probability of entering into a structural adjustment agreement with the World Bank (Abouharb and Cingranelli 2004a; 2005), but conflict, domestic or international, has not played a significant role in the loan determinations of the International Monetary Fund.

Hypotheses

A number of competing theoretical perspectives provide the same expectations about the conditions under which countries are more likely to enter into structural adjustment agreements over the 1981–2003 historical period. Classical economic theory and those who critique the Bank while still using a classical economic perspective have the same expectations concerning the importance of economic factors affecting the probability of entering into these agreements. Both proponents and critics argue the importance of economic factors: debt, foreign currency shortages, overvalued exchange rates, poverty, economic decline, and low levels of international trade are all likely to increase the probability of entering into these agreements.

There is an overabundance of theory (Ikenberry 1999), with multiple theoretical explanations for similar outcomes. For example, classical economic theory, its critics, and those theorizing from a dependency perspective argue that countries which have lower levels of international trade are more likely to receive a structural adjustment package, though the reasoning, as we have already noted, is very different. If relationships with multiple theoretical explanations prove significant, the next stage of theory development would be to provide discriminating tests between these competing perspectives (Schultz 2001). The theoretical perspectives also provide a number of discriminating hypotheses concerning the impact of physical integrity and labor rights, and to a lesser extent the impact of democracy on the probability of entering into a structural adjustment agreement. Dependency theorists and proponents of two-level games both argue that democracies are less likely to receive a structural adjustment package. In addition, dependency theorists would argue that these international financial institutions are more likely to enter into agreements with governments that are allied with the United States, had a colonial or dependent relationship with one of the key backers of these institutions, and have lower levels of respect for the physical integrity and worker rights of their citizens. If significant, these hypotheses will provide a stronger basis from which to adjudicate between the competing theoretical perspectives.

Research design

This study uses a cross-national, annual time-series data set comprised of 131 developing countries, each with a population of at least 500,000 in 1981, which were in existence for the entire period under examination. The data spans the time period from 1981 to 2003. Table 4.5, above, provides a summary of the operationalization of variables.

Results

Table 5.1 displays the probability of entering into either a World Bank or IMF structural adjustment agreement during the period 1981–2003. A number of similarities exist across the selection criteria of both the World Bank and International Monetary Fund. Countries were more likely to enter into agreements when they were in debt and had low levels of trade with the rest of the international economic system,

Table 5.1. *Which governments enter into structural adjustment agreements with the World Bank and IMF 1981–2003, all developing countries (logit equation)*

	World Bank SAA direction of coefficient	IMF SAA direction of coefficient
Economic factors		
Debt as a proportion of GNP	.074*** (.022)	.086*** (.015)
GDP per capita	−.00001 (.00004)	−.0001* (.00005)
Exchange rate value	9.15e−07 (7.83e−07)	7.42e−07 (9.19e−07)
Average foreign currency reserves	−.0254 (.0234)	−.027 (.031)
Extent of international trade	−.0128*** (.003)	−.011*** (.003)
Change in GDP per capita	.001 (.001)	−.0007 (.001)
Human rights		
CIRI: physical integrity rights index	.054^ (.04)	.084* (.043)
Level of respect: worker rights	.12^ (.095)	−.141^ (.102)
Physical quality of life index	.001 (.006)	.003 (.006)
International political factors		
Log of population	.167*** (.05)	.021 (.055)
Cold War	.14 (.14)	−.562*** (.15)
Alliance with United States[1]	.031 (.158)	.057 (.169)
Domestic political factors		
Level of democracy	−.016 (.021)	.03^ (.023)
Conflict proneness factors		
Rebellion	−.012 (.075)	.053 (.085)
Interstate conflict	−.005 (.145)	−.315^ (.22)
International financial institution factors		
Number of countries under an SAA that year	.019** (.007)	.043*** (.008)
Constant	−4.689*** (1.071)	−3.82*** (1.153)
N	1673	1671
Pseudo R^2	.09	.10

Note: P>|z .1^.05*, .01**, .001***

[1] The model also included factors indicating whether a country had a previous colonial or dependent relationship with Japan, France, or the United Kingdom. French colonial heritage increased the probability of IMF loan receipt, while UK colonial heritage increased the probability of World Bank loan receipt at the .05 level of confidence. None of the other colonial indicators were significant. Models are estimated with robust standard errors, with one-tailed significance tests. Cubic splines were used to control for temporal dependence.

significant at the .001 level of confidence. Likewise, governments that have higher levels of respect for the physical integrity rights of their citizens are more likely to receive loans from these institutions, significant at least at the .10 level of confidence. Finally, governments are more likely to enter into these agreements when the sovereignty costs are lower, indicated here by larger numbers of other countries also under these programs in a particular year, significant at the .001 level of confidence.

While the results indicate many similarities in the loan-selection criteria of the World Bank and IMF, there are also some differences. The IMF appears to pay more attention to economic factors in its decision-making. Countries which have lower levels of GDP per capita were more likely to enter into a structural adjustment agreement, significant at the .05 level of confidence. Also the end of the Cold War made it more difficult for developing countries to gain additional financial assistance from the IMF as competition increased from many of the, now independent, former Soviet republics, significant at the .001 level of confidence. A number of marginally significant results indicated that there was some evidence that the IMF was more likely to enter into structural adjustment agreements with governments that had more democratic institutions, but had lower levels of respect for worker rights, significant at the .10 level of confidence. Involvement in interstate conflict reduced the probability of entering into these agreements, significant at the .10 level of confidence. In comparison, populous countries were more likely to receive World Bank structural adjustment loans, significant at the .001 level of confidence. There was also some evidence that the World Bank was more likely to enter into structural adjustment agreements with governments that had higher levels of respect for worker rights, significant at the .10 level of confidence.

Table 5.2 examines the probability of entering into any structural adjustment agreement. A number of economic factors have a significant impact on the probability of structural adjustment receipt. Countries that have higher levels of debt and low levels of international trade are more likely to receive a structural adjustment loan, significant at the .001 level of confidence. As before, governments that have higher levels of respect for physical integrity rights are more likely to become loan recipients, significant at the .01 level of confidence.

A number of political variables also change the probability of structural adjustment receipt. Populous countries are more likely to receive a

Table 5.2. *Which governments enter into structural adjustment agreements 1981–2003, all developing countries (logit equation)*

	Coefficient	Robust standard error
Economic factors		
Debt as a proportion of GNP	.097***	.015
GDP per capita	−.00004	.00004
Exchange rate value	5.01e−07	8.72e−07
Average foreign currency reserves	−.024	.024
Extent of international trade	−.012***	.003
Change in GDP per capita	.0003	.001
Human rights		
CIRI: physical integrity rights index	.09**	.037
Level of respect: worker rights	−.071	.088
Physical quality of life index	−.001	.005
International political factors		
Log of population	.121**	.048
Cold War	−.178^	.133
Alliance with United States[1]	.011	.142
Domestic political factors		
Level of democracy	.015	.02
Conflict proneness factors		
Rebellion	.073	.071
Interstate conflict	−.082	.152
International financial institution factors		
Number of countries under an SAA that year	.031***	.006
Constant	−3.572***	1.011
N		1673
Pseudo R^2		14

Note: P>|z .1 ^.05*, .01**, .001***

[1] The model also included factors indicating whether a country had a previous colonial or dependent relationship with Japan, France, or the United Kingdom. UK colonial heritage increased the probability of loan receipt, significant at the .10 level. None of the other colonial indicators were significant. Models are estimated with robust standard errors, with one-tailed significance tests. Cubic splines were used to control for temporal dependence.

loan from either the World Bank or International Monetary Fund, significant at the .01 level of confidence. Governments were also more likely
to enter into these agreements as the sovereignty costs dropped, indicated here by a greater number of developing countries under structural
adjustment agreements in a particular year, and was significant at the
.001 level of confidence. There was some evidence that the end of the
Cold War also made it more difficult for developing countries to receive
structural adjustment loans as competition for assistance increased; it
was marginally significant at the .10 level of confidence.

Conclusions

In this chapter, the factors that increased or decreased the probability of
a government receiving a World Bank or IMF structural adjustment
loan over the period from 1981 to 2003 were identified. Four different
and partly contradictory theoretical perspectives were advanced that
could be used to describe or explain the selection criteria of the World
Bank and IMF: classical economic theory (Van de Laar 1980); the
theory of two-level games in international affairs (Putnam 1988; Milner
1997); the logic of credible commitments (Leeds 1999; Martin 2000);
and dependency theory (Palast 2003; Pion-Berlin 1984). Hypotheses
were derived from each of these perspectives and tested.

The results provided support for the idea that the Bank and Fund's
operations are based on classical economic theory and guide loan-
selection decisions. Those in financial difficulty, who were in debt,[8] and
had low levels of international trade were more likely to enter into these
agreements. The Bank and Fund were clearly promoting their policies
to advance development through export-led economic growth.

One of the most important political questions examined in the chapter
was whether the selection processes of the Bank and Fund were biased
against democratic regimes. This question is important for both theoretical and practical reasons. Putnam's theory of two-level games led us
to expect that democracies would be less likely to be selected. The idea
that democratic regimes can make more credible commitments in
international negotiations implied that democracies would be more
likely to be selected. Mainstream critics of the bank have argued that the
World Bank and International Monetary Fund pay little attention to

---

[8] To be sure, dependency theory arguments which we examine next provide some support
for an alternative explanation based on maintaining a core–periphery relationship
between the industrialized states and developing economies.

nurturing democracies, implying that democracies would be neither more nor less likely to receive loans from the Bank and Fund.

The findings indicate a slight preference on the part of the IMF to work with more democratic regimes, a result we have found in previous work (Abouharb and Cingranelli 2004a). The findings for the impact of regime remained insignificant in estimating when governments enter into either a structural adjustment agreement with the World Bank or the joint model estimating entering into an agreement with either institution. One reason for this finding might be that commitments made by democratic governments to implement economic reforms are much more credible than commitments made by civilian authoritarian or military governments (Dollar and Svensson 2000). Our findings simply suggest that the officials at the Bank and Fund either have not recognized that fact in the past or have refused to take it into account in the loan-selection process. If the Bank and Fund were more biased towards democratic regimes in the loan-selection process, there would be fewer cases where reform commitments would not be honored by loan recipients.

One of the strongest findings to emerge from our study was that countries with larger populations were much more likely to receive structural adjustment agreements. While it is possible to treat population size as a technical control variable, we think that the bias towards large countries is political. More populated countries like India and Indonesia carry greater weight in the international system, and it is likely that preferences towards such countries in the selection process are due to this fact.[9]

Dependency theory received some support. The "bad motives" arguments of dependency theorists led us to expect that the World Bank and IMF would provide a disproportionate share of their loans to governments allied with the United States that were in debt, that had little international trade, authoritarian governments, and governments that did not protect the physical integrity rights and worker rights of their citizens. There was some support for the arguments about the impact of colonial and dependent relationships on the probability of SAA receipt. French and UK colonial and dependent relationships increased the probability that these countries would receive an SAA from the IMF and

---

[9] Low correlations between population size and other factors that might also be proxies for international influence – such as GDP correlated at .04 and debt as a proportion of GNP correlated at the .12 level – indicate that large countries do generate more attention in the negotiations process with the World Bank and IMF, and that this is different from other indicators of international influence.

World Bank, respectively significant at the .05 level of confidence. There was some marginal evidence that US-dependent relationships increased the probability of receipt of a structural adjustment agreement from either institution, significant at the .10 level of confidence. Furthermore, countries in debt were much more likely to enter into structural adjustment agreements with both the World Bank and IMF, significant at the .001 level of confidence. Purely economic explanations would also indicate that countries in debt were more likely to enter into these agreements. A number of the results also limited the amount of support that can be given to dependency theory arguments. There was no support for the arguments that repression of physical integrity rights increased the probability of receiving a structural adjustment package from either institution, and the findings about worker rights were both mixed and marginal. While individual examples have sought to connect structural adjustment receipt and repression, these examples do not seem to hold in a wider comparative context.

Understanding the selection criteria of the World Bank and IMF is of crucial practical importance to any estimation of the effects of structural adjustment agreements. Having identified these selection factors we are now in a position to answer the questions about the impact of structural adjustment: All other things being equal, was it the SAA or the pre-existing situation that accounts for the impacts attributed to World Bank and IMF structural adjustment programs?

Part III

Findings

6   Economic and social rights

Introduction

In 2000, the World Bank and IMF, the Organisation for Economic Co-operation and Development, and the United Nations published a jointly prepared document titled *A Better World for All*. In it, the world's two most important international financial institutions guaranteed that, in partnership with others, they would make substantial progress in reducing world poverty by 2015. The report proposes measuring poverty reduction in seven areas: world poverty (the percentage of people living on the equivalent of 1 US dollar or less per day), gender gaps in school enrollment, primary school enrollment, infant mortality and maternal mortality (Sadasivam 1997), access to health services, and sustainable development. Among other specific goals mentioned in the report, the promises include decreasing rates of infant mortality by two-thirds and maternal mortality by three-fourths, providing access to all that need health services, and ensuring that all children are enrolled in primary school. Taken together, the goals in the report are commonly referred to as the "Millennium Development Goals."

This report and these promises made in it were necessary because there is a growing consensus that most of the countries we usually refer to as "developing economies" are not developing at all or are not developing as quickly as had been hoped. Jeffrey Sachs, an economist who directs the Millennium Development Project, notes that, according to World Bank estimates, 1.1 billion people or about one-sixth of the world's population live in extreme poverty (Sachs 2005). This does, however, represent an improvement from 1.5 billion people living in extreme poverty in 1981. Asia leads in numbers of impoverished people, but, proportionately, Africa is worst off, with nearly half of its population living on less than the equivalent of 1 US dollar per day (Sachs 2005).

Some think that it is wrong for the World Bank and IMF to be making promises about poverty alleviation, because they see these institutions as primarily responsible for the lack of progress towards these goals in the past. The common charge is that the conditions associated with structural adjustment programs insisted upon by the World Bank and IMF have actually slowed economic development in the developing economies – not increased it. Since neither institution has promised a meaningful change in its structural adjustment strategy, critics think that achievement of the ambitious goals outlined in *A Better World for All* is highly unlikely. Critics believe that structural adjustment actually worsens poverty and inequality in developing economies because compliance with structural adjustment conditions usually requires loan-recipient governments to take actions that increase economic and social hardships for their citizens.

The debate over these questions is complicated, in part, because there is controversy concerning how to measure progress in combating poverty in the developing economies. Should the focus be on improvements or declines in aggregate wealth, usually measured as Gross Domestic Product per capita or in outcomes that reflect how that wealth has been used to improve the quality of life for most citizens? The emerging consensus is that structural adjustment programs have not contributed to aggregate economic growth (Przeworski and Vreeland 2000; Vreeland 2003). If one chooses to emphasize development outcomes as the World Bank and IMF have done in their recent guarantees, it is less clear what role structural adjustment conditionality has played in progress or lack thereof in achieving those goals.

We cannot reliably know whether the consequences of IMF (or World Bank) policies were worse than what the alternative would have been (Stiglitz 2002). However, we can compare progress in outcomes for countries with many years of experience under structural adjustment with countries having little or no experience under structural adjustment. Joseph Stiglitz and most others make such comparisons in an ad hoc fashion. China, the world's most populous country, for example, has dramatically reduced poverty (according to some calculations) over the last quarter of a century. Stiglitz argues that China's success is due to the fact that it has accepted relatively few structural adjustment loans, and has insisted upon gradually liberalizing its economy instead of taking the more rapid, shock-therapy approach advocated by the IMF. A study sponsored by the Heritage Foundation shows that the ten largest recipients of World Bank and IMF structural adjustment loans have made little progress in liberalizing their economies or in improving their GDP per capita since receiving their first loans (Eiras 2003).

A nuanced approach is required to rule out the possibility that worse outcomes were the result of the selection practices of the Bank and Fund. Perhaps these institutions have worked longest with countries such as Jamaica and Argentina, for example, because their economies were worst off in the first place. Thus, their lack of progress in reducing poverty may be the result of those problems more than the result of structural adjustment conditions. It is also necessary to control for the effects of other factors such as civil war, which worsen the economic and social situation for the poorest in society, that might have been experienced by some country groupings more than others. The statistical analysis indicates, that even after controlling for issues of selection, structural adjustment conditionality has worsened government levels of respect for economic and social rights in developing economies, not improved them.

Basic human needs or basic human rights?

The line between satisfying basic human needs and promoting human rights has been semantic ever since economic and social rights were formally recognized in international human rights law. Economists tend to discuss the effort by governments to satisfy basic human needs. By this, they mean the needs all human beings have for a minimal level of food, shelter, water, housing, education, and health care if they are to survive and, hopefully, enough to allow them to live a life of dignity. Political scientists and human rights activists refer to these human needs in terms of economic and social human rights. Governments representing most of the world's peoples and cultures have formally agreed to respect human rights to a minimal standard of living. The most basic of all international agreements is the United Nations Universal Declaration of Human Rights (UDHR), approved by the General Assembly in 1948. Together with the International Covenant on Economic, Social and Cultural Rights (ICESCR) and the International Covenant on Civil and Political Rights (ICCPR), both concluded in 1966, these three documents comprise what is commonly referred to as the International Bill of Human Rights. The purpose of the two 1966 covenants is to make legally binding the rights listed in the UDHR, as the UDHR is a non-binding resolution. Among other economic and social rights, the UDHR recognizes the rights to an existence worthy of human dignity (Article 23), to a standard of living adequate to maintain health and well-being, to food, clothing, housing, and medical care, to necessary social services (Article 25), to free elementary education, and to higher education on the basis of merit (Article 26). Similarly, the ICESCR recognizes the right to a decent standard of living, to adequate food, clothing, and housing, to continuous improvement of living conditions (Article 11), to medical care (Article 12), and to education (Articles 13 and 14).

Despite the recognition of economic and social rights in international human rights law, until recently international nongovernmental human rights organizations such as Amnesty International and Human Rights Watch focused their reports and activities almost exclusively on identifying and remedying government violations of civil and political rights. Now there is a move towards an "integrated human rights approach" that reflects a belief in the complementarity, universality, and indivisibility of all rights. As interpreted by the Deputy Executive Director of Amnesty International USA, an integrated human rights approach:

> means that we recognize and act on the firmly held belief that people have a right to food, to clean water, and to a safe and adequate place to live as much as they are entitled to the right to peacefully express their opinions or exercise their religion; the right of a woman to have access to credit is as much of, and as important a right, as her right to be free from violence in the home; children have a right to education and basic healthcare as much as they have a right not to be sentenced to death; indigenous communities have a right to live and work on their ancestral lands as much as they have the right to be free from extra-judicial slaughter. (Goering 2007: 214)

The international recognition of basic economic and social human rights does not guarantee every human being the full enjoyment of those rights no matter where he or she lives. However, international law does *legally obligate* all governments to do the best they can, within their resource constraints, to satisfy those rights for their people. Clearly, there is great variance in the degree of efforts different governments are making towards these ends, and participation in structural adjustment programs may restrict the effort made by some governments.

In the current policy debate over appropriate strategies for helping developing economies, the distinction between using the terms "basic human needs" and "economic and social human rights" is an important one. Shue (1980) and Pogge (2007) have argued that economic and social rights are the most basic or important of all human rights, though there is much debate on this point (e.g., Cranston 1964). If all human beings have a right to safe drinking water as implied by the explicit rights guaranteed in the International Bill of Human Rights, then privatizing water and denying it to those who cannot afford it cannot be justified under international law. If all human beings simply have a basic need for water, privatization is more justifiable.

How structural adjustment agreements reduce respect for economic and social human rights

As governments attempt to bring their budgets into balance and to reduce the role of the state in the economy, as structural adjustment programs require, massive layoffs of public sector workers and substantial cuts in the wages and retirement packages of public employees have been common. Morocco's cuts in public service employees in the wake of its 1981 Extended Fund Facility (EFF), for example, contributed to a 60 percent rise in unemployment between 1982 and 1984. A similar process occurred in the Ivory Coast where public sector layoffs followed a 1981 EFF (Cavanagh, Anderson, and Pike 2005). These public sector layoffs to accommodate Bank and Fund structural adjustment requirements have been documented in many case study accounts.

Another way structural adjustment loan recipients have attempted to reduce public expenditures is to cut public subsidies and raise fees for social programs in areas such as health, education, income support, and housing. Ghana entered into more structural adjustment agreements than any other African country between 1983 and 1990. Yet, during the 1980s, education spending remained at half of its 1975 level, and overall enrollment rates declined from 1983 to 1987. Costa Rica began its structural adjustment experience in 1981. Its expenditures for health services decreased during the 1980s. By 1985, its Ministry of Health reported significant increases in the occurrence of intestinal parasitic diseases, rheumatic fever, and alcoholism (Cavanagh, Anderson, and Pike 2005). In his article in *Time* magazine (March 14, 2005), economist Jeffrey Sachs wrote "For a quarter century and changing only recently, the main IMF prescription has been budgetary belt-tightening for patients much too poor to own belts." In an interview with journalists, Sachs elaborated:

Now, the IMF and the World Bank basically don't block increases in health spending, if donors come forward ... In private they know that there is a silent tsunami, silent holocaust underway in rural Africa with mass death. But, they don't say in public that the United States and other donor countries should therefore do more to save the millions of lives that could be saved ... What they say is to the governments, "Well, so sorry you have what you have; now live and in fact die, within your meager means ..." That is why IMF, World Bank programs often have health systems that have four or five dollars per person per year as the total spending. That is what you get in an impoverished country if you don't get help. You get a few dollars per person per year in the health sector. Compared with our country with more than $5,000 per person per year. It is one of the most shocking facts on our planet, because in effect it is a mass death sentence and the IMF and the World Bank should be standing up country by country and declaring this.[1]

---

[1] Telephone press briefing for journalists (as reported to the authors by Nancy Anderson) with Jeff Sachs to discuss the G8 Summit, June 15, 2005.

The Bank and Fund have also pressed some countries to stop the rise in wages to limit inflationary tendencies within their economies and to reduce protections of workers to attract foreign investment. A World Bank loan approved for Nicaragua in 1994, for example, required the Nicaraguan government to remove some non-monetary benefits from labor agreements (Cavanagh, Anderson, and Pike 2005). An IMF bailout for Argentina in 2001 came with the condition that the government remove the protections that limited the employer's ability to terminate employees (Lloyd and Weissman 2001).

Another favorite target of IMF and World Bank structural adjustment policies are price subsidies that some developing economies have provided for basic necessities such as gasoline, foodstuffs, and public transportation. Mozambique, for example, received its first IMF structural adjustment facility in 1987. By 1988, prices of basic commodities had shot up 300–500 percent (Cavanagh, Anderson, and Pike 2005). Nigeria, the world's sixth largest oil producer, has been urged to deregulate its oil industry, which will lead to higher domestic prices for gasoline and less access to gasoline for Nigeria's poor. Under a World Bank SAP negotiated in 2005, the Yemini government agreed to reduce subsidies on petroleum products. The elimination of price subsidies has been so devastating for poor people that it has led to riots and bloodshed in some developing countries (see Chapter 7).

Many developing countries also have been pressured to sell off public enterprises such as water provision, airlines, power utilities, and train services to private investors. Allegedly, many of the sell-offs have been tainted by corruption and have led to the transfer of assets from citizens to wealthy individuals or foreign corporations, thereby increasing inequalities within those societies. In addition, critics contend that privatization of natural monopoly services reduces the responsiveness of service providers to public wants and needs with no likely improvement in efficiency or effectiveness of service delivery (Lloyd and Weissman 2001).

An important study by infrastructure expert Antonio Estache (2005) helps to establish the track record of public–private partnerships in infrastructure (PPPI) over the 1984–2004 time frame. This is significant because about 40 percent of the total volume of Bank lending is devoted to infrastructure. The study finds that, in PPPs, the public sector assumed more costs than benefits. As percentages of total investment, private sector commitments, public sector investments, and development aid represented about 22%, 70%, and 8%, respectively. Any gains in efficiency were achieved at the cost of increased burdens imposed on the lowest income groups. In general, the private sector engages in "cream-skimming." It serves the paying customers and leaves the rest. Since there are now no internationally agreed fiscal accounting and reporting standards for PPPs, risks of poor performance and corruption have increased.

In the 1990s, the World Bank and IMF adopted a policy of water privatization and full-cost water pricing. The concern was that the world is running out of freshwater sources at an alarming rate and that conflict over what remains is inevitable. Also, the Bank argued, governments of poor countries have failed to deliver water to their populations efficiently (Alexander 2005). More recently, in response to criticism concerning the takeover of water services by transnational corporations in some countries, the World Bank has argued that public–private partnerships (PPPs) for water can help efficiently fulfill the human right to water. However, according to critics, the World Bank and IMF have contributed to governmental failure in this area because they have ended most cross-subsidies between profitable sectors – telecommunications and electricity – and the unprofitable water sector. Cross-subsidies are illegal under World Trade Organization rules (Alexander 2005).

Following IMF and World Bank advice, the government of Bolivia sold the public water system for a city with more than half a million people to a subsidiary of the Bechtel Corporation. Local water users were almost immediately hit with rate hikes of 100 percent or more. In a country where the minimum wage was US$100 a month, the poorest families were asked to pay water bills of $20 or more (Shultz 2000). Increases in water prices of this magnitude have been common. Policy conditions attached to IMF and World Bank loans led to privatization of the urban water system in Ghana and a 95 percent increase in water fees in 2001, with additional price hikes expected. Public Citizen, an international NGO, reported that, in 2002, about 35 percent of the Ghanaian population lacked access to safe water and 68 percent lacked sanitation services (Raja 2002).

The link between access to safe and affordable water and public health is generally acknowledged by the community of health professionals. According to one estimate, over 2 million children die each year of diarrhea, a disease related to the lack of access to clean water. More than 1 billion people lack access to clean drinking water and approximately 2.5 billion have no sanitary means for disposing of human waste. Yet a review of forty randomly selected IMF loan agreements reached in 2000 revealed that the IMF included provisions for water privatization in twelve of them – Angola, Benin, Guinea Bissau, Honduras, Nicaragua, Niger, Panama, Rwanda, Sao Tome and Principe, Senegal, Tanzania, and Yemen (Grusky 2001). The author concluded that it was African countries and the smallest, poorest, and most debt-ridden countries that were being subjected to IMF conditions on water privatization.

Through adjustment lending by the IFIs and project lending by the Bank, trade liberalization has been a high priority. Trade liberalization, by its nature, cuts budget revenue from trade taxes which, in some countries, has accounted for a third to one-half of all budget revenue. When these cuts led to high budget deficits, the IFIs promoted budget targets that necessitated deep cuts in public investment for basic services (health care, education, water) and infrastructure.

Previous research

The most widely used measure of the degree to which government policy results in satisfying basic human needs and basic human rights to unpolluted air, water, food, education, clothing, shelter, and health care is the physical quality of life index (PQLI). Morris (1979) developed the PQLI under the auspices of the Overseas Development Council. It is a composite of three indicators: infant mortality per thousand live births; life expectancy at age one; and the adult literacy rate. The ranges for the first two indicators are transformed to a zero to 100 scale, and then the index is computed by taking the unweighted arithmetic mean of all three indicators.

The PQLI is a reasonable measure of the past attainment of the desired development outcomes outlined by the Bank and Fund in *A Better World for All*. Some Millennium Development Goals developed by the Bank and Fund refer to inputs, while others refer to outcomes. For example, reducing the percentage of the population who live on less than the equivalent of 1 US dollar per day is not an ultimate objective of development. Achievement of this instrumental or intermediate goal should lead to important ultimate development outcomes such as better health, adequate shelter, and a longer life. However, as a number of authors have noted, societies having the same level of wealth often have widely divergent development outcomes (Morris 1979; Sen 1999).

There are other composite indices measuring the quality of life of the poor within societies. The human development index developed by the United Nations Development Programme is a well-known alternative measure. It includes two components of the PQLI: life expectancy at birth and adult literacy rate. It does not include the infant mortality rate, and it adds the combined gross enrollment ratio for primary, secondary, and tertiary schools and GDP per capita. Thus, this measure indicates both the total wealth available in a society (as indicated by GDP per capita) and how it is used to help the poor (United Nations Development Programme 2004).

Previous research has shown that the average HDI and PQLI scores for developing and economically developed countries advanced at a modest pace from 1960 to 1990 (Morris 1996), from 1975 to 1994 (Van der Lijn 1995), and from 1976 to 1996 (Callaway and Harrelson-Stephens 2004). Not surprisingly, the average PQLI scores (Callaway and Harrelson-Stephens 2004; Morris 1996; Van der Lijn 1995) and HDI scores (Van der Lijn 1995) were much lower, on average, for developing countries. The regional breakdown showed that HDI and PQLI had improved in all regions, but countries in Africa had made the least progress in improving their economic and social human rights conditions (Van der Lijn 1995). There is a growing literature seeking to explain variations among governments around the world in meeting the basic human needs of their people. Of particular interest is research that has examined the relationship between the degree of liberalization of a country's economy and its performance in meeting the basic human needs of its citizens as measured by the physical quality of life index. Though the relationship has received considerable attention, there is no consensus in the findings. Some studies have shown more liberalized economies are associated with higher PQLI scores (Callaway and Harrelson-Stephens 2004; Milner 2000), while others have found them to be associated with lower PQLI scores (Moon 1991).

However, it is clear that wealthier societies do tend to have higher PQLI scores. The most widely reported finding is that the greater the aggregate wealth of a country (as measured by its GNP or GDP per capita or the log of GDP per capita) the greater the level of provision for basic human needs (Callaway and Harrelson-Stephens 2004; Milner 2000; Moon and Dixon 1985; Morris 1979; Park 1987; Poe et al. 2004; Rosh 1986). This relationship appears to be curvilinear (Morris 1979). Increases in aggregate wealth produce increases in PQLI up to a point. After that point, there are decreasing marginal returns on investments, so it is exceedingly difficult to reach the best possible outcomes on all three component indicators of the physical quality of life index.

There is unanimous support for the idea that, other things being equal, more democratic governments do a better job of providing for the basic human needs of their citizens (Callaway and Harrelson-Stephens 2004; Milner 2000; Moon 1991; Moon and Dixon 1985; Poe et al. 2004; Rosh 1986; Spalding 1986). So, with the rapid democratization of the developing world in the 1990s, one would have expected significant advances in PQLI scores.

There is also some evidence that countries with higher PQLI scores have a higher population density and have had a British colonial experience (Poe *et al.* 2004). Surprisingly, previous research has found no relationship between whether a country is experiencing civil conflict or whether it is engaged in international war and its PQLI score (Poe *et al.* 2004). Research has shown that domestic and international conflict tends to be associated with less respect for other types of human rights (Poe and Tate 1994; Poe, Tate, and Keith 1999), and evidence from many case studies suggests that conflict takes its toll on the poor. This discussion leads to our hypotheses about the patterns in respect for economic and social rights over time and the impact of structural adjustment agreements upon them.

The critics of structural adjustment suggest that governments that have operated under structural adjustment conditions have experienced more poverty and inequality than governments that have not (Garuda 2000). We expect that the greater the number of years of structural adjustment conditionality experienced by a country the lower its protection of the economic and social rights of its citizens. We believe that the effect of structural adjustment is a cumulative one, with changes in the PQLI taking place relatively slowly. We do not think that the PQLI will change perceptibly on a yearly basis as a result of structural adjustment, but a cumulative debilitating effect of structural adjustment on the ability of governments to provide for the economic and social rights of their citizens we think will become evident over time.

Research design

To test these hypotheses, we examined the 131 developing economies that have existed throughout the 1981–2003 period as described in Chapter 3. The dependent variable of interest is the physical quality of life index, which is our measure of government respect for the economic and social rights of its citizens and is explained in more detail below. We also note the importance of controlling for issues of selection and briefly discuss some other factors that have been associated with differing levels of government respect for economic and social rights, which are included as controls to better isolate the impact of structural adjustment agreements.

Indices and PQLI

The human development index (see above) was considered for use in this research. It is available for most countries of the world since 1996.

However, the HDI and other measures are more complex, whereas the PQLI is easy to compute and its scores are easy to understand. Other studies have emphasized that governments of equal aggregate wealth make very different decisions about how to use that wealth to help the poor in their societies (Sen 1999). We are more likely to be able to develop useful theories of development if we keep this in mind and leave for separate investigation the relationship between total wealth available in a society and how it is put to use.

Other available indices mix inputs with outcomes, while the PQLI, as noted above, focuses exclusively on outcomes. To be sure, the PQLI does not measure all development outcomes, but it does measure attainment of outcomes that are universally desired, and for which data are available for almost all countries of the world – even the poorest, where bureaucratic infrastructures for data collection and analysis are not well developed. Thus it can be used to measure change over relatively long periods of time extending into the past. Other advantages of the PQLI as a measure is that it does not assume that there is only one pattern of development; it reflects the distribution of social results, and it facilitates international comparison (Morris 1979: 21).

The most common criticism of the PQLI is that there is no theoretical basis for assigning equal weights to the three components (Bayless and Bayless 1982; Goldstein 1985; Hicks and Streeten 1979). While this is true, Morris notes that there is no good theoretical basis for weighting the three components differently either, so equal weights are appropriate. Some scholars have analyzed each component separately to deal with this criticism (Poe *et al.* 2004). However, for the sake of simplicity, we use the aggregate index. The PQLI is not the only good measure of development outcomes, but it is an excellent measure for examining whether structural adjustment agreements have resulted in more or less poverty and inequality within developing economies.

We updated and expanded the coverage of existing measures of PQLI, which had previously ended in 1996, through to 2004. We also sought to fill in missing values where possible with new data sources. Any remaining missing cases were interpolated. The component indicators do not fluctuate widely from year to year, so the straight-line interpolation method was used to estimate the values for missing years.[2] While PQLI is an appropriate indicator of government respect for

---

[2] We wish to thank Rhonda Callaway and Wesley Milner who provided their data sets containing the component indicators for the PQLI and the calculated PQLI scores from 1976 through 1996. We filled in figures for years where the scores for one or more

economic and social rights, it is important to make sure that any consequences attributed to structural adjustment are due to these programs and not preexisting factors which make some countries more likely to enter into them.

Controlling for the effects of selection

It is important to control for the selection effects of these international financial institutions in any analyses undertaken. Previous work has indicated that these institutions have preferences for entering into agreements with particular kinds of countries (Abouharb and Cingranelli 2004a; 2005; 2006; Przeworski and Vreeland 2000; Vreeland 2003). These preferences mean that countries with particular levels of respect for economic and social rights are more likely to become loan recipients. In order to assess the impact of these structural adjustment agreements on government respect for the economic and social rights of their citizens, it is important to control for these selection effects.

Other factors associated with government respect for economic and social rights

A number of factors have been found in previous research to affect government respect for the economic and social rights of their citizens. It is also important to control for these factors, when trying to assess the impact of structural adjustment. These factors include higher levels of democracy, wealth, population density, and countries with a British colonial heritage.

Higher levels of democracy are expected to have positive impacts on government respect for economic and social rights. Citizens can elect to replace governments which poorly provide for the economic and social welfare of their citizens (Bueno de Mesquita *et al.* 2003; Moon 1991; Moon and Dixon 1985; Rosh 1986; Spalding 1986). More wealthy countries are also more likely to have higher levels of respect for the economic and social welfare of their citizens. Previous work has found that more wealthy countries better provide for the needs of their citizens (Moon and Dixon 1985; Park 1987; Rosh 1986). The density of population within a country is also thought to affect the level of respect for economic and social rights. Countries that are densely populated put additional stress on resources within the country and on the ability of

indicators were widely spaced over time and updated their data set through 2004. The same original sources were used wherever possible.

governments to respond and fulfill the needs of their citizens. The consequence is to lower levels of respect for economic and human rights in
comparison to situations where the density of the population is lower
(Henderson 1993; Poe and Tate 1994). Finally, countries with a British
colonial heritage are expected to better fulfill the needs of their citizens. The
consequences of a British colonial past were to generate bureaucracies and
civil servants that could more efficiently and effectively respond to the
wishes of the government and the needs of the population as a whole.

Findings

Implementation of World Bank and IMF structural adjustment agreements reduces government respect for the economic and social welfare
of their citizens, significant at the .01 level of confidence in the selection-
corrected findings presented in the first column of Table 6.1. Economic
growth has a positive impact on government respect for economic and
social rights, significant at the .05 level of confidence. To our surprise
the findings indicated that British colonial heritage lowered respect for
these rights. Since the physical quality of life index changes slowly over
time, much of the variance in it is explained by lagging the dependent
variable, which means that many of the variables we expect to be significant remain insignificant for statistical reasons.

  As noted, this study advances our understanding of the human
rights consequences of structural adjustment by correcting for the
effects of selection. It is possible that the worsened economic and
social rights outcomes observed and reported in previous studies
resulted from the poor economic conditions that led to the imposition
of the structural adjustment conditions rather than the implementation
of structural adjustment conditions themselves. In other words, the
hardships for the poor might have gotten worse whether or not a
structural adjustment agreement (SAA) had been implemented. In
addition, as our selection-corrected results show, some of the factors
that increase the probability of entering into an SAA – such as having a
large population and being relatively poor – are also associated with an
increased probability of economic and social hardship. For these reasons,
one must disentangle the effects of selection before estimating the
human rights impacts of structural adjustment agreements. The reader
will recall that, in order to control for the effects of selection, a two-
stage analysis was undertaken. In the first stage of the analysis, the
factors affecting World Bank and IMF decisions concerning which
governments receive SAAs were identified. In the second stage, the
impacts of implementing SAAs on governmental respect for human

Table 6.1. *The impact of World Bank and IMF structural adjustment agreements on government respect for economic and social rights 1981–2003, all developing countries (ordinary least squares)*

	Selection corrected	Selection not corrected
Number of years under a World Bank or IMF structural adjustment agreement	−.016** (.007)	−.013* (006)
Economic factors		
GDP per capita	−.00001 (.00003)	−.5.83–06 (.00001)
Change in GDP per capita	.001* (.004)	.001** (.003)
Trade as a proportion of GDP	.002 (.001)	.001 (.001)
International political factors		
Log of population	.033 (.029)	.025 (.026)
Domestic political factors		
Level of democracy	.007 (.013)	.003 (.011)
United Kingdom colonial heritage	−.239** (.091)	−.176** (.07)
Population density	3.61e−08 (1.57e−07)	3.61e−08 (1.26e−07)
Conflict proneness factors		
Interstate conflict	.11 (.095)	.091 (.068)
Rebellion	.005 (.031)	.004 (.031)
Control variables		
World Bank and IMF selection effects	−.062 (.251)	–
Respect for economic and social rights lag	.989*** (.005)	.987*** (.003)
Constant	.888* (.449)	1.028** (.391)
N	1673	2062
R^2	.99	.99

Note: P>|z .1^ .05*, .01**, .001***
Models are estimated with robust standard errors, clustered on country with one-tailed significance tests.

rights were examined, while controlling for the indirect effects of World Bank and IMF selection criteria concerning which types of countries were more likely to receive such loans.

In this analysis, the probability of each country negotiating an SAL in each year was calculated and then entered as an independent variable in the selection-corrected equation. This independent variable was left out of the equation that yielded the results reported in column two of Table 6.1. The variable titled "World Bank and IMF selection effects" was not significant in the selection-corrected results. Thus, correcting for selection made little difference to the findings reported. Had we not controlled for the effects of selection we would have reached the same conclusion about the effects of exposure to structural adjustment, but the results would have been statistically significant only at the .05 level of confidence.

Conclusions

The findings presented indicate that the consequences of the World Bank and IMF structural adjustment agreements lowered levels of government respect for economic and social rights, contributing to a deterioration in the situation for the mass of the population in these countries. The impacts of these agreements have been detrimental to those countries entering into them, even accounting for the selection effects of these institutions. In the debate over how best to promote the Millennium Development Goals, the path undertaken by the World Bank and IMF of neoliberal rapid economic liberalization appears to be having the opposite of the intended effect. Instead of promoting high-quality or equitable economic growth that lifts the poor out of poverty and social misery, the consequences of these programs have been to perpetuate these conditions.

7   Civil conflict: demonstrations, riots, and rebellion

Introduction

The causes of why people engage in anti-government protest and rebellion are multifaceted (e.g., Fearon and Laitin 2003; Regan and Henderson 2002; Regan and Norton 2005; Sambanis 2004a; 2004b). The reasons for these actions fall into two broad categories. The first concerns groups that take action for political reasons, choosing their moment to take advantage of governmental weakness. Second, groups take action against their government because they have fared poorly under its economic policies. This research demonstrates that the consequences of World Bank and International Monetary Fund involvement in the governance of developing countries increase the probability of anti-government protest and rebellion along two dimensions already highlighted in the civil conflict literature. The first describes how the involvement of these international financial institutions constitutes a marker of government weakness increasing the probability of rebellion as opposition groups sanction violent attacks to take advantage of this situation for their own political advantage. The second concerns the deleterious economic consequences of these agreements on developing countries. The consequences of these programs increase levels of hardship for many people in countries undergoing structural adjustment. Many more citizens, as a result, have been harshly treated by their governments leading to greater amounts of anti-government protest and rebellion as people try to change government policy to improve their personal circumstances.

The evidence presented later provides support for these arguments linking the negotiation of structural adjustment agreements with an increased probability of rebellion. Even after accounting for the loan-selection criteria used by these institutions concerning which countries enter into these agreements and the factors previously associated with rebellion, this research generates evidence that entering into structural adjustment agreements increases the probability of rebellion.

Opposition groups view entering into these agreements as an indication of governmental weakness. These groups engage in rebellion to take advantage of this situation for their own political gain.

Implementation of structural adjustment agreements, which often necessitated cutbacks in government spending and reduced protection for the economic and social rights of many citizens within the country, generated sufficient grievances among the population for it to lead to greater civil conflict. The empirical findings indicate that countries which undertook the most neoliberal reforms of their economies have endured the most amount of anti-government demonstrations, riots, and rebellion over this period.

There are a number of theoretical and policy implications that flow from this work. From a theoretical perspective the argument links the actions of international financial institutions to processes within states beyond matters of economic growth or decline. The research indicates an important and novel transnational source of conflict within countries. Most of the previous research has concentrated either on domestic sources of rebellion – such as wealth, ethnic diversity, or institutional configurations like the extent of democracy (Fearon and Laitin 2003; Sambanis 2004b) – or on broader international processes such as the impact of globalization (Barbieri and Reuveny 2005; Hegre, Gissinger, and Gleditsch 2003). From a policy perspective, the findings cast additional doubt on the value of the neoliberal approach towards the promotion of economic development and domestic stability within developing countries. The following sections examine some of the literature that pertains to this topic, indicate a number of hypotheses, discuss issues of selection that need to be accounted for, present a research design, findings, and some conclusions about the contribution of this work to our knowledge about the probability of rebellion, when countries are likely to experience greater periods of civil conflict, and some of the broader policy implications for governments trying to promote economic development.

Background: international economic processes and their impact on domestic stability

Most of the quantitative literature which has examined how international economic processes affect domestic stability has focused on the larger topic of globalization (e.g., Barbieri and Reuveny 2005; Hegre, Gissinger, and Gleditsch 2003). The findings of existing work have been mixed. Some have found that increased integration into the international economic system has reduced the probability of anti-government violence (Esty *et al.* 1998; Hegre, Gissinger, and Gleditsch 2003; Barbieri and Reuveny 2005). Other work has found economic integration increases the probability of anti-government protest and violence within countries (Polanyi 1957; Walton and Seddon 1994). Finally, some research has found economic integration to be unrelated to the probability of civil conflict (Fearon and Laitin 2003).

A number of qualitative case studies have looked more closely at the domestic impact of structural adjustment agreements. They concur in their conclusions: the consequences of these structural adjustment agreements have been to cause domestic instability (Di John 2005; Keen 2005). As Di John (2005: 114) writes:

A few weeks after the announcement of [structural adjustment] reforms, Venezuela experienced the bloodiest urban riots since the urban guerrilla warfare of the 1960s. The riots, known as the "Caracazo," occurred in late February 1989. A doubling of gasoline prices, which were passed on by private bus companies, induced the outburst … The riots that ensued were contained by a relatively undisciplined military response that left more than 350 dead in two days.

Others have linked the consequences of IMF structural adjustment conditions to rioting, urban violence, the dissolution of social fabric (Auyero 2001; Stigltiz 2002: 36), ethnic conflict in Indonesia (Stiglitz 2002), and rebellion in Sierra Leone (Keen 2005). The approach taken here incorporates these insights and builds a theoretical framework which weaves the choices of governments to enter into and implement structural adjustment agreements within the larger framework of theories predicting anti-government protest and violence.

Structural adjustment and its impact on anti-government protest and violence: a theoretical framework

Entering into structural adjustment agreements and the probability of rebellion

To the extent that entering into a structural adjustment agreement signifies political instability within a country, groups opposed to the incumbent government may seek to take advantage of the situation for their own purposes. Such a signal may increase the probability of rebellion. This argument falls within a broader literature that has examined governmental weakness generally (Skocpol 1979; Snyder and Tilly 1972; Tilly 1978) and the weakness of governments in less developed countries (Ayoob 1995; Goodwin and Skocpol 1989; Job 1992;

Mason 2004). A variety of arguments have been forwarded to explain this weakness, ranging from the consequences of colonialism (Mason 2004) to the domestic political choices of governing elites (Bates 1981; Bueno de Mesquita *et al.* 2003). Weak states often lack the institutional strength – such as civilian control over the armed forces – and financial capabilities to ameliorate the economic difficulties of groups within the state that have fared poorly (Mason 2004: 134–136).

Groups opposed to the government will often seek to take advantage of any situation where the incumbent government is faltering. Governments may become unstable for a variety of reasons. Of particular interest here is the effect of economic mismanagement on the abilities of government to remain in office. Economic decline has a variety of deleterious consequences. It makes office retention more difficult in industrialized democracies (Powell and Whitten 1993), and increases the probability that governments collapse (Bueno de Mesquita *et al.* 2003) and that countries become involved in civil conflict (Blomberg and Hess 2002). Governments tend to enter into structural adjustment agreements when they are in economic difficulty (Abouharb and Cingranelli 2004a; 2005; 2006; Joyce 1992; Przeworski and Vreeland 2000; Vreeland 2003). Economic trouble may lead governments into political difficulties because of the constraints they face in providing private benefits to their supporters (Bueno de Mesquita *et al.* 2003).

If governments are in sufficient economic difficulty that they need assistance from these international financial institutions then entering into agreements may serve as a signal to opposition groups that this is a period of particular governmental weakness. This argument complements previous research which has found that political instability increases the probability of anti-government violence (Gasiorowski 1998; Snyder and Tilly 1972). By choosing their moments carefully, these groups believe that they are more likely to successfully accomplish their objectives. The demands made by these groups include more services from central government, autonomy, secession, or even control of the state itself (Gurr 2000; Tilly 1978). Regardless of the groups' specific aims, they will be more likely to rebel at times of governmental weakness, when their actions are more likely to succeed. One signal of governmental weakness is the need for international financial assistance.

The need of governments to seek assistance is often viewed with indignation (Vreeland 2003). For example, the Shagari administration in Nigeria had assiduously avoided entering into an IMF agreement despite great need because the general public's view towards the IMF was one of "vehement popular antipathy" (Callaghy 1990: 269).

The government avoided entering into negotiations with the IMF until winning reelection. Having been safely reelected, the administration decided to enter into structural adjustment negotiations with the IMF. The consequence: a military coup that toppled the civilian administration (Vreeland 2003: 37). If groups opposed to the government interpret entering into an agreement with the IMF or World Bank as a signal of governmental weakness, then we should expect there to be an increased probability of anti-government rebellion during these years. While entering into structural adjustment agreements increases the probability of anti-government rebellion for political reasons, there is considerable reason to expect that the negative economic consequences of these programs increase the prevalence of civil conflict.

Implementation of structural adjustment agreements on the prevalence of civil conflict

There are three related mechanisms, identified in the literature on civil conflict, through which the implementation of structural adjustment agreements increases the prevalence of civil conflict within a society. The first is that these programs generate economic decline, increasing levels of hardship within countries through their failure to promote export-led economic growth. The second is that these programs promote rapid economic restructuring, generating social dislocation. The third is that there is good reason to believe that these programs increase perceptions of relative deprivation.

Hardship The literature on hardship and civil conflict makes the argument that poor countries with high levels of poverty are more likely to become involved in conflicts over these limited resources (Arat 1991; Blomberg and Hess 2002; Fearon and Laitin 2003; Gurr 2000; Lindstrom and Moore 1995). Research has found that economic recessions increase the probability of civil war (Blomberg and Hess 2002). When resources are in high demand, and the supply of them is limited, resolution over which groups obtain these goods and which go possibly hungry, thirsty, or needy in some way can often turn violent (Auyero 2001; Walton and Seddon 1994). Governments tend to be the focal points of such violence because they are generally the most important actor in deciding the distribution of scarce resources, especially in less developed countries (Bates 1981; Mason 2004). Structural adjustment programs fit within this broader literature on hardship and violence because governments were often mandated to make cutbacks in public spending on social and welfare programs (Chipeta 1993; Fields 2003; Handa and King 1997; Johnson and Salop 1980; Meyer 1998; Sisson 1986; Sowa 1993; World Bank 1992; Zack-Williams 2000). Some studies have emphasized the disproportionate negative economic human rights consequences of these cutbacks for women (Buchmann 1996; Commonwealth Secretariat 1989; Elson 1990; Riphenburg 1997; Sadasivam 1997; Tanski 1994), for public sector employees, and low-wage workers (Daddieh 1995). The poor and those in the public sector saw their wages fall in real terms (Daddieh 1995; Klak 1996; Munck 1994), while at the same time they faced increased living costs due to the removal of price controls and subsidies for essential commodities (Zack-Williams 2000).

Greater levels of hardship may increase the likelihood that adversely affected groups become involved in civil conflict in order to change government policy. The cutbacks in social and welfare spending that accompanied most structural adjustment agreements increase hardship for broad swathes of the population and generate grievances against the government (Collier 2000). A number of different studies have argued that these cutbacks in social and welfare spending increase unorganized violence like looting and rioting (Auyero 2001; Chua 2003; Fording 2001; Walton and Seddon 1994). These cutbacks also made it easier for political entrepreneurs (DeNardo 1985) to widen their base of support and continue their rebellious activities (Mason 2004). Examples from Sierra Leone indicate that the government tried to reduce the size of the state to fulfill its structural adjustment agreement. Civil servants previously employed by the state often lent support to the rebels because a change of regime was expected to improve their chances of future employment and thus improve their personal circumstances (Keen 2005). Likewise, when the government reduced spending on education, youths who would otherwise be in school, having been harshly treated by their government, were now more amenable to rebellion. They were encouraged by the rebel leadership in Sierra Leone to attack elite private educational establishments, whose funding did not depend on the government (Keen 2005).

Rapid economic change   Higher levels of wealth have been associated with lower probabilities of civil conflict (e.g., Fearon and Laitin 2003; Hegre *et al.* 2001). In contrast, the process by which that wealth is created, economic change, often generates domestic instability (Mason 2004; Polanyi 1957). Increased integration into the international economic system is one source of this economic change. The detrimental consequences on society of rapid economic change have been examined by Piven and Cloward (1993: 5), who argue that "the two main sources of catastrophic changes that distinguish capitalism are depression and rapid modernization." Rapid modernization in its latest iteration has arrived in the form of rapid economic liberalization.

The continual nature of change that underlies capitalism and the fluctuating labor requirements that stem from this not only generate unemployment as people, at a minimum, shift from one labor market to another, but they may also become permanently excluded from the labor market as a result of shifting labor demands. Indeed, according to Piven and Cloward's argument, the maintenance of a civil and stable society depends on secure employment. Mass unemployment breaks these social bonds of stability and civil behavior. The impact of mass unemployment is usually one of civil disorder, "crime, mass protests, riots – a disorder that may even threaten to overturn existing social and economic arrangements" (Piven and Cloward 1993: 7).

Structural adjustment programs are such a source of rapid economic change. Some SAPs have been variously described as "shock therapy" (Stiglitz 2002). These programs often involve governments quickly removing barriers to fully functioning free markets within their countries and between themselves and other states. While each structural adjustment program is negotiated by representatives of the Bank and Fund and the Finance Ministry of the recipient country, common provisions to promote rapid restructuring of the domestic economic system include privatizing state-owned industries and utilities, maintaining a low rate of inflation and price stability, shrinking the size of its state bureaucracy, maintaining as close to a balanced budget as possible, eliminating and lowering tariffs on imported goods, getting rid of quotas and domestic monopolies, increasing exports, deregulating capital markets, making its currency convertible, and opening its industries and stock and bond markets to direct foreign ownership and investment (Meyer 1998).

Rapid restructuring of the economy generates hardship and instability for large sections of the population, increasing resentment against the incumbent regime, which often spills over into anti-government violence (Gasiorowski 1998; Olson 1963; Vreeland 2003). Another mechanism by which these structural adjustment agreements increase the prevalence of civil conflict is the extent to which they increase levels of relative deprivation.

Relative deprivation   The connection between the impact of structural adjustment agreements and relative deprivation explanations of civil conflict stems from the policy choices mandated by the World

Bank and IMF for the restructuring of national economies. The concept of relative deprivation describes the differences between what an individual expects, and whether these expectations are satisfied (Davis 1969; Feierabend and Feierabend 1966; Gurr 1968). When these expectations are not satisfied an individual feels relatively deprived; often their reaction is violence (Gurr 1968), generating instability within a country (Feierabend and Feierabend 1966). To be sure, there is some debate as to what constitutes a sufficient temporal period of personal dissatisfaction to comprise being in a state of relative deprivation. This ranges from discussion that frames the generation of relative deprivation as phenomena which take place over longer periods of time. When there are increasing differences between expectations and gratification, especially after a prolonged period when both had been rising, these can lead to violence (Davies 1969: 547). Others have made the argument that a sense of relative deprivation can take place without the need for a prolonged period of rising expectations. Instead, any barrier, whether social or physical, providing the individual is cognizant of this interference, can generate feelings of relative deprivation increasing the willingness of individuals to respond with violence (Gurr 1968: 253–254). Indeed, the examples given indicate that relative deprivation can occur from the "failure to obtain an expected promotion or the infidelity of a spouse" (Gurr 1968: 254).

There is good reason to believe that the policy changes mandated by the World Bank and IMF may have increased levels of relative deprivation because of the cutbacks in government social and welfare spending, which have often lowered people's incomes, as well as increased levels of domestic unemployment. These policy changes also quickly open up domestic businesses and industries to foreign competition, many of which close, unable to compete with competition from industries in more developed economies. Individuals compare their present situation to that if there had not been any cutbacks in government spending and when they had greater security about their employment. Where these cutbacks have worsened people's situations they will feel relatively deprived. The formation of grievances which flow from feelings of relative deprivation is a key factor which increases the willingness of people to become involved in civil conflict (Collier 2000; Gurr 1970; 2000).

Structural adjustment programs frequently involve reductions in the numbers of people working for the government, while often raising the costs of living for most citizens. Not only do many become unemployed but the reductions in welfare provision also generate greater differences between individuals' expectations had they been employed, in comparison to their new situation due to structural adjustment: both unemployed and with little welfare assistance from the government (Daddieh 1995; Frausum and Sahn 1996; Friedman 2000; Handa and King 1997). Cutbacks in government spending on a variety of programs push the poor to the margins of existence and make them more amenable to organization by political entrepreneurs to engage in civil conflict against their government (Regan 2005).

The discussion has posited three different mechanisms that connect the consequences of neoliberal adjustment on the prevalence of civil conflict. The implication of this discussion is that, all else being equal, the detrimental consequences of these programs are greatest for those governments that have engaged in the most neoliberal reforms. Thus, the longer periods of time countries have spent under structural adjustment agreements restructuring their economies along neoliberal lines, the more prevalent civil conflict.[1]

There is considerable reason to believe that the types of countries which enter into agreements with the World Bank and International Monetary Fund constitute a non-random sample of all possible countries. Some of the factors which make countries good candidates for structural adjustment agreements – such as being poor or in economic difficulty – mean that they are also more likely to experience civil conflict. Thus, it is important to control for the selection criteria of the World Bank and International Monetary Fund in order to assess the direct impact of structural adjustment on the probability of rebellion and the prevalence of civil conflict.

The argument that was laid out described how both entering into and implementing structural adjustment agreements increase the probability and prevalence of civil conflict through a number of different mechanisms: an indication of governmental weakness, increased hardship, rapid economic restructuring, and relative deprivation. When examining the impact of structural adjustment agreements on the probability of rebellion and the prevalence of civil conflict, it is important to control for existing arguments that are pertinent to the discussion. To be sure, an agreed-upon list of "standard" control variables has yet to materialize (Sambanis 2004b). The next section briefly examines some existing arguments about the probability of civil conflict which need to be

---

[1] Other work has examined the role of minority groups who benefit from the free-market system more generally to the detriment of broader swathes of society (Chua 2003). These narrowly distributed benefits are also a source of conflict within these countries against the market system, the wealth of these privileged minorities, and sometimes violence against the minorities themselves.

accounted for when trying to estimate the impact of structural adjustment agreements on civil conflict. These factors include the impact of government respect for the economic welfare of its citizens, the wealth, demographic change, topography, natural resources, political structure, ethnic heterogeneity, and political change within regimes.

Other important factors affecting civil conflict

Government respect for citizens' economic welfare

Research has linked lower levels of government respect for the economic welfare of their citizens to civil conflict (Poe and Tate 1994; Poe, Tate, and Keith 1999). Everything else being equal, those countries which provide greater respect for the economic welfare of their citizens should have a lower probability of civil conflict. In comparison, those countries that provide relatively poorly for the economic welfare of their citizens generate grievances among their populations and increase the probability of civil conflict as a means to improve government respect for these rights (Regan 2005).

Wealth

Previous research has highlighted the importance of wealth reducing the probability of civil conflict (De Soysa 2004; Fearon and Laitin 2003; Hauge and Ellingsen 1998; Hegre *et al.* 2001; Hibbs 1973; Sambanis 2004a). A number of different theoretical arguments have been made which link higher levels of wealth to lower levels of civil conflict, especially lower levels of anti-government violence. One line of argument suggests that higher levels of wealth reduce conflict over scarce resources making negotiated outcomes easier (e.g., Hibbs 1973; Hegre *et al.* 2001). Others argue that higher levels of wealth provide the state with additional capabilities to strengthen itself through higher levels of coercive force (Fearon and Laitin 2003). Higher levels of wealth also increase the economic opportunity costs of civil conflict (Fearon and Laitin 2003) and make it easier for governments to provide alternative sources of income to those considering engaging in rebellion (Heath *et al.* 2000).

Demographic change

Some have argued the importance of demographic stress on the probability of civil conflict (Davies and Gurr 1998). When countries experience rapid demographic change, like a fast-growing population increasing level of population density, these changes can strain government resources to adequately provide for the welfare of their citizens but they also bring people into closer contact with each other. Both consequences make it easier for political entrepreneurs to take advantage of these circumstances and recruit supporters for their cause, increasing the probability of anti-government protest and rebellion.

Topography

Arguments about the topography of countries and how it affects the onset of civil conflicts have also been made (Fearon and Laitin 2003). Countries that are mountainous contain more inhospitable terrain: these difficult conditions make it easier for rebel groups to organize away from the purview of the state.[2]

Natural resources

Of interest has been the argument put forward by Collier and Hoeffler (2001) that resource-rich countries are more likely to be targeted by rebel groups who wish to take over control of the state for their own personal gain. While the argument forwarded by Collier and Hoeffler is appealing, recent work has questioned the validity of their measures and the robustness of their findings (Fearon 2005). The previous findings, which showed that countries with greater natural resources were more likely to become the target of organized rebellion, were not robust to updated measures of the variables of interest and changes in how the measure was calculated moving from five-year averages to annual indicators (Fearon 2005). The fact that these findings are not robust to changes in measurement may indicate that the issue in question may not be natural resources per se but rather the fairness in how the proceeds from these resources are distributed within societies. Aggregate measures such as the level of natural resources within a country do not address this issue and warrant further investigation.

Political structure

A number of studies have linked anocracies or mixed regimes – those exhibiting both authoritarian and democratic traits – to an increased

---

[2] To be sure, others have noted the spuriousness of correlations between conflict and measures which tend to vary very little within countries over time – such as income inequality or topographical measures (unless the boundaries of the state change) – but do vary between them. The correlation between the two is a statistical artifact rather than a causal relationship (Mason 2004: 32).

probability of civil conflict (DeNardo 1985; Francisco 1995; Hegre *et al.* 2001; Muller and Weede 1990). The argument made in the literature suggests that governments repress when they perceive serious threats to their hold on power (Most and Starr 1989; Pion-Berlin and Lopez 1991; Regan and Henderson 2002; Starr 1994; Simon and Starr 1996). Repression may lead to a series of interactions between opposition and government that can become increasingly vicious if the government responds to peaceably made demands with violence (Mason 2004; Moore 1998). The perception of what constitutes a serious threat depends upon the vulnerability of the incumbent government (Davenport 1995).

Where governments rule on the basis of unreliable support, many more threats are viewed as destabilizing. In democratic systems, political leaders represent a wide range of viewpoints. Extremists not incorporated into the system will tend to form only a very small part of the political spectrum. Therefore any threat they pose will tend not to be viewed as credible to the incumbent government (Regan and Henderson 2002: 123). In authoritarian systems, the opposition is generally cowed into submission when faced with overwhelming coercive force (Fein 1995; Gartner and Regan 1996; Regan and Henderson 2002). These systems then tend to be less likely to experience civil conflict than their mixed-regime counterparts (Hegre *et al.* 2001). The combination of democratic and authoritarian traits exhibited in mixed regimes is one that "invites protest, rebellion, and other forms of civil violence" (Hegre *et al.* 2001: 33). The mix of repression, which generates grievances, with an openness that allows groups to organize against the government is an explosive one that can end in civil conflict. Those facing a mixed regime are sometimes allowed to protest governmental actions, while in other situations they are repressed by their government for demonstrating their unhappiness with government policy. Such government behaviour radicalizes the opposition away from the continued use of peaceful protest, while the reluctance of these regimes to be consistently repressive on a broad-enough scale allows groups to organize in violent opposition (Regan and Henderson 2002).

Ethnic heterogeneity

A number of different arguments exist which posit that ethnically heterogeneous countries are more likely to experience civil conflict than homogeneous societies (Horowitz 1985; Fearon and Laitin 2003). These arguments include primordial explanations of behavior which maintain that connections of blood to kith and kin generate in-group/ out-group behavior favoring those more closely related (Salter 2001;

Van den Berghe 1978; Vanhanen 1999). At the other end of the
spectrum are instrumental arguments, which suggest that individuals
will promote ethnic attachments when it provides them with economic
or political benefits (Eller 1999). Particular cultural traits often provide
the basis of entitlement. A third position argues that it is not differences
between groups that lead to conflict, rather violence is triggered when
there is competition over political and economic resources that fall
along ethnic lines (Mousseau 2001; Petersen 2002; Ross 1993).

Institutional change

Finally, there are some discussions about the frequency and magnitude
of changes in political institutions, and their impact on domestic stability. Political change, whether democratization or autocratization,
generates domestic instability (Hegre *et al.* 2001) and increases the
probability of civil conflict (Fearon and Laitin 2003). Political change
has the impact of deconsolidating institutions, increasing the probability of anti-government protest rebellion as groups opposed to the
incumbent regime seek to capitalize on such fluid situations where the
issue of which groups are going to benefit and which are going to be
made worse off by such changes may be unclear (Hegre *et al.* 2001;
Sahin and Linz 1995; Tarrow 1994).

Research design

Issues of selection

The empirical models account for what have been described as issues of
selection, which refer to the factors that change the probability of a
government entering into a structural adjustment agreement with either
the World Bank or International Monetary Fund (e.g., Abouharb and
Cingranelli 2004a; 2005; 2006; Joyce 1992; Przeworski and Vreeland
2000; Stone 2004; Vreeland 2003). Chapter 5 identified a number of
important factors which relate to the economy, politics, human rights,
and conflict proneness of countries that affect the probability of entering
into a structural adjustment agreement with the World Bank and IMF.

Many of the factors that make countries candidates for World Bank
and IMF structural adjustment agreements – such as being poor and in
economic difficulty – have also been linked to civil conflict in previous
research (Blomberg and Hess 2002; Fearon and Laitin 2003; Sambanis
2004a; 2004b). Thus the pool of countries that enters into these
agreements is non-random. In order to tease out the consequences of

structural adjustment on civil conflict it is important to account for these underlying selection criteria of the Bank and Fund. Indeed, the IMF has made a point of defending its record in using structural adjustment agreements to promote economic growth (Rogoff 2003). In response to criticism of their policies, they have noted that their assistance has been targeted at countries in economic difficulty and that the outcomes would have been worse had the IMF not become involved (Rogoff 2003). A two-stage model is the most appropriate method to capture the conceptual framework presented. A two-stage approach accounts for the selection effects concerning which types of countries tend to go under structural adjustment agreements. It is important to control for these selection effects before assessing the direct impact of structural adjustment on the probability of rebellion (Abouharb and Cingranelli 2004a; 2005; 2006; Collier 1991; Gujarati 1995; Przeworski and Vreeland 2000; Vreeland 2003).

The analyses separately examine the consequences of entering into structural adjustment agreements on the probability that a rebellion takes place and, second, the implementation of structural adjustment agreements on the prevalence of civil conflict. The temporal domain of the model spans 1981–1999. The unit of analysis is the country year. The analysis includes several measures of civil conflict: the incidence of rebellion and prevalence of anti-government demonstrations, riots and rebellion. The rebellion measure is taken from Strand, Wilhelmsen, and Gleditsch (2005), while the measures of anti-government demonstrations and riots come from Banks (2005). These are elaborated upon below.

The first stage refers to the equation which estimated the factors affecting entering into a structural adjustment agreement with the World Bank or International Monetary Fund. The first-stage equation results were presented in Chapter 4. The second stage refers to equations predicting either the incidence of rebellion or the prevalence of anti-government demonstrations, riots, and rebellion. Predicted probabilities from the structural adjustment agreement equation described in Chapter 4 were included in both the models estimating the impact of structural adjustment on the probability of rebellion and the prevalence of civil conflict to account for the selection effects of the World Bank and IMF.

Model One examines the incidence of rebellion and uses a logit equation. Model Two has three separate dependent variables: the prevalence of demonstrations, riots, and rebellion. Given our interest in the prevalence of civil conflict, an event count model is the most appropriate estimation technique. Other research has found that events of civil conflict are not independent from one another. For example, a country which endures a rebellion is much more likely to endure another (e.g., Regan 2005). An event count model which accounts for this over-dispersion is a negative binomial regression event count technique (Long 1997). To be sure, if over-dispersion is not present, the model reduces to a Poisson event count model, which assumes that the mean and variance in the event counts are the same. Tables 4.5 and 4.8 in Chapter 4 provide a summary of the operationalization of the independent variables used in the first and second stages of the analysis.

Dependent variables

Rebellion[3] The underlying framework used to code the incidence and prevalence of rebellion stems from Gleditsch *et al.* (2002). A civil conflict is defined as one where armed force is used to promote the parties' general position in the conflict. Any materials can be used as weapons in the conflict. The coding decisions used by Strand, Wilhelmsen, and Gleditsch (2005) describe the parties that participate in an armed conflict. The government is the party that controls the capital, and the opposition is any nongovernmental group of people that has announced a name for its group and uses armed force. The state is either an internationally recognized sovereign government controlling a specified territory, or a government not recognized internationally but which controls a specified territory whose sovereignty is not disputed by another internationally recognized sovereign government previously controlling the same territory. The issues over which the parties are fighting range from incompatibilities as stated by the parties over government or territory, such as secession or autonomy, to incompatibilities over the political system, such as the replacement of the central government or a change in its composition.

Incidence of rebellion This measure is taken from the Strand, Wilhelmsen, and Gleditsch (2005) civil war data set. It is a dichotomous measure where a value of "1" indicates where there was a rebellion with at least twenty-five battle deaths during that year and a value of "0" indicates that no rebellion took place.

Prevalence of civil conflict Each one of the prevalence measures is constructed the same way. Each separate measure counts the number

---

[3] For an excellent discussion of the drawbacks of different coding schemes in drawing up lists of civil wars see Sambanis (2004b).

of consecutive years a country has experienced anti-government demonstrations, riots, or rebellion. Thus, for a country that has experienced eighteen years of rebellion, the prevalence measure will increase by one each consecutive year that a rebellion takes place. If the country experiences three years of rebellion between 1981–1984 and then remains peaceful, the count will go from one to three and then revert to zero for the rest of the period. Demonstrations describe any peaceful public gathering of at least 100 people for the primary purpose of displaying or voicing their opposition to government policies or authority, and are taken from Banks (2005). Riots describe any violent demonstration or clash of more than 100 citizens involving the use of physical force, and are also taken from Banks (2005).

Findings

The results provide strong support for both arguments. Countries that entered into structural adjustment agreements with the World Bank or IMF faced an increased probability of rebellion. Likewise, the consequences of structural adjustment implementation increased the numbers of years governments endure anti-government demonstrations, riots, and rebellion. The longer governments have spent under structural adjustment agreements, the more years these countries have endured states of anti-government protest and violence. Both sets of results report findings that do and do not account for selection issues. We report both but believe the models that account for selection to be more accurate. To be sure, the findings are consistent across both the models that do and do not account for selection. Only in the model displaying the impact of structural adjustment on the prevalence of anti-government demonstrations do the findings differ; in the model accounting for selection, SAA implementation now has a significant impact.

Table 7.1 displays the results concerning the impact of entering into a structural adjustment agreement on the probability of rebellion. When governments enter into these agreements it appears to signal weakness to opposition groups within the country. Rebel groups were more likely to launch rebellions when governments entered into structural adjustment agreements with the World Bank and IMF, significant at the .05 level of confidence. The results provide support for existing arguments about the probability of rebellion. Countries with higher levels of population density and more ethnically heterogeneous populations faced an increased probability of rebellion. The findings about the impact of primary commodity exports support recent research (Fearon 2005) indicating that countries which were primary commodity exporters were

Table 7.1. *The impact of entering into structural adjustment agreements on the probability of rebellion 1981–1999, all developing countries (logit)*

	Selection corrected	Selection not corrected
Entering into a structural adjustment agreement	.392* (.249)	.538** (.195)
Control variables		
Physical quality of life index	−.005 (.009)	−.006 (.009)
GDP per capita	2.21e−06 (.00008)	9.06e−06 (.00005)
Population density	8.16e−07* (3.92e−07)	3.01e−07 (4.14e−07)
Mixed-regime POLITY score	−.245 (.43)	−.245 (.40)
Ethnic heterogeneity	.008** (.003)	.01** (.003)
Regime durability	.004 (.01)	.002 (.008)
Log of primary commodity exports	−.327* (.156)	−.657*** (.189)
Log of fuel exports	.008^ (.005)	.009* (.005)
Log of mountainous states	.312*** (.088)	.218** (.085)
World Bank and IMF selection effects	−.842 (.696)	−
Constant	−.228 (.754)	−1.62 (.739)
N	1288	1791
Pseudo R²	.59	.52

Note: P>|z .10^ .05*, .01**, .001***
Models are estimated with robust standard errors with one-tailed significance tests. Cubic splines were included to control for temporal dependence.

less likely to face rebellion, while those that were exporters of fuel were in greater danger of such acts.

Table 7.2 displays the results concerning the impact of structural adjustment implementation on the prevalence of anti-government protest and violence. These results provide support for the argument that longer exposure to structural adjustment does not improve matters in these countries but rather makes them worse. Countries that have been under these programs the longest have endured the greatest number of years of anti-government demonstrations, riots, and rebellion. Yet, the logic of neoliberal arguments would indicate that countries that have undertaken the most restructuring of their economies would benefit the most from increased levels of economic growth and wealth generation reducing conflict within these countries.

Table 7.2. *The impact of implementing structural adjustment agreements on the prevalence of anti-government demonstrations, riots, and rebellion 1981–1999, all developing countries (negative binomial regression)*

	Demonstrations selection corrected	Demonstrations selection not corrected	Riots selection corrected	Riots selection not corrected	Rebellion selection corrected	Rebellion selection not corrected
Number of years under a World Bank or IMF structural adjustment agreement	.019^ (.015)	.012 (.015)	.032** (.013)	.034**(.013)	.08*** (.012)	.096*** (.012)
Control variables						
Physical quality of life index	−.019*** (.004)	−.017*** (.004)	−.012** (.005)	−.006^ (.004)	.002 (006)	.006 (005)
GDP per capita	9.66e−06 (.00005)	.00003 (.00002)	.001** (.00005)	.00005** (.00002)	.00006^ (.00004)	.0001*** (.00002)
Population density	−8.44e−07*** (2.39e−07)	−7.31e−07** (3.13e−07)	−7.43e−07*** (3.06e−07)	−7.27e−07* (3.79e−07)	−9.31e−07*** (3.06e−07)	−5.80e−07^ (3.95e−07)
Mixed-regime POLITY score	−.09 (.21)	−.107 (.202)	.116 (.17)	.133 (.162)	.453** (.188)	.5007** (.182)
Ethnic heterogeneity	.0005 (.003)	.002 (.003)	−.001 (.002)	−.0006 (.002)	−.005* (.003)	−.005* (.003)
Regime durability	.004 (.005)	.006 (.005)	.006 (.005)	.003 (.005)	.002 (.006)	.004 (.005)
Log of primary commodity exports	.169* (.105)	.197* (.105)	.143^ (.108)	.162^ (.105)	.098 (108)	.133 (108)
Log of fuel exports	−.003 (.002)	−.002 (.002)	−.008** (.003)	−.003 (.003)	.001 (.003)	−.001 (.003)
Log of mountainous states	−.059 (.054)	−.043 (.048)	−.035 (.047)	−.019 (.046)	−.07 (.057)	−.088 (.057)
World Bank and IMF selection effects	−.72** (.292)	—	−.873*** (.244)	—	−.487* (.291)	—
Constant	3.15*** (.465)	2.667*** (.4245)	2.698*** (.452)	2.099*** (.402)	1.756*** (.521)	1.187*** (.467)
N	1287	1789	1287	1788	1288	1791

Note: P>|z| .10^ .05*, .01**, .001***
Models are estimated with robust standard errors, with one-tailed significance tests.

The results provide some interesting findings about how factors linked to the probability of rebellion affect the numbers of years governments have endured anti-government protest and violence during the 1981–1999 period. A number of control variables were found to have a consistent impact as indicated by their statistical significance in two or more models. Our indicator of respect for economic and social rights, the physical quality of life index (PQLI), shows that higher levels of PQLI reduce the number of years governments face anti-government demonstrations and riots. Greater levels of wealth, indicated by our GDP per capita measure, appeared to lengthen conflicts, perhaps increasing the level of resources available to anti-government groups. Countries with more dense populations appeared to spend fewer years enduring each type of anti-government protest and violence. Taken together with the earlier results this may indicate that countries with dense populations are more likely to undergo rebellions and other types of anti-government action, but that these instances are short-lived. Being a primary commodity exporter appeared to lengthen the period of time governments face anti-government demonstrations and riots but did not impact the length of rebellion. Finally, the selection criteria of the Bank and Fund appear to favor governments that are less likely to endure anti-government demonstrations and riots. These empirical results provide no support for arguments about the beneficial consequences of structural adjustment agreements.

Conclusions

The results provide support for arguments about the importance of transnational sources of civil conflict and complement some of the existing research on the impact of economic integration on civil conflict (Barbieri and Reuveny 2005; Mason 2004). The theoretical value of this research is to provide a framework that links the impact of specific transnational forces, in this case the actions of international financial institutions, to the potential for anti-government protest and rebellion within countries. The argument we have made links entering into and implementing structural adjustment agreements with the World Bank and International Monetary Fund to increases in the probability of anti-government protest and rebellion along a number of existing dimensions identified in the civil conflict literature. Entering into agreements with these institutions appears to signal governmental weakness that opposition groups will try to take advantage of for their own political ends, increasing the probability of anti-government rebellion. This work also assesses the impact of these international financial institutions' neoliberal policy framework on the domestic stability of countries undertaking these programs. Instead of promoting development and increasing levels of stability within developing countries, the consequences of these policies increased the periods of time governments were faced with anti-government demonstrations, riots, and rebellion. When taken together with the findings that government respect for human rights worsened during periods of structural adjustment implementation, this work dovetails with previous research about the deleterious consequences of these programs (Abouharb and Cingranelli 2006).

The policy implications of this research are clear. The consequences of structural adjustment agreements as presently framed by the World Bank and IMF have detrimental effects on the stability of developing countries. They have not only failed to promote economic development but the consequences of the economic decline and damage wrought upon the social fabric of these countries have increased the amount of time governments are faced with anti-government demonstrations, riots, and rebellion. These are worrying findings given the importance that the international community has placed upon the promotion of economic development, the maintenance of domestic political and economic stability in developing countries, and the avoidance of generating more failed states in the international system, especially since such states have often been found to harbor transnational terrorist organizations.

8 Torture, murder, disappearance, and political imprisonment

Introduction

Dramatic scenes of anti-government protest and rioting, which were met with acts of government-sponsored repression, took place across Morocco in the summer of 1981. These protests and the government's violent response came in the midst of an economic slump caused by lower levels of international demand for phosphates, fruits, and vegetables, Morocco's main exports (Paul 1981: 30). The bleak economic situation was worsened by austerity measures imposed by the International Monetary Fund, which called for the removal of food price subsidies and cuts in government spending (Paul 1981: 30). Paul (1981) describes in detail the violent repercussions of government-spending reductions which led to spontaneous demonstrations. Many students responded to reductions in education funding mandated by the IMF with rioting. The government responded to this first round of action with arrests of members of the former communist party and socialist parties in Morocco. Demonstrators were arrested and brought to trial for "endangering public order."

Organized labor responded to the removal of price controls with calls for action. The Moroccan Trade Union Confederation called for a strike, which turned out to be very successful. The effect of this strike almost entirely shut down Morocco's largest city, Casablanca. Two days after this strike union leaders asked all citizens to join the protest. Demonstrators poured into the streets in all parts of the country, turning over buses, smashing cars and windows, setting things on fire, often targeting banks in the process. Local police were unable to control the riots so the army, with tanks and helicopters, attempted to quell the unrest which went on into the next morning. Special army units were sent in and Casablanca was sealed off from the countryside. Gunfire was heard and the fighting between army and demonstrators continued for thirty-six hours. Afterwards large-scale arrests were undertaken targeting opposition political and trade union leaders. The police also went to the offices of many newspapers and searched and seized numerous documents and letters. They shut down the newspaper produced by the Socialist Union of Popular Forces political party. The riots were unofficially estimated to have left 600 dead (Paul 1981); the army and its heavy-handed approach, it seems, extrajudicially killed hundred of civilians, leaving thousands more wounded and arrested. The austerity measures insisted upon by the IMF as part of any financial assistance package touched off much of the violence.

Were these events in Morocco unusual, or do the austerity measures associated with structural adjustment packages often lead government leaders to use repression, as the Moroccan government did, to squash dissent and maintain their hold on political office? As we have shown in previous chapters, countries under structural adjustment for a relatively long period tend to have governments that provide lower than expected levels of respect for economic and social rights (Chapter 6). The deprivations caused by structural adjustment conditions are generally unpopular in less developed countries: anti-government demonstrations occur more often (Chapter 7). Sometimes these protests become violent, increasing the occurrence of riots and organized rebellion (Chapter 7). In this chapter, we demonstrate that governments often respond to these challenges to their authority by increasing the repression of physical integrity rights.

World Bank and International Monetary Fund structural adjustment conditions require loan-recipient governments to rapidly liberalize their economies. According to previous research, these economic changes often cause at least short-term hardships for the poorest people in less developed countries. The Bank and IMF justify the loan conditions as necessary stimuli for economic development. However, research has shown that implementation of structural adjustment conditions actually has a negative effect on economic growth (Przeworski and Vreeland 2000; Vreeland 2003). While there has been less research on the human rights effects of structural adjustment conditions, most studies agree that the imposition of structural adjustment conditions on less developed countries worsens government human rights practices (Franklin 1997; Keith and Poe 2000; McLaren 1998; Pion-Berlin 1983; 1984). This chapter focuses on the effects of structural adjustment conditions on the extent to which governments protect their citizens from extrajudicial killings, torture, disappearances, and political imprisonment.

A summary of the results

Empirically, this study advances our understanding of the human rights consequences of structural adjustment by correcting for the effects of selection. It is possible that the worsened human rights practices observed and reported in previous studies might have resulted from the poor economic conditions that led to the imposition of the structural adjustment conditions rather than the implementation of the structural adjustment conditions themselves. In other words, the human rights practices of loan-recipient governments might have gotten worse whether or not a structural adjustment agreement had been implemented. In addition, as our results will show, some of the factors that increase the probability of entering into an SAA, such as having a large population and being relatively poor, are also associated with an increased probability of human rights violations. For these reasons one must disentangle the effects of selection before estimating the human rights impacts of structural adjustment agreements. In order to control for the effects of selection, a two-stage analysis was undertaken. In the first stage of the analysis, the factors affecting World Bank and IMF decisions concerning which governments receive SAAs were identified. In the second stage the impacts of implementing SAAs on government respect for human rights were examined.

Chapter 5 examined the selection criteria of the Bank and Fund, and the first-stage results demonstrated that the Bank and Fund do give SAAs to governments that are poor and experiencing economic trouble, but the Bank and Fund also employ a wide variety of noneconomic loan-selection criteria. The noneconomic selection criteria examined in the first stage demonstrate that the Bank and Fund prefer to give loans to governments that provide greater protection for the physical integrity rights of their citizens. Earlier research had shown that democracies were at a disadvantage when negotiating an SAA from the IMF (Przeworski and Vreeland 2000; Vreeland 2003), a finding consistent with expectations generated by Putnam's (1988) theory of two-level games. Our findings indicate that democracies are neither advantaged nor discriminated against when negotiating with these international financial institutions. After controlling for selection effects and other explanations of respect for physical integrity rights, the findings of the second-stage analysis show that governments that have spent greater periods of time under structural adjustment conditions have worsened levels of government respect for the physical integrity rights of their citizens.

The theoretical links between structural adjustment and repression

The competing arguments laid out in Chapter 3 indicated two very different expectations about the connection between structural adjustment and government respect for the physical integrity rights of their citizens. The neoliberal perspective argues that the conditions associated with structural adjustment stimulate high-quality economic growth, generate wealth, and promote economic development. From this perspective, the more liberal changes that governments make to their economies the greater the benefits that will accrue as the economy grows, wealth is generated, and economic development takes place. The consequences of wealth generation and higher levels of economic development, according to previous research, should lead to increased levels of respect for human rights.

In contrast, the critical perspective indicates that, in practice, structural adjustment conditions almost always cause hardships for the poorest people in a society, because they necessitate some combination of reductions in public employment, elimination of price subsidies for essential commodities or services, and cuts in expenditures for health, education, and welfare programs. These hardships often cause increased levels of civil conflict that present substantial challenges to government leaders. Some governments respond to these challenges by becoming less democratic, as in the case of Peru under President Fujimori in the 1980s (Di John 2005). Increased civil conflict and decreased democracy are associated with higher levels of repression (e.g., Poe, Tate, and Keith 1999). The majority of the existing research presents more evidence for the critical perspective. The case of Venezuela provides an illustration of the role of structural adjustment in producing increased civil conflict, a weakened democratic system, and repression (Di John 2005: 114; see above, p. 152). Although Venezuela's democratic system has been maintained, over the period of this study dissatisfaction with economic policies has played a part in three attempted coups, multiple general strikes, and two presidential-assassination attempts, and has led to several states of emergency being imposed. Even today, debate over structural adjustment policies in Venezuela remains heated. President Hugo Chavez sustains his popularity largely based on his opposition to the kind of unregulated economic liberalization advocated by the World Bank and IMF (Banks, Muller, and Overstreet 2003).

The fairest way to assess the impact of structural adjustment is over the longer period. If structural adjustment generated the benefits argued for by its proponents then those governments that have been under structural adjustment the longest should see the greatest improvements in their human rights situations. In comparison, if the consequences of structural adjustment are as deleterious as laid out by its critics then we should expect that governments under structural adjustment the longest will tend to be faced with increased levels of violent anti-government protest. Government leaders will be tempted to violate the physical integrity rights of citizens to maintain their hold on office.

Previous research linking structural adjustment to human rights practices

As noted in Chapter 3, government abuse of physical integrity rights has, thus far, been the phenomenon of chief theoretical interest in most empirical studies of the determinants and consequences of government abuse of human rights.[1] The results of previous research explicitly focusing on the effects of SAAs on government respect for physical integrity rights are consistent with the expectations of the critical perspective (Fields 2003; Franklin 1997; Keith and Poe 2000; McLaren 1998). Keith and Poe (2000) evaluated the human rights effects of getting an SAA from the IMF by comparing the human rights practices of governments with and without such loans while controlling for other factors reliably associated with good or bad human rights practices by governments. They focused on a global sample of countries between 1981 and 1987, and found some evidence indicating an increase in the level of repression of physical integrity rights during the implementation of a structural adjustment agreement. Using a cross-sectional analysis, Franklin (1997) also found some support for the argument that governments implementing IMF agreements were likely to become more repressive of the physical integrity rights of their citizens.

The limitation of the previous research is that these studies have not controlled for the selection criteria employed by the Bank and Fund when deciding with which countries to enter into structural adjustment agreements. Thus, estimating the human rights effects of structural adjustment requires the use of a two-stage econometric model. Chapter 4 detailed the need for a selection model in order to properly estimate the relationship between structural adjustment and government respect for human rights. Previous research that we have undertaken controlled for issues of selection and examined the impact of World Bank structural adjustment agreements on freedom from torture, political imprisonment, extrajudicial killing, and disappearance (Abouharb and Cingranelli 2006). The findings indicated that implementation of World Bank structural adjustment agreements had significant negative impacts on government respect for freedom from torture, extrajudicial killing, and

---

[1] For an excellent review of the econometric research explaining cross-national variation in government respect for physical integrity rights, see Poe (2004).

disappearance. Here we estimate the joint impacts of IMF and World Bank structural adjustment programs.

Hypotheses

In order to test hypotheses about the human rights impacts of SAAs, one must first account for the effects of World Bank and IMF loan-selection criteria. As noted, previous research suggests that economic, political, conflict, and human rights factors help determine the probability of receiving an SAA and also impact subsequent human rights practices. Since these selection issues were addressed in Chapter 5, the hypotheses concentrate on the human rights impact of structural adjustment conditionality. Our expectation is that governments which spend greater periods of time under structural adjustment conditions have lower levels of respect for physical integrity rights.

Other studies have demonstrated that wealthier countries, more democratic countries, and countries with a British colonial experience tend to have governments that provide more respect for the physical integrity rights of their citizens. Countries with relatively large populations, relatively large population increases, high levels of civil conflict, and involvement in interstate war tend to have governments that provide less respect for the physical integrity rights of their citizens (Poe 2004; Poe, Tate, and Keith 1999). These factors will be included as control variables in the analysis.

Research design

Chapter 4 details the research design used. The first-stage model predicting entering into a structural adjustment agreement and the impact of structural adjustment implementation on respect for physical integrity rights were linked by using predicted probabilities. These probabilities were generated from the first-stage model predicting entering into a structural adjustment agreement and were included as an independent variable in the second-stage ordinary least squares model. Tables 4.5 and 4.7, found in Chapter 4, describe the variables used in each equation.

Measuring respect for physical integrity rights

The measure of respect for physical integrity rights used in this analysis is the CIRI physical integrity rights index. This is an additive index that includes four human rights practices, each of which is scored from "zero" to "two." Thus the index score for each country in each year could range from "zero" to "eight." Cingranelli and Richards (1999a) have demonstrated the unidimensionality of this scale. In other work (Abouharb and Cingranelli 2006), we have examined the effects of structural adjustment on each of the scale's components. Here, we only look at the effects on overall government respect for physical integrity rights. The four components of the index are torture, political imprisonment, extrajudicial killing, and disappearances. Each was scored based on a count of the number of instances of violations of each right in each country year. We illustrate this procedure using the example of torture.

According to Cingranelli and Richards (2006), torture refers to the purposeful inflicting of extreme pain, whether mental or physical, by government officials or by private individuals at the instigation of government officials. Torture includes the use of physical and other force by police and prison guards that is cruel, inhuman, or degrading. This also includes prison conditions, including whether conditions meet minimum international standards, and deaths in custody due to negligence by government officials. Torture can be anything from simple beatings, to other practices such as rape or administering shock or electrocution as a means of getting information, or a forced confession. Torture also takes into account mental abuse and ill-treatment of those in state custody such as: unsanitary conditions, denial of adequate meals or no meals at all, and inadequate medical attention.

The coding scheme   Torture is:

(0) Practiced frequently
(1) Practiced occasionally
(2) Not practiced
(9) Not mentioned

The coding scores above were based on the number of instances of torture (persons tortured) that occurred in a country during the calendar year (and *only* in that year). These numbers and their corresponding coding score are:

Coding score	Number of instances
0	50 or more
1	From 1 to 49
2	Zero

Coders were instructed to code instances where violations were described by adjectives such as "gross," "widespread," "systematic," "epidemic," "extensive," or "wholesale" as "zero" (practiced frequently). In instances where violations were described by adjectives such as "numerous" or "many," coders were instructed to use their best judgment after reading both the Amnesty International Report and the US State Department's *Country Reports on Human Rights Practices*. Such cases might be coded as a "one" (practiced occasionally) or a "zero" (practiced frequently). When Amnesty International's evaluation of the government's performance explicitly differed from the one provided by the US State Department, coders were instructed to treat the Amnesty International evaluation as authoritative. The other three components of the CIRI physical integrity rights index were coded in the same way. The definitions of each of these human rights practices as provided by Cingranelli and Richards (2006) follow.

Political imprisonment refers to the incarceration of people by government officials because of: their speech; their nonviolent opposition to government policies or leaders; their religious beliefs; their nonviolent religious practices including proselytizing; or their membership in a group, including an ethnic or racial group.

Disappearances are cases in which people have disappeared, political motivation appears likely, and the victims (the disappeared) have not been found. In most instances, disappearances occur because of a victim's political involvement or knowledge of information sensitive to authorities. Often, victims are referred to by governments as "terrorists," and labeled a threat to national security. Knowledge of the whereabouts of the disappeared is, by definition, not public knowledge. However, while there is typically no way of knowing where victims are, it is typically known by whom they were taken and under what circumstances. In many instances, victims are taken under false pretense, such as having been taken away for questioning due to suspicion of some political action that is in opposition to the government. There are some cases of persons that are held under the circumstance of "clandestine detention." These are prisoners that are known to be in custody but their whereabouts are not known. Since the whereabouts of clandestine detainees are not known, they should be counted among the disappeared.

Extrajudicial killings are killings by government officials without due process of law. They include murders by private groups *if* instigated by government. These killings may result from the deliberate, illegal, and excessive use of lethal force by the police, security forces, or other agents of the state whether against criminal suspects, detainees, prisoners, or others. Death resulting from torture was counted as extrajudicial killing, since death occurred while the prisoners were in the custody of the government or its agents. In most cases, the US State Department (USSD) and Amnesty International (AI) indicate cases of political killings by explicitly referring to these killings as "political." A victim of politically motivated killing is someone who was killed by a government or its agents as a result of his or her involvement in political activities or for supporting (implicitly or explicitly) the political actions of opposition movements against the existing government.

Independent variables

The independent variable of chief theoretical interest is the "number of years a country has been under a World Bank or IMF structural adjustment agreement." Other studies have demonstrated that wealthier countries, more democratic countries, and countries with a British colonial experience tend to have governments that provide more respect for the personal integrity rights of their citizens. Countries with military governments, relatively large populations, relatively large population increases, high levels of domestic conflict, and involvement in interstate war tend to have governments that provide less respect for the personal integrity rights of their citizens (Poe 2004; Poe, Tate, and Keith 1999). These factors were included as control variables in the analysis. The dependent variable is lagged one year, so the effective dependent variable is the annual change in respect for physical integrity rights.

Findings

First-stage results: entering into a World Bank and IMF structural adjustment agreement

Table 5.2 presented in Chapter 5 provided the results of the first-stage equation predicting which governments enter into structural adjustment agreements with the World Bank or International Monetary Fund. The economic factors shown to have a significant impact on entering into a structural adjustment agreement included being in greater debt and having relatively little trade. We also found that governments with higher levels of respect for the physical integrity rights of their citizens were more likely to receive a structural adjustment package. More populous countries had a greater impression with the Bank and Fund, increasing the probability of SAA receipt. In our sample of developing

Table 8.1. *Impact of entering into World Bank and IMF SAA and its implementation on respect for physical integrity rights 1981–2003, all developing countries (ordinary least squares)*

	Selection corrected	Selection not corrected
Number of years under a World Bank or IMF structural adjustment agreement	−.012* (.007)	−.003 (.006)
Economic factors		
GDP per capita	.0001*** (.00002)	.00002* (9.47e−06)
Percentage change in GDP per capita	−.001* (.0005)	−.0004 (.0004)
Trade as a proportion of GDP	.003** (.001)	.001^ (.001)
Domestic political factors		
Democracy	.053*** (.012)	.048*** (.01)
Log population	−.249*** (.03)	−.225*** (.024)
Population density	1.70e−08 (1.04e−07)	1.09e−08 (9.02e−08)
UK dependent/colonial experience	.110^ (.0755)	.01 (.069)
Physical quality of life index	−.007** (.003)	−.004^ (.002)
Conflict proneness		
Interstate conflict	.072 (.115)	.048 (.082)
Rebellion	−.463*** (.058)	−.452*** (.049)
Control variables		
World Bank and IMF selection effects	1.24*** (.167)	–
Respect for personal integrity rights lag	.522*** (.029)	.554*** (.026)
Constant	5.825*** (.574)	5.756*** (.486)
N	1606	2062
R^2	.68	.99

Note: P>|z .1^ .05*, .01**, .001***
Models are estimated with robust standard errors, with one-tailed significance tests.

countries in existence for the whole period, the end of the Cold War has increased competition for assistance from these institutions from the newly independent post-Soviet states, reducing the probability of receiving a structural adjustment package. Finally, the greater the numbers of countries under structural adjustment in a particular year the more likely a government will enter into an agreement since the sovereignty costs are lowered as more countries become involved in the process.

Second-stage results: the human rights impact of structural adjustment

The second human rights impact stage results in Table 8.1 show both the selection corrected effects of structural adjustment agreements on government respect for physical integrity rights (column 1) and the effects we would have discovered if we had not controlled for the effects of selection (column 2). The selection-corrected effects show that governments which have spent longer periods of time under structural adjustment conditions have lower levels of respect for physical integrity rights, significant at the .05 level of confidence. In general, the control variables at the second human rights impact stage behave as one would have expected given the results of previous research.

Economic factors found to improve levels of government respect for physical integrity rights included our measure of wealth, higher levels of GDP per capita, significant at the .001 level of confidence. These findings dovetail with the previous research (Poe, Tate, and Keith 1999). We also find support for previous arguments about the beneficial impacts of increased trade on government respect for physical integrity rights, significant at the .01 level of confidence (Richards, Gelleny, and Sacko 2001). Also of interest is the finding that rapid economic growth, measured here as the percentage change in GDP per capita, has a negative impact on respect for physical integrity rights, significant at the .01 level of confidence. These findings also provide additional evidence for previous arguments about the destabilizing effect of rapid economic growth (Olson 1963; Poe, Tate, and Keith 1999).

A number of domestic political factors also were associated with variation in levels of government respect for the physical integrity rights of their citizens. More democratic regimes had higher levels of respect, significant at the .001 level of confidence, as did former colonies of the United Kingdom, significant at .10 level of confidence. Countries with larger populations had lower levels of respect for physical integrity rights, significant at the .001 level of confidence. One puzzling finding was that our indicator of respect for economic and social rights, the physical quality of life index, was negatively associated with greater levels of respect for physical integrity rights, significant at the .01 level of confidence. One possibility is that this indicator is showing some kind of diminishing level of beneficial returns. Respect for economic and social rights improves levels of government respect for physical integrity rights by lowering the possibility that people protest against their governments' public policies, but after a certain point improvements in these rights fail to have any further significant impact in improving respect for physical integrity rights.

Higher levels of rebellion, our measure of civil conflict, indicate that when governments are faced with armed opposition they are more likely to repress their citizens, significant at the .001 level of confidence. The findings indicate little support for some previous arguments linking involvement in international conflict with lower levels of respect for physical integrity rights at home. Finally, our selection effects control measure indicated that the criteria used by the World Bank and IMF overall make them more likely to enter into agreements with countries that have higher levels of respect for physical integrity rights, significant at the .001 level of confidence. These selection-corrected effects bear out our findings in Chapter 5 that representatives of key countries on the boards of the Bank and Fund prefer to make agreements with governments that respect the human rights of their citizens.[2]

In this analysis, the probability of each country negotiating an SAL in each year was calculated and then entered as an independent variable in the selection-corrected equation. This independent variable was left out of the equation that yielded the results reported in column two of Table 8.1. The variable titled "World Bank and IMF selection effects" was significant in the selection-corrected results. Thus, correcting for selection made a substantial difference in the findings reported. Had we not controlled for the effects of selection we would have found that the number of years under a World Bank or IMF structural adjustment agreement was not associated with worse levels of respect for physical integrity rights.

Conclusions

The most important substantive finding of this study is that the longer the period that countries have spent under structural adjustment agreements the worse are levels of government respect for physical integrity rights. This finding is generally consistent with the findings of previous comparative and case study research on the human rights effects of IMF structural adjustment agreements. It is stronger, but generally supportive of the finding reported by Keith and Poe (2000) regarding the effects of IMF structural adjustment conditions.

---

[2] An alternate model was estimated using the Political Terror Scale (Gibney and Dalton 1996). The sign was in the expected positive direction, indicating that longer periods of structural adjustment implementation increased levels of political terror, but was statistically insignificant.

The findings presented here have important policy implications. There is mounting evidence that national economies grow fastest when basic human rights are respected (Kaufmann 2004; Kaufmann, Kraay, and Mastruzzi 2005; Sen 1999). Structural adjustment agreements place too much emphasis on instituting a freer market and too little emphasis on allowing the other human freedoms necessary for rapid economic growth to take root and grow. By undermining the human rights conditions necessary for economic development, the Bank and Fund are damaging their own mission.

9 Worker rights

Introduction

As we have shown in previous chapters, countries under structural adjustment for a relatively long period tend to have governments that provide lower than expected levels of respect for economic and social rights (Chapter 6). The deprivations caused by structural adjustment conditions are generally unpopular in less developed countries: anti-government demonstrations occur more often (Chapter 7). Sometimes these protests become violent, increasing the occurrence of riots and organized rebellion (Chapter 7). Governments often respond to these challenges to their authority by increasing the repression of physical integrity rights (Chapter 8). Many country studies have also provided evidence that structural adjustment conditions have led to reduced government respect for worker rights.

For example, comparative case studies conducted by the Structural Adjustment Participatory Review International Network (SAPRIN) took a close look at the effects of structural adjustment programs on workers in Ecuador, El Salvador, Mexico, and Zimbabwe (SAPRIN 2004). The study's findings showed how a combination of labor-market reforms, layoffs resulting from privatizations and civil service reform, and the shrinking of labor-intensive productive sectors had severely undermined the position of workers. Employment levels had dropped, jobs had become more precarious, real wages had deteriorated, income distribution had become less equitable, and worker rights and unions had been weakened. Structural adjustment reforms had allowed employers greater flexibility in establishing the terms and conditions of work, and public enterprises had been privatized without adequate regulation (SAPRIN 2004, Chapter 4; also see Heredia and Purcell 1996; Lloyd 2001). The SAPRIN report includes many specifics of how labor law reforms in all four countries designed to make the economy more business friendly had limited the rights of workers to organize and to strike (SAPRIN 2004: 106–107). The rights to form and join labor unions and to collectively bargain with employers are two of the most important internationally recognized worker rights (ILO 2003). Other studies report that a de facto condition associated with structural adjustment loans is reducing wages or wage increases to make exports more competitive (Bello 1996; Heredia and Purcell 1996).

The World Bank has begun to respond to these criticisms. The International Finance Corporation (IFC), the arm of the World Bank that provides loans and guarantees as well as taking equity positions in private enterprises, under persistent pressure from the SAPRIN, the International Trade Union Confederation (ITUC), and other groups in civil society, in 2006 adopted new standards for projects carried out by private businesses. These new standards require businesses working on IFC-financed projects to respect the core labor standards established by the International Labour Organization (ILO). These ILO standards require that workers be allowed to form unions and collectively bargain. They prohibit child labor, forced labor, and discrimination. In addition, the new IFC standards oblige IFC clients to protect contract workers and observe good health and safety practices. Gus Ryder, ITUC General Secretary, would like to see governments that accept funds from other branches of the World Bank bound by the same standards. "This is not a matter of asking the Bank to do the job of the ILO, governments or anyone else. It is a matter of asking the Bank to ensure that all of its operations abide by internationally-recognized workers' rights' standards" (ITUC 2006). On December 13, 2006, World Bank President Paul Wolfowitz announced that the Bank would take further steps to protect worker rights by guaranteeing that all future infrastructure projects funded by the Bank would be required to respect all of the core labor standards of the International Labour Organization. Approximately 8 billion US dollars' worth of projects per year will be affected by this decision (Union Network International 2006).

Scholars have yet to perform rigorous, systematic, scientific studies of the relationship between implementation of structural adjustment programs and respect for worker rights. This chapter begins to fill that void. In Chapter 5, we examined the impact of government respect for worker rights on the probability of entering into a structural adjustment agreement with the World Bank or International Monetary Fund. Those results were weak and inconsistent. World Bank-financed agreements were more prevalent with governments that had a relatively high level of protection of worker rights than those that did not (see Table 5.1). With IMF-financed agreements, we found the opposite was true (see Table 5.1). Not surprisingly, when we considered the overall effect of strong protections of worker rights on the likelihood of entering into a structural adjustment agreement, there was no statistically significant effect (see Table 5.2).

In this chapter, we begin by defining worker rights. We argue that worker rights are human rights, and respect for worker rights is of central importance to any strategy of equitable economic development. We then review studies that have examined the consequences of respect for worker rights on the distribution of income in society, the development and maintenance of democracy, and the ability of a country to engage in international trade. All of these topics have been the subjects of previous research. The results of these studies illustrate the important political and economic consequences that follow from respect or lack of respect for worker rights. We also review the previous research seeking to explain government respect for human rights, in general, and worker rights in particular. Our purpose is to identify plausible alternative explanations for different levels of government respect for worker rights. Then we introduce a new measure of respect for worker rights, and we present findings showing that the longer a country has been under structural adjustment conditionality the greater the repression of worker rights.

Worker rights

Two international human rights agreements – the Universal Declaration of Human Rights (UDHR) and the International Covenant on Economic, Social and Cultural Rights (ICESCR) – acknowledge worker rights as human rights. The UDHR recognizes the right to just and favorable conditions of work, to protection against unemployment, to equal pay for equal work, to an existence worthy of human dignity (Article 23), to rest and leisure, to reasonable limitation on working hours, to periodic holidays with pay (Article 24), and to security in the event of unemployment (Article 25). The ICESCR recognizes the right to work, to equal remuneration for work of equal value, to a decent standard of living, and to reasonable working hours (Article 7). The ICESCR also recognizes many rights that depend mainly on income gained through work such as adequate food, clothing, and housing, to continuous improvement of living conditions (Article 11), to medical care (Article 12), and to education (Articles 13 and 14).

The worker rights included in international human rights documents are elaborated in more detail in the 185 Conventions and 195 Recommendations of the oldest international governmental human rights organization in the world – the International Labour Organization, the

UN agency that focuses on labor issues (ILO 1998b: 46). In most instances, ILO Conventions preceded the development of the acknowledgments of worker rights in the UDHR and ICESCR human rights documents. The Declaration on Fundamental Principles and Rights at Work (ILO 1998b) is a modern initiative of the International Labour Organization requiring all ILO members to "respect, to promote and to realize, in good faith" five core rights (recognized in previously ratified ILO Conventions) that are considered fundamental human rights. They are: freedom of association; the effective recognition of the right to collective bargaining; the elimination of all forms of forced or compulsory labor; the effective abolition of child labor; and the elimination of discrimination in respect of employment or occupation (ILO 1998b; 2003). The worker rights examined in this chapter closely parallel the rights in this list.

For all of the other human rights examined in this book, agents (employees) of the government are directly responsible for protecting or violating rights. Soldiers, police, or prison guards are most likely to engage in torture or extrajudicial killing. The executive and judicial branches identify political opponents and decide whether they should be imprisoned for their views. The relationship between government practices and respect for worker rights is different. It is indirect. Most commonly, government policies affect, protect, or violate worker rights indirectly by regulating the relationship between employers and employees. Those regulations may guarantee that employers provide a minimum wage, safe and healthy working conditions, or paid vacations. Governments also can prohibit employers from discriminating in hiring and treatment at the workplace, from requiring mandatory overtime work, or from arbitrarily terminating employment. Another way government policies can affect worker rights is through legislation that helps workers directly, for example the provision of national unemployment insurance.

Providing more respect for the rights of workers may have important political and economic consequences for societies. Changes in respect for worker rights may lead to similar changes in respect for other human rights. Indeed, the status of workers in a country seems to be a bellwether for the status of human rights in general (Leary 1996). Governments rarely will respect other human rights if they do not respect worker rights (Leary 1996). This may indicate that respect for worker rights is a leading indicator or precursor of changes in the level of respect for other human rights in society. Research has shown that more respect for worker rights is associated with a more equitable distribution of income in society, more international trade and investment in developing countries, and more respect for procedural democratic rights. Perhaps it is because government policies towards workers are so pivotal that labor organizers are often the targets of human rights abuse in developing countries. Suppression of trade unions is a common form of human rights violation that regularly occurs in both democratic and authoritarian political systems (Weisband and Colvin 2000).

Consequences of respect for worker rights

A more equitable distribution of income

Previous research has shown that there is a more equitable distribution of income in society if governments protect the rights of workers, because workers with rights to form labor unions and to bargain collectively will tend to have higher wages and more generous benefits (Blanchflower and Slaughter 1999). Since most citizens are workers, higher wages will produce a more equitable distribution of income. Having an equitable distribution of income means that the gains associated with economic growth have been distributed widely in society rather than consumed by a small elite (Chu, Davoodi, and Gupta 2000). This wider distribution of income should translate into better social and economic rights protection. If there is sufficient income to be distributed, an equitable distribution of income will help to build and maintain a middle class. One enduring characteristic of less developed countries is the absence of a large middle class. Much of the democratization literature stresses the importance of a middle class to the development of democracy (Lipset 1959; Moore 1966). The middle class has the education and leisure time to monitor the activities of government leaders and engage in the political process on a regular basis.

The World Bank's own 2006 *World Development Report* (2005a), titled *Equity and Development*, stresses the importance of respecting core labor standards and presents a generally positive assessment of the role that trade unions play in equitably distributing the benefits of economic growth. In that report, which the Bank defines as its annual "flagship" research report, the Bank investigated the link between equity and prosperous development, acknowledging that labor regulations and strong protection of worker rights are key factors in achieving equitable growth and development. These conclusions sharply contradict the conclusions of recent editions of another World Bank publication, the widely publicized *Doing Business in 2006* (and *Doing Business in 2007*), which ranks countries according to their friendliness to business, based on criteria that penalize countries for enforcing any sort of labor regulation.

Of course, there are other things besides respect for worker rights that affect the distribution of income within societies. Research on this subject has been limited by the absence of reliable information about the degree of income inequality that exists in many developing countries. When less developed countries have been included, sample sizes have been small. At the risk of oversimplification, previous research indicates that the distribution of income tends to be more equitable if the regime is democratic (Burkhart 1997; Muller 1988; Simpson 1990). Progressive tax and expenditure policies also produce a more equitable distribution of income (Chu, Davoodi, and Gupta 2000). Higher minimum wages (Blanchflower and Slaughter 1999), higher levels of union density (Blanchflower and Slaughter 1999), and low levels of foreign direct investment also were found to produce a more equitable distribution of income (Beer 1999).

The decline in union density, or the percentage of workers who belong to trade unions, has been an important explanation of rising income inequality in some OECD states (Blanchflower and Slaughter 1999; Rueda 2005). Unions reduce inequality by standardizing pay rates among workers. In states where workers can easily form or join trade unions, the threat of unionization encourages nonunion employers to raise pay or benefits to keep unions out. Thus, strong protection of worker rights produces strong unions, and the presence of strong unions generally means less inequality in society (Blanchflower and Slaughter 1999: 82).

Relatively low levels of respect for worker rights in the United States in comparison with other OECD countries have led to declines in union density and the real value of the minimum wage (Blanchflower and Freeman 1992; Dubofsky 1994). Approximately one-third of the total increase in income inequality in the United States can be attributed to declines in unionization and the real minimum wage along with economic deregulation (DiNardo, Fortin, and Lemieux 1996). Decentralized wage-setting mechanisms in the United States, because of deference to the individual member states, also have contributed to a greater rise in male wage inequality in the United States than in other countries (Blau and Kahn 1996).

International trade and direct foreign investment

The relationship between respect for worker rights and involvement in international trade is complex. Two studies conducted by the

Organisation for Economic Co-operation and Development (1996; 2000) show that respect for labor rights is not an impediment to international trade and investment. However, the OECD studies also note that China has been the most successful developing country in attracting foreign investment and thereby expanding its international trade over the past two decades. China has done so with relatively poor protection of worker rights. Thus, the argument that developing countries can succeed in integrating into the global economy while upholding high standards for worker rights is not fully convincing. The efforts of the World Bank and IMF to convince governments of developing countries to develop more business-friendly laws and policies also imply that policies that tilt towards workers instead of employers will be detrimental to the efforts of governments to attract foreign investment and trading partners.

Government respect for procedural democratic rights

As noted, greater respect for worker rights – especially a minimum wage – facilitates a more equitable distribution of income in society, and, with a sufficient level of economic development, a larger middle class. The existence of a middle class may pave the way for a successful transition from an authoritarian to a democratic system and from an unstable to a stable democracy (Burkhart 1997). When workers possess rights such as freedom of association at the workplace, they are empowered to challenge a political and economic regime if they choose. One well-known example of workers leading the fight for democracy in an authoritarian regime was Poland's Solidarity movement in the 1980s. Students and workers are often in the forefront of social movements pressing for progressive political reforms in many parts of the world in both authoritarian and recently democratized regimes. In many developing countries, labor unions and church organizations are the backbone of civil society. The existence of voluntary organizations that can interact with government policy-makers is important to a well-functioning democracy, because they provide a forum for advocating demands and an organized way to communicate those demands to political leaders.

Greater respect for worker rights facilitates the development of democracy, and democracy, in turn, promotes greater respect for worker rights. There have been numerous case studies and careful comparisons of small groups of cases concluding that democratization is associated with greater government respect for worker rights. However, most of the previous research on the subject has focused on historical developments in the advanced industrial economies (Adams 1993; Jacobs 1986;

Rimlinger 1977). Does more procedural democracy lead to more respect for worker rights in developing countries? The answer seems to be "yes." Though there has not been much scientific research on this point, the existing global, comparative studies of developing countries have found support for the "democracy–worker rights" linkage (Cingranelli 2002; Cingranelli and Tsai 2002; Mosley and Uno 2007; Mosley 2006; Rodrik 1998).

However, there are some useful counter-examples. If workers are not an important part of the movement to create democracy in an authoritarian state, the policies of the newly democratic state may not be favorable to workers (Huang 2000). South Korea and Taiwan both achieved democratic transitions without the strong support of organized labor. As a consequence, the democratic governments of both countries have been hostile to organized labor (Huang 2000). For example, in 1997, the South Korean government made revisions in the Labor Standard Law, giving employers greater flexibility in terminating workers and in assigning working hours. Similarly, the ruling and opposition parties ignored workers' protests during Taiwan's democratization (Huang 2000).

Given the history of industrial and labor relations in the advanced economies, repression of workers in less developed democratic countries is not surprising. Even the long-established democratic governments of Europe and North America suppressed the trade union movements in their countries in the first fifty years of trade unionism (Jacobs 1986; Rimlinger 1977). According to Jacobs, "one may say that before 1850 labour relations in European countries were characterized by repression. In all these countries trade unions were at first illegal, as were the industrial struggles conducted by workers" (1986: 195). In the United States, repression of trade unions continued well into the early part of the twentieth century (Dubofsky 1994; Goldstein 2001). If the developing economies follow this same path, then one should expect a reduction in respect for worker rights during the early stages of rapid development – even in democratic systems.

The effects of economic globalization on worker rights

A particular country is more or less "economically globalized" to the degree that it participates in worldwide economic interactions beyond some minimum threshold level. Economic globalization is not new. Nations have been involved in economic transactions for thousands of years. However, the rapid increase in economic interconnectedness is new. For some, globalization refers to far more general phenomena. For example, as defined by Held *et al.* (1999: 2), it is a "widening, deepening and speeding up of world interconnectedness in all aspects of contemporary social life, from the cultural to the criminal, the financial to the spiritual."

Changes at the highest level of aggregation, in this case the operations of the world economic system, will affect the behaviors of all of the constituent parts of the system, in this case nation states and the workers within them. At the level of the world economic system, there has been a sharp increase in the amount of economic activity that takes place between people who live in different countries relative to the amount of economic activity among people who live in the same country (Held *et al.* 1999). The extent to which different countries participate in global international transactions is not uniform. Some countries are deeply involved in transnational economic activities of many kinds. Others are hardly involved at all. Thus, if globalization has an impact on worker rights, in general, its impact should be greatest in countries that have the greatest involvement in or experience the greatest increase in transnational economic activities (Cingranelli 2002).

The richer countries of Europe and North America along with Japan, Australia, and New Zealand have long been major exporters of industrial products and services. They have been major participants in the world economy for a long time. They now are able to extend their economic relations in a more vigorous way to more states. Workers in these countries have experienced the consequences of both the highest level of involvement in international economic activities and the greatest amount of increase in those activities since 1990 (Anderson, Cavanagh, and Lee 2000). Most of the economic interactions of the richer countries are with each other (Anderson, Cavanagh, and Lee 2000). About sixty countries included in this study, mostly in Africa, are so poor that their economic interactions with the rest of the world are very limited. In many instances, much of their meager export earnings is generated from one or two agricultural or mineral products (Anderson, Cavanagh, and Lee 2000).

There are two schools of thought on the nature of the relationship between globalization and worker rights. One is the neoliberal school of economics, which posits that a more globalized economy creates more aggregate wealth, and that workers directly benefit from the trickle-down effects of that wealth (Aggarwal 1995; Bhagwati 2002; 2004). The more a particular country participates, the greater the benefits to its workers. Workers in less developed countries would be likely to gain the most from participation in the global economy, because there will tend to be more investment where pay and benefits are low, and working conditions are poor. Once capital investments have been made in these countries, workers will gain more advantage to improve their rights relative to employers.

This might lead to a "leveling-up" effect as worker rights in less developed countries catch up with worker rights in the more advanced economies. In essence, this would be the opposite of what is expected from the race-to-the-bottom thesis. However, there are many possibilities and little convincing evidence so far. Workers in less developed countries may not benefit much from the movement of capital and increased trade that economic globalization brings. Unemployment rates are so high in developing countries that willing workers are easy to find no matter how poor the working conditions (Tonelson 2002). Even if there is a benefit in the early stages of increased trade and investment, once workers organize and press for more rights and higher compensation business may relocate to countries where labor is less well organized and less protected by government policies (Silver 2003). Still another view is that increased competition among nations might lead to a convergence of respect for worker rights in all countries whose national economies significantly participate in the global economy. The convergence hypothesis suggests that workers in the more advanced economies will lose some rights and workers in the less advanced economies will gain some. The convergence will take place somewhere in the middle.

Critical theorists emphasize the class-conflict elements of the world economy. They see the interests of multinational corporations (MNCs) as completely at odds with the interests of workers (Parenti 1989). Globalization, in their view, primarily benefits MNCs to the detriment of workers. The more a particular country participates in the global economy, the greater the suffering of its workers (Carleton 1989). Since capital can move easily in the more global economy, but workers cannot, capital will always seek the lowest-cost labor, and capitalists will move their factories whenever workers seek greater protections for their rights (Moses 2000). This will inevitably lead to what some critical theorists refer to as a "race to the bottom" as the governments of nation states compete to provide the most favorable business climate. A favorable business climate is one that strengthens management prerogatives at the expense of workers. The intense competition, in and of itself, leads to a deterioration of worker rights in all countries that seek greater national economic integration into the global economy. According to critical theory, the least economically developed capitalist countries are likely to have the dubious distinction of being the winners of this race to the bottom partly because of their dependence on foreign assistance from institutions like the IMF and World Bank. Critical theorists note that Western bilateral foreign aid and multilateral official development assistance are often conditioned upon the recipient adopting certain free-market initiatives.

How structural adjustment affects worker rights

Earlier we described the kinds of policies that countries under structural adjustment have adopted to comply with the conditions of structural adjustment agreements. The purpose of those policies is to help the governments of developing countries attract foreign direct investment and to participate in international trade by increasing exports. Some contend that the World Bank has had a long-standing commitment to maintaining government respect for some labor standards (Nelson 2000). World Bank officials have even argued that respect for three core labor standards – against child labor, forced labor, and discrimination in hiring and treatment at work – actually promotes economic growth (Sensor 2003).

The theoretical links between structural adjustment agreements and protections of worker rights are clear-cut at a high level of abstraction. As noted in Chapter 3, one argument is that a relatively limited government as required by SAAs is fundamental to all human freedoms. Limited government reduces barriers to the functioning of the free market, allowing human beings to pursue their own interests in their own ways and allowing them to pursue opportunities that are likely to be lost if human freedom is restricted (Friedman 1962; Hayek 1984). Consistent with this line of thought, Cranston (1964) has argued that respect for most human rights only requires forbearance on the part of the state. In contrast, we argue that respect for worker rights requires substantial government regulation of the employer–employee relationship. Structural adjustment programs worsen protections for worker rights because they encourage a smaller role of the state in the economy. A reduced role of the state in capitalist economies gives employers more discretion in the employer–employee relationship. More employer discretion over the terms and conditions of work leads to greater abuse of worker rights.

Once one moves beyond this high level of abstraction to the details of SAAs things get much more complicated, since the particular provisions of structural adjustment agreements vary from state to state and over time. Economists argue about the effects of different common provisions in both the short and the long term. Many provisions are expected to have positive effects in the long term even though the short-term effects on workers are likely to be negative. Moreover, whether the effects on workers are expected to be positive or negative depends upon the economic sector in which they work. For example, the effects of increased international trade should increase wages and decrease unemployment in the long term, but in previously protected sectors of the economy, wages are likely to decrease and unemployment may increase (Vreeland 2003; Handa and King 1997).

Reduction in public expenditures is the most common of structural adjustment agreements. After analyzing ninety-four IMF agreements between 1980 and 1984, for example, Sisson (1986) reported that 91 percent of them contained some promise of spending reductions. Most commonly these reductions in government spending are achieved through removal of subsidies for goods, services, food, or credit, and some combination of reductions in public employment, wage freezes, or reductions in employee benefits (Vreeland 2003; Sisson 1986). Several studies have concluded that the negative effects of IMF structural adjustment agreements on economic growth "are paid for by the least well-off in a country" (Vreeland 2003: 151; see also Garuda 2000; Pastor 1987a; 1987b).

Most previous empirical research has focused on the effects of structural adjustment agreements on employment, wages, and employee benefits. These outcomes are relevant to assessing the effects of SAAs on the rights of workers to a decent job and to a minimal standard of living. However, as noted above, "worker rights" is a much broader concept. No previous large-n empirical research project has assessed the effects of SAAs on such core labor rights as freedom of association at the workplace or collective bargaining. One assumes that reductions in public employment, wages, and benefits are achieved, in part, by reducing the voice and power of workers in the public sector. Reductions in these and other labor standards constitute at least one strategy a government could adopt to attract more foreign direct investment and to engage in more international trade.

There are some preliminary research results on the effects of international trade and foreign direct investment on government respect for worker rights. These studies are relevant to the evaluation of the impact of SAAs on government respect for worker rights, because expansion of international trade – especially exports – and attracting more foreign direct investment are two important elements of the neoliberal economic reforms advocated by the IMF and the Bank through their structural adjustment programs. However, it is important to remember that long-term participation in structural adjustment programs by a developing country does not mean that the country has been successful in significantly increasing either its international trade or the amount of its foreign direct investment. With that in mind, early research results indicate that international trade and foreign direct investment have opposing effects on workers. Trade worsens respect for worker rights in developing countries. Foreign direct investment may improve it.

Trade

Several studies have shown that worker rights are less protected in developing countries that trade more internationally (Cingranelli and Tsai 2003; Gereffi and Korzeniewicz 1994; Mosley 2002; 2006; Murillo and Schrank 2005; Neumayer and De Soysa 2006). One of the reasons that international trade is associated with less protection of worker rights is that export processing zones (EPZs) are often created at the urging of the World Bank and IMF to facilitate export-led economic growth. Frequently labor rights are restricted in these zones (Klak 1996: 358; Moran 2002). Democracy and international trade seem to exert opposite effects on government respect for worker rights. The rights of workers in countries that have both democratized and engaged in more international trade have not been significantly affected one way or the other. Most negatively affected were countries, like China, where there had been significant economic globalization, but little or no progress towards democracy (Cingranelli and Tsai 2003).

Foreign direct investment

There is less consensus concerning the effects of foreign direct investment (FDI) on human rights, in general, and on worker rights, in particular. Most research results suggest that foreign direct investment has a positive effect on government respect for physical integrity rights in developing countries (Blanton and Blanton 2007; Garcia-Johnson 2000; Richards, Gelleny, and Sacko 2001; Richards and Gelleny 2003). Others have reached the opposite conclusion (Meyer 1996; 1998). The effects of foreign direct investment on worker rights have received less attention. Most studies have reported a positive relationship (Elliott and Freeman 2001; Aggarwal 1995; Busse 2003; Mosley and Uno 2007; Mosley 2006), while some suggest the opposite (Brady and Wallace 2000). The effects also may be localized, since much FDI occurs in export processing zones, where labor laws may be different from those that prevail elsewhere in the country.

Research design

As in other chapters, this analysis uses a cross-national, annual time-series data set. The data span the time period from 1981 to 2003. The unit of analysis was the country year. The measure of worker rights used in the analysis was ordinal with three values, so ordered logit was the estimation technique used. Here we describe the measure of the dependent and independent variables. Again, we employ a selection model, because some of the same factors that were found to affect which countries enter into structural adjustment agreements were expected to affect government respect for worker rights. For example, if a country was not much involved in international trade, it was much more likely to negotiate a structural adjustment agreement with the Bank or Fund. Table 4.5 includes a description of the control variables used in this chapter. The effect of foreign domestic investment on labor standards is not evaluated here because of missing data problems.

Measuring respect for worker rights

Information about the level of respect governments around the world provided for important worker rights was taken from the US State Department's annual *Country Reports on Human Rights Practices*. This report, published since 1974, includes descriptions of respect for worker rights in each country. The worker rights reported on are those included in Section 502(a) of the United States Trade Act of 1974. These are: freedom of association, the right to collective bargaining, the elimination of all forms of forced or compulsory labor, the effective abolition of child labor, and acceptable conditions of work with respect to minimum wages, hours of work, and occupational safety and health. This list is much the same as the ILO's list of five core labor rights except that the last element on the list concerning "acceptable conditions of work" is not among the core rights recognized by the ILO, and one of the core rights recognized – the elimination of discrimination in respect of employment or occupation – is not included in the State Department analysis. The State Department report emphasizes the responsibility of all governments to see that all workers should have the right to join a trade union in order to exercise their rights as workers. Workers should have the right to association, the right to bargain collectively, and freedom from governmental influence. The coding for each country-year is based on a three-point scale.

Worker rights are:

(0) Not protected by the government
(1) Somewhat protected by the government
(2) Protected by the government

Coders were instructed to code a particular country for a particular year as zero if that government did not allow workers to form trade unions or prohibited strikes. If a government allowed workers to form trade unions and to use strikes against employers, but the State Department report mentions other problems with government respect for worker rights such as the abuse of child labor or tolerance of unsafe working conditions, then the country was coded as a one. If a government ensured that workers had the freedom to form unions and collectively bargain and there was no mention of other problems with government practices towards workers, the country was coded as a two for that year.

The application of these rules is best illustrated using some examples. In 1981, the Congo received a score of zero largely based on the following language in the *Country Reports*: "The Congolese confederation of trade unionists (CSC) represents workers but, as an appendage of the state, is restricted in its right to strike, bargain collectively and lobby" (US State Department [Congo-1981] 70). Another example of a country that did not respect the rights of its workers in 1981, and therefore received a score of zero for that year, was Angola. According to the *Country Reports*: "There is a government sponsored trade union movement, the national union of Angolan workers (UNTA). Traditionally labor union activities and rights are tightly restricted by government. Strikes are prohibited by law as a crime against the security of the state" (US State Department [Angola-1981] 17). Many governments prevent the police, military, emergency medical personnel, and firefighters from forming unions. If other workers can form unions and strike and there are no other problems with government treatment of workers, then the country was coded as two. If the police, military, emergency medical personnel, and firefighters are allowed to form unions but are not allowed to strike, this fact also was not used as evidence of lack of respect for worker rights. This is because international law recognizes the right of governments to prohibit strikes of employees whose work is essential to the public's safety.

The *Country Reports* were used as the source of information about actual government respect for different worker rights because they cover a long period of time, report on almost all countries in the world, and report on government practices protecting or violating a fairly wide range of worker rights. Some would argue that the *Country Reports* are a potentially biased source of information about worker rights. According to this point of view, governments allied to the United States would be likely to receive better treatment in the reports than neutral countries or those allied with adversaries (Mitchell and McCormick 1988). The reports prior to 1981 are not used in this analysis largely because of such criticisms. However, there is widespread agreement that the reports since that date are objective and accurate. Poe, Carey, and Vazquez (2001) compared the *Country Reports* with the annual reports produced by Amnesty International and found few discrepancies in the evaluations of government human rights practices made by the two sources.

An illustration of the lack of bias in the *Country Reports* is Angola, which was communist in 1981. According to the "bias" argument, the negative evaluation of worker rights in Angola that year may have been influenced by that fact. However, in 1992, Angola held democratic elections, and has been relatively democratic since. Despite this fact, the US State Department's review of the level of government respect for worker rights in Angola continued to be very negative.

The Amnesty International reports do not discuss worker rights. The ITUC has produced some reports on freedom of association at the workplace and the right to collective bargaining, but the formats of the reports are not consistent, most countries of the world are not included, and they have only been produced since 1995.

The amount of information about worker rights included in the *Country Reports* has grown dramatically over time. Until the mid-1980s, the rights of freedom of association, collective bargaining, freedom of trade unions from government control or serious interference, and the right to strike were discussed consistently. Other worker rights were discussed less consistently. They were mentioned only when the US State Department wished to emphasize worker rights problems. Since 1993, however, there are sections in the report discussing the situation in all six areas of worker rights.

Independent variables

The independent variable of chief theoretical interest is the "number of years a country has been under a World Bank or IMF structural adjustment agreement." Other studies have demonstrated that wealthier countries, more democratic countries, and countries with a British colonial experience tend to have governments that provide more respect for the human rights of their citizens. Countries with military governments,

relatively large populations, relatively large population increases, high
levels of domestic conflict, and involvement in interstate war tend to have
governments that provide less respect for the human rights of their citizens (Poe 2004; Poe, Tate, and Keith 1999). These factors were included
as control variables in the analysis. Previous research has also shown that
the amount of international trade a country engages in affects government
respect for worker rights, so this factor was included as an independent
variable in this analysis. The dependent variable is lagged one year, so the
effective dependent variable is the annual change in respect for worker
rights.

Limitations

There are some weaknesses in the research design we employ here.
First, this analysis of government respect for worker rights is incomplete
in the sense that it ignores unemployment rates and wages. These are
two outcomes of great interest to workers and of great relevance to the
race-to-the-bottom thesis. Second, the design ignores the plight of
workers in the informal economy. The informal economy consists of
"the exchange of goods and services in the black market not regulated
or taxed by state authorities" (Ness 2005: 8). The informal economy in
wealthy democracies is relatively small. It is found mainly in the private
transportation, domestic, and food service industries (Ness 2005). The
measures employed in this study only reflect the rights of workers in the
formal economy. Only the formal economy is regulated by government
policies and practices. Workers in the informal economy have no rights,
and in many developing countries the majority of workers, especially in
rural areas, fall outside the formal economy. Finally, the scores for each
country assume that the government's labor practices are the same
whether the worker is located within or outside an export processing
zone. This is a necessary oversimplification, because the source material
does not always mention whether national labor laws are upheld within
those zones. Thus, the results presented here should be viewed as a
preliminary exploration of an important question.

Findings

Table 9.1 presents the results of the empirical analysis. Column one of
the table presents the selection-corrected effects. These are the results
that we trust the most. Column two shows the effects without controlling
for the effects of selection. Most important, the selection-corrected
results show that, even after controlling for the effects of other plausible

Table 9.1. *The impact of World Bank and IMF structural adjustment agreements on government respect for worker rights 1981–2003, all developing countries (ordered logit)*

	Selection corrected	Selection not corrected
Number of years under a	−.02* (.011)	−.005 (.011)
World Bank or IMF structural		
adjustment agreement		
Economic factors		
GDP per capita	.0001** (.00004)	.0001 (.00002)
Change in GDP per capita	−.001** (.0005)	.0003 (.0004)
Trade as a proportion of GDP	−.001 (.002)	−.0003 (.001)
Domestic political factors		
Level of democracy	.119*** (.022)	.131*** (.021)
Population density	5.28e–08 (1.71e-07)	5.78e–08 (1.37e–07)
Physical quality of life index	−.01* (.006)	−.003 (.005)
United Kingdom colonial heritage	.393** (.175)	.231ˆ (.145)
Conflict proneness		
Interstate conflict	−2.17 (.184)	−2.1ˆ (.157)
Rebellion	−.019 (.069)	−.073 (.064)
Control variables		
World Bank and IMF selection effects	1.00*** (.307)	–
Lagged respect for worker rights	1.802*** (.096)	1.95*** (.102)
N	1608	1973
Pseudo R²	.23	.26

Note: P>|z .ˆ .05*, .01**, .001***
Models are estimated with robust standard errors, with one-tailed significance tests.

explanations of respect for worker rights, the larger the number of years under structural adjustment, the lower the protection of worker rights in a country. As expected, the governments of wealthier countries and countries with democratic governments treated workers better. Other less important but statistically significant findings showed that: countries selected by the IMF and World Bank tended to have higher respect for worker rights, the previous year's level of support for worker rights was a good predictor of the level of protection a year later, and the governments of former colonies of the United Kingdom tended to have more respect for worker rights than others. Rapid economic growth indicated by large changes in GDP per capita had worsened government levels of respect for worker rights; the findings provide support for previous arguments about the destabilizing societal effects of rapid economic growth on society (Olson 1963).

To our surprise, higher scores on the physical quality of life index – our measure of respect for economic and social rights – were associated with worsening levels of government respect for worker rights. We think that higher levels of respect for economic and social rights do have a positive impact on respect for workers. However, we think a threshold effect exists. Like previous research indicating that regimes have to achieve high levels of democracy before there is substantial improvement in respect for physical integrity rights (Davenport and Armstrong 2004), the same may be true for economic and social rights, which have to achieve a particular level before there is a concomitant improvement in respect for worker rights. These relationships warrant further investigation.[1]

The reader will recall that, in order to control for the effects of selection, a two-stage analysis was undertaken. First, the probability of each country negotiating an SAL in each year was calculated and then entered as an independent variable in the selection-corrected equation. This independent variable was left out of the equation that yielded the results reported in column two of Table 9.1. The variable titled "World Bank and IMF selection effects" was positive and significant in the selection-corrected results, indicating that, overall, the Bank and Fund tend to negotiate agreements with countries that have a relatively high level of respect for worker rights. Thus, correcting for selection made a big difference in the findings concerning the effects of adjustment. Had we not controlled for the effects of selection we would have concluded that exposure to structural adjustment had no statistically significant effect on respect for worker rights.

Conclusions

The longer a developing country participated in structural adjustment programs, the weaker the government protections of its workers. The critical theory interpretation of this finding is that the Bank and Fund, through their structural adjustment agreements, are helping to fund the "race to the bottom" by encouraging the governments of developing countries to develop policy environments that are often hostile to the rights of workers. A more circumspect conclusion is that countries

---

[1] We were unable to estimate the impact of foreign direct investment due to a large number of non-randomly missing cases. Inclusion of this measure reduced our sample size by 20 percent (from 1,608 cases to 1,286). Future research needs to address these limitations when trying to assess the impact of these processes on government respect for worker rights.

under structural adjustment are attempting to make their economies more friendly to domestic and international business. Policy-makers in developing countries recognize they must attract investment, and thus they do things like weaken labor standards or the enforcement of labor standards or both. The result, in sum, is that these policy decisions tilt the balance towards employers and against workers.

10   Democracy and civil liberties

Introduction

Developing countries are likely to have a higher rate of economic growth if they have democratic political institutions and if their citizens have protections of their civil liberties (Kaufmann 2005; Kaufmann and Pritchett 1998; Sen 1999). Critics of the World Bank and IMF have contended that structural adjustment agreements undermine institutional democracy and protections of civil liberties. There were four main variants to this "undermining democracy" argument. The first three critiques focus on the deleterious effects of structural adjustment on the development of democratic institutions and democratic methods for selecting leaders. We find no evidence in support of this critique. In fact, we find considerable evidence to the contrary. Countries undergoing structural adjustment were more likely to develop democratic institutions and democratic human rights than those not undergoing structural adjustment.

The fourth argument suggesting that the implementation of structural adjustment programs undermines democratic rights is not about procedural democracy. It is about substantive democracy or the extent to which the actual policies produced in a society reflect what most people want. It's an important contention, and we will return to it later, but it is not an argument that can be tested using the kinds of evidence available for large-scale comparative analysis of the type we have conducted in this project.

The first argument was that the World Bank and IMF allegedly were more willing to negotiate with authoritarian governments than with democratic governments, because authoritarian governments were more likely to implement unpopular policies (Pion-Berlin 1984; 1989; 1997; 2001). Deprived of foreign capital, democratic regimes floundered, and were replaced by more authoritarian regimes. In Latin America, this occurred most often through military coups. Consistent with this argument, previous research had shown that democracies were less likely to receive structural adjustment loans from the IMF (Vreeland 2003; Przeworski and Vreeland 2000). However, our research results presented in Chapter 4 showed that democratic governments were about as likely to enter into structural adjustment agreements as were authoritarian governments.

Other studies of the selection biases of the World Bank and the IMF, using different samples of countries, measures of democracy, control variables, and periods of time, have found a weak, but statistically significant, bias both against and in favor of democracies (Abouharb and Cingranelli 2004a; 2006). These inconsistent findings among studies show that the relationship is not robust to minor variations in research design. Thus, the safest interpretation is that there is no clear pattern of selection bias for or against democracies.

Second, it is commonly alleged that, during the Cold War, the IMF and World Bank provided assistance to brutal dictatorships as long as they were allied to the United States, the largest contributor to the Bank and Fund, and they were committed to the fight against communism (Berkeley 2001). To examine the validity of this idea, all of the analyses presented in this book were broken down into the period that was part of the Cold War (1981–1991) and the period that occurred after the Cold War ended (1992–2003). We do not present those results here, because there were no differences in selection criteria or in the effects of structural adjustment on respect for democratic rights that were consistent with this argument. As noted, authoritarian regimes were not more likely to enter into agreements with the Bank and Fund, and the factors that affected the likelihood of entering a structural adjustment agreement did not change much when the Cold War ended. However, if our examination had focused on the *volume*, or amounts, of loans rather than the number of loans made to developing countries, we may have reached a different conclusion – namely, that there was a greater probability that large SALs were made to dictatorial regimes such as those of Mobutu (Zaire), Suharto (Indonesia), Marcos (Philippines), and Pinochet (Chile).

Finally, critics note that major economic changes associated with structural adjustment conditions often caused discontent among the citizens of affected countries. Governments sometimes responded to this discontent with curtailment of democratic rights. As noted in Chapter 1, even after making a transition to democracy, President Rawlings of Ghana, according to some critics, continued to behave as a dictator (Kwame 1999). We include brief descriptions of the stories of the alleged negative impact of structural adjustment conditions on democratic rights in Peru and Egypt as other cases illustrating this argument.

President Fujimori of Peru was perhaps the most notorious example of a democratically elected leader who often behaved in an authoritarian way to put neoliberal economic reforms into practice. After taking office in 1990, President Fujimori inherited a country in economic crisis and tormented by civil war with the Shining Path. President Fujimori quickly ended the civil war. He also moved rapidly to get the country back into the good graces of the IMF. While some adjustment measures were implemented during the 1980s, structural adjustment began in earnest in Peru within two weeks of President Fujimori's inauguration with the introduction of what became known as the "Fujishock" (Pion-Berlin 1989).

President Fujimori used many extra-constitutional measures to consolidate his authoritarian regime. In 1992 he used the army to shut down the Congress and five years later he paved the way for reelection by sacking the country's highest court after its justices ruled that he could not run for a third term. The National Intelligence Service (Servicio de Inteligencia Nacional, SIN) was widely blamed for harassing opposition candidates, and manipulating the press, the courts, and the electoral bodies to secure President Fujimori's reelection (Human Rights Watch 2001). Critics contended that the US government generally turned a blind eye to these dictatorial measures, in large part because of President Fujimori's strong commitment to the structural adjustment programs advocated by the IMF and World Bank (Chossudovsky 1997; Pion-Berlin 1991).

In Egypt, the period of structural adjustment also coincided with increased repression of civil liberties. In his book, *A Grand Delusion: Democracy and Economic Reform in Egypt*, Kienle (2001) contends that painful economic reforms necessitated by structural adjustment conditionality have slowed the transition from an authoritarian to a democratic political system. Egypt began its structural adjustment reforms in 1987. According to the annual human rights reports issued by the US Department of State, prior to 1989 the government showed substantial respect for such civil liberties as freedom of assembly and association, and freedom of speech and press. During the structural adjustment period, the government adopted laws making it difficult for new parties to get access to the ballot, interfered with voting at the polling places, engaged in fraudulent vote counts, utilized military courts to get rid of political opponents, and limited freedom of speech and press. When the press became too critical of structural adjustment reforms, some journalists were punished and some periodical publications were put out of business (Kienle 2001). According to *Aljazeera*, the parliamentary elections of 2005 showed a similar pattern of "violence, allegations of widespread fraud and annulled results" (Al-Atraqchi 2005).

Structural adjustment may even be fuelling the rise of Islamist movements in Egypt and elsewhere in the Middle East where more secular and democratic governments are emerging (Lubeck 2000). Structural adjustment policies provided a convenient target for Islamist opposition groups who blame their own governments for making agreements with Western imperialist institutions that do not serve majority interests in society. The Muslim Brotherhood, the principal opposition group to the government in Egypt, opposes the structural adjustment policies of the government (Kienle 2001). Members of the Brotherhood have been the main target of physical integrity rights abuse by the Egyptian government, including torture, political imprisonment, and extrajudicial killing.

The Ghana, Peru, and Egypt examples notwithstanding, the democratic development of most other countries under structural adjustment has been better. The results presented in this chapter will show that countries that have been under structural adjustment conditionality the longest have better-developed democratic institutions, have elections that are freer and fairer, have more freedom to form and join organizations, and have more freedom of speech and press than countries with less exposure to structural adjustment conditionality. These things are true after controlling for the effects of selection. Even Bolivia, a country we used as an example of the economic failure of structural adjustment policies in Chapter 1, has experienced substantial increases in procedural democracy over the past few decades.

The 2005 national elections in Bolivia were widely acknowledged as free and fair. Evo Morales of the Movement Toward Socialism (MAS) Party won the election with 54 percent of the vote, an absolute majority. His opponent conceded defeat, and, in January of 2006, Morales was sworn in for a five-year term. His win marked the first election of an indigenous head of state in Bolivia (Democracy Now 2006). He campaigned vigorously against the structural adjustment policies of the IMF and World Bank and against the policies of the US government. During the election campaign, he pledged to increase state control over Bolivia's vast natural gas resources and to protect coca plantations. The Bush administration criticized Morales for his close ties to Venezuelan president Hugo Chavez and Cuban president Fidel Castro as well as his opposition to neoliberal economic policies. During the election, Morales appealed to voters, in part, by declaring that his election would be a nightmare for the United States (Democracy Now 2006).

The final "undermining democracy" critique is not about procedural democracy. According to this perspective, structural adjustment agreements are negotiated between the executive branch of the government of the loan-recipient country and representatives of the Bank or Fund. The legislature, the heart of any democracy, is not formally a part of the negotiation process (Alexander 2006a). Thus, the normal democratic process is not used to make some of the most important economic decisions affecting the societies of developing countries. When decisions do not reflect what most people in a society want, there is a lack of "substantive democracy." The argument that structural adjustment conditions have undermined substantive democracy is one of the main conclusions of the Structural Adjustment Participatory Review International Network (SAPRIN) evaluation of the economic effects of structural adjustment programs (2004). The authors of the SAPRIN study noted that, "while procedural democracy has been promoted ... real democratic choice for both civil society and governments in the arena of economic policy has been severely limited by the IFIs and their Northern Board members. Governments have been urged to improve their governance, but not so that they will better respond to the interests of their own people" (2004: 221). Paradoxically, structural adjustment may have led, simultaneously, to advances in procedural democracy and a decline in substantive democracy. The results of this study do not bear upon this argument that structural adjustment programs undermine substantive democracy.

In the remainder of this chapter, we discuss the elements that are part of procedural democracy. We argue that procedural democracy is a human right. Most, but not all, of the elements of procedural democracy are considered directly or indirectly in the analyses we will present later. Countries with high levels of procedural democracy have been shown to provide greater protections of other human rights and economic growth. However, liberal democracy, a special type of procedural democracy, is more important as a facilitator of other human rights protections and equitable economic development. We briefly review the literature on the correlates of democratic development in order to construct a statistical model that reveals the effect of structural adjustment while controlling for the effects of other plausible explanations of democratic outcomes. Finally, after presenting the results outlined above, we discuss some reasons why structural adjustment has led to higher levels of government respect for procedural democracy in developing countries.

The meaning of procedural democracy

Procedural democracy refers to the method citizens use to choose their leaders and influence government policies. Typically, procedural democracy exists if, at a minimum, citizens are given a choice among rival political leaders who compete for their votes. Between elections, those who were elected, the politicians, make decisions. At the next election, citizens can choose to keep or change their elected leaders. If these institutional arrangements are in place, a country has procedural democracy (Schumpeter 1942) or "government by the people." Some have argued that this kind of "thin" definition of procedural democracy, when employed by policy-makers, can do more harm than good (Herman and Brodhead 1984). We will return to this point later.

As a result of this kind of skepticism and as a way of providing guidance to new democracies, a number of governmental and nongovernmental organizations have proposed standards that a government should meet before it should consider itself to be fully procedurally democratic. In 1976, the Commission on Security and Cooperation in Europe (CSCE), an independent US government agency, was created to address and assess democratic, economic, and human rights developments in the countries participating in the Organization for Security and Co-operation in Europe (OSCE). The Commission consists of nine members of the US House of Representatives, nine from the US Senate, and one member each from the Departments of State, Defense, and Commerce. The OSCE's Office for Democratic Institutions and Human Rights (ODIHR) is the lead agency in Europe in the field of election observation. It co-ordinates and organizes the deployment of thousands of observers every year to assess whether elections in the OSCE area are in line with international standards for democratic elections and other democratic political institutions.

The 1990 Copenhagen Document, adopted by the Organization for Security and Co-operation in Europe, was the first attempt by the international community to stipulate in detail the requirements that should be met in any national political election. Since then, numerous organizations have undertaken the effort – including the United Nations, the Organization of American States, the Council of Europe, the Parliamentary Assembly of the Commonwealth of Independent States, the UN Human Rights Committee, and other international or regional governmental and nongovernmental organizations. The most detailed statement produced thus far was by the Organization for Security and Co-operation in Europe (2003). Today, policy-makers think in terms of "extent" of procedural democracy, because there is now a much longer list of criteria that must be met before one would argue that full procedural democracy exists.

This list of criteria was needed because being procedurally democratic has become a condition of membership in important international

Table 10.1. *International standards for a free national political election*

A free political election is one that protects:
• freedom from violence, intimidation, or coercion;
• freedom of speech and expression by voters, parties, candidates, and the media;
• freedom of assembly, to hold political rallies, and to campaign;
• freedom of access to and by voters to transmit and receive political and electoral information messages;
• freedom of access to the polls by voters, party agents, and accredited observers;
• freedom to question, challenge, and register complaints or objections without negative repercussions;
• freedom of association: that is, freedom to form organizations such as political parties and nongovernmental organizations;
• freedom to register as a voter, a party, or a candidate; and
• freedom to exercise the franchise in secret.

organizations such as the European Union, the North American Treaty Organization, and the Organisation for Economic Co-operation and Development (OECD). Good governance also has become a criterion for the distribution of foreign aid by OECD donor countries. There is a growing international consensus on standards for what constitutes a free, fair, and genuine national political election. The standards are numerous, but realistic, since they were designed to help evaluate democratic elections in countries with a wide variety of institutional arrangements and economic endowments. They distinguish between features that make an election free and features that make an election fair. A "free" electoral process is one where fundamental human rights and freedoms are respected. Table 10.1 summarizes the international standards for a free political election.[1]

According to international standards for political elections, a "fair" electoral process is one where the contest is reasonably level and accessible to all voters, parties, and candidates. In many countries, elections

---

[1] The benchmark standards for procedural democracy used in this chapter are based on international standards for free and fair elections that have been developed and promulgated by governmental and nongovernmental organizations. See, especially, OSCE (1990), (2003), and Inter-Parliamentary Union (1994). International nongovernmental organizations (INGOs) have promulgated similar principles such as the guidelines developed by the International Foundation for Election Systems (www.ifes. org); Common Borders (www.commonborders.org), and the Administration and Cost of Elections Project (www.aceproject.org). Information about election standards also can be found on the websites of the International Institute for Democracy and Electoral Assistance (IDEA) at www.idea.int, and the National Democratic Institute for International Affairs (NDI) at www.ndi.org.

Table 10.2. *International standards for a fair national political election*

A fair national political election is one that has:

- an independent, non-partisan electoral organization to administer the process;
- guaranteed rights and protection through the constitution and electoral legislation and regulations;
- equitable representation of voters provided through the legislature;
- clearly defined universal suffrage;
- secrecy of the vote;
- equitable and balanced reporting by the media;
- equitable opportunities for the electorate to receive political and voter information;
- accessible polling places;
- equitable treatment of voters, candidates, and parties by elections officials, the government, the police, the military, and the judiciary; and
- an open and transparent ballot-counting process.

are free, but unfair. For example, governing political parties in many countries use nonviolent means to gain advantages over challenging parties. The governing party, as an excuse to limit the circulation of opposition newspapers or literature, may restrict access to newsprint or may use unfair advantages to raise an abnormally large campaign fund. Such practices create an unfair election contest. Table 10.2 summarizes the international standards for a fair national political election.

Procedural democracy as a human right

The right to free and fair elections is a de facto human right in the modern world. The principle that all national governments should hold democratic political elections was set forth in the Universal Declaration of Human Rights in 1948 and the International Covenant on Civil and Political Rights in 1966. While there is no explicit human right to choose leaders through an election, it is implied by the right to participation in government, since there is no other reasonable way to ensure popular participation in national politics other than through a representative government. Many of the components of procedural democracy listed in Tables 10.1 and 10.2 are internationally recognized human rights. The International Bill of Human Rights (IBHR) specifically mentions freedom of opinion and expression, freedom of assembly, freedom of association, the right to participation in government, nondiscrimination, and access to an independent and impartial tribunal. Other rights and freedoms listed in Tables 10.1 and 10.2 such as clearly defined universal suffrage, secrecy of the vote, and an open and transparent ballot-counting process are suggested by the implied right to choose leaders through an electoral process. Other human rights, though not explicitly concerned with democratic practices, also cover some of the rights and freedoms listed in Tables 10.1 and 10.2. For example, the IBHR guarantees physical integrity rights, and these rights would protect voters from violence, intimidation, or coercion during election campaigns.

Procedural democracy promotes respect for other human rights and economic growth

Almost every empirical study of human rights practices has shown that more democratic societies have better human rights practices of all types (e.g., Davenport and Armstrong 2004; Mitchell and McCormick 1988; Poe, Tate, and Keith 1999). In previous chapters, our own results have shown that more democratic governments provide greater protection of physical integrity rights and worker rights. Most previous research has shown that more democratic societies also provide greater protection of economic and social rights (e.g., Poe *et al.* 2004). In some respects, this is simply evidence of the interdependence of all human rights. As noted above, there is an implicit right to procedural democracy in the International Bill of Human Rights. Since respect for some rights is dependent upon respect for others, many human rights tend to advance or decline together. The real question is which human rights are the leading indicators of better human rights practices in other areas. We know more about interdependence than we do about sequence or causal ordering.

A "leading indicator" human right is one that, if government protection is increased or decreased, will cause government protection of other human rights to increase or decrease. There are good theoretical and empirical reasons to believe that procedural democratic rights are leading indicator human rights. When citizens have more procedural democratic rights such as freedom of speech and press, and free and fair elections, they are empowered to affect government decision-making. Once empowered in this way, they will use their voice to encourage leaders to increase respect for other human rights to such things as education, housing, and health care. They will also use their political power to increase their freedom from abuses of their person, such as torture. Empirically, we know that there is a positive statistical relationship between most indicators of procedural democracy and respect for most other human rights.

However, procedural democracy does not guarantee respect for other human rights. Many procedurally democratic states have poor human rights records. While democratic institutions of all types have been shown to facilitate better respect for human rights than authoritarian institutions, some democratic institutional arrangements are much better than others. The Holocaust showed that democracies can elect evil people to office, and those people can commit terrible human rights violations on a large scale. In fact, there is a lot of variation in the human rights practices of democratic states, so it is clear that democratic institutional arrangements do not ensure good human rights practices (Sobek, Abouharb, and Ingram 2006). As Donnelly (2003: 192) writes, "the will of the people, no matter how it is ascertained, often diverges from the rights of individual citizens. Electoral democracies often serve the particular interests of key constituencies. Direct democracy, as Athens dramatically illustrates, can be remarkably intolerant."

The best type of democracy for the advancement of human rights is liberal democracy (Donnelly 2003). Liberal democracies guarantee that all citizens have equal rights and they limit the range of democratic decision-making to protect individual and minority rights. Schumpeter's (1942) thin concept of a procedural democracy did not involve any such guarantees. The modern notion of free and fair elections, which builds upon Schumpeter's original idea, specifies what would be necessary to have full procedural democracy. It requires protections of certain civil liberties such as freedom of speech, association, and press. However, a country where procedural democratic rights are fully respected could still choose by majority vote to violate the rights of the minority. Only a liberal democracy with a bill of rights and an independent judiciary to uphold it can prevent tyranny of the majority.

Unfortunately, many of the democracies formed in the 1990s in less developed countries were not and are not liberal democracies. Some have argued that the end of the Cold War has encouraged the creation of too many "illiberal democracies" (Zakaria 1997). These countries appear to be democratic, because they hold regular elections. However, neither the elections, nor the institutions of government, are truly democratic, because there are too few constitutional limits on the power of leaders and insufficient guarantees of basic rights and freedoms to the people. These regimes, meeting only the "thin" definition of procedural democracy, even have been called "demonstration democracies" (Herman and Brodhead 1984), because they were allegedly created only to please the United States government, the IMF, and the World Bank. Some of the basic human rights commonly not protected by these new democracies were freedom of speech, a free press, freedom of organization of intermediate groups such as unions, freedom to form political parties and field candidates, and freedom from government-sponsored terror (Herman and Brodhead 1984).

The presence of so many illiberal democracies in the world today is one of the main reasons why there are so many countries, like Egypt and Peru, that meet the minimal definition of procedural democracy, but continue to have significant violations of many other human rights. Though there has been a substantial advance in the number of nations in the world having achieved what most would consider the minimum threshold level of procedural democratic practices, there has been no similar dramatic advance in the number of nations of the world with good records of protections of physical integrity rights or economic and social rights (Human Security Centre 2006).

Our evidence demonstrates that the implementation of structural adjustment conditions does not simply lead to more "demonstration democracies." The results show that, besides democratic institutions, countries that have been under structural adjustment conditionality the longest also have elections that are more free and fair, have more freedom to form and join organizations, and have more freedom of speech and press than countries with less exposure to structural adjustment conditionality. These are some of the most important features one would expect in a fully developed procedural democracy. As was discussed in Chapter 1, they are also the types of rights that have been shown in previous work to facilitate economic growth.

Correlates of procedural democracy

The implementation of structural adjustment programs is just one important factor affecting whether a government will be democratic or authoritarian. To isolate and evaluate the effects of structural adjustment on procedural democratic development, one must control for the effects of other important influences. By far the most important of these is the level of economic development of a state. Lipset's now famous and often-tested thesis was that: "The more well-to-do a nation, the greater the chances it will sustain democracy" (1959: 319). Besides wealth, literacy, urbanization, and mass media are other factors that facilitate the development of procedural democracy (Lipset 1959). Other elements such as political culture (Huntington 1984), the existence of a middle class (Moore 1966), and transnational factors also affect the probability of democracy. Transnational factors are those forces in the international environment that impinge upon the processes that take place in single countries. These factors include international war, colonialism, international norms, and international financial constraints like structural adjustment.

In one of the most ambitious and methodologically sophisticated studies of transitions from authoritarianism to democracy for all countries of the world from 1940 to 1990, it was found that national wealth, as measured by per capita income, was the most important explanation for the survival of democracies (Przeworski *et al.* 2000). The authors also found that having a British colonial experience was associated with a greater likelihood of making the democratic transition. This is probably because the British used a model of indirect rule over their colonies, thus giving colonized populations some limited experience with democratic self-government.

Other studies have demonstrated that wealthier countries and countries with a British colonial experience tend to have governments that provide more respect for the human rights of their citizens. In contrast, countries with relatively large populations, high levels of civil conflict, and involvement in interstate war tend to have governments that provide less respect for the human rights of their citizens (Poe 2004; Poe, Tate, and Keith 1999). Rapid economic growth has also been theorized to have a disruptive impact on social stability (Olson 1963), negatively impacting government respect for human rights (Poe, Tate, and Keith 1999). We argued in Chapter 3 that respect for economic and social rights led to less civil conflict, thus promoting respect for other human rights. These factors will be included as control variables in the analysis.

Research methods

Some of the factors that make countries candidates for World Bank and IMF structural adjustment agreements such as experiencing economic difficulty have been shown to impede democratic development in previous research (Lipset 1959; Przeworski *et al.* 2000). Thus the pool of countries that enters into these agreements is non-random. In order to tease out the consequences of structural adjustment on democracy and democratic rights it is important to account for these underlying selection criteria of the Bank and Fund. To account for these selection issues the analyses used two-stage econometric models. The results of the selection model were reported in Chapter 5. The selection equation was utilized to generate predictions about the likelihood that each country would enter into a structural adjustment loan in a particular year. This probability was then used as an independent variable to control for the selection criteria of these institutions in the equation results reported here. The independent variable is listed as "World Bank and IMF selection effects" in the table of findings. The standard control variables we have used in this chapter are described in Table 4.6.

Institutional procedural democracy

One dependent variable in this analysis is a measure of democratic institutional development, the POLITY IV score for democracy. This is an eleven-point scale that ranges from "0," no institutional democratic development, to "10," full institutional development. This measure indicates how well a government meets Schumpeter's (1942) thin definition for procedural democracy. If a country gets a score of 10, it has a legislature that has enough power to check the chief executive, political parties have easy access to the ballot, there are at least two competitive parties, and there are regular elections.[2]

Three other dependent variables used in the analysis assess other aspects of the modern definition of full procedural democracy as described in Tables 10.1 and 10.2 above. The dependent variables for this part of the study were taken from the Cingranelli and Richards (CIRI) Human Rights Project. Information about these human rights practices of governments was gathered through a content analysis of information in the annual US Department of State's (USSD) *Country Reports on Human Rights Practices*. While these measures do not include every criterion listed in Tables 10.1 and 10.2, they are the same variables that were used by Kaufmann (2005) to show that democratic procedural rights were associated with higher rates of economic growth. These variables include freedom of assembly and association, freedom of speech and the press, and free and fair elections. Full descriptions of the coding procedure for each variable are included in the CIRI coding guide.[3] Brief descriptions follow.

Freedom of assembly and association It is an internationally recognized right of citizens to assemble freely and to associate with other persons in political parties, trade unions, cultural organizations, or other special-interest groups. This variable evaluates the extent to which the freedoms of assembly and association are subject to actual governmental limitations or restrictions (as opposed to strictly legal protections). Despite the international recognition of the right to assembly and association, in some countries citizens are prohibited by government from joining, forming, and participating in political parties of their

---

[2] We use the 0–10 democracy scale based on Gleditsch and Ward's (1997) discussion.
[3] The CIRI coding guide is available at www.humanrightsdata.org.

choice. Citizens in many countries are prohibited from protesting or publicly criticizing government decisions and actions. In more than a few countries, organizations critical of a government or those that are perceived to have hostile political agendas are not allowed to hold demonstrations, and their activities are severely curtailed and closely monitored by the state. This variable and the other two from the CIRI data set have three values. Coders were asked to characterize the citizens' rights to freedom of assembly and association as: severely restricted or denied completely to all citizens "0"; limited for all citizens or severely restricted or denied for select groups "1"; and virtually unrestricted and freely enjoyed by practically all citizens "2." Coders were reminded that it was the actual practices of governments, and not the legal protections that existed, that were being coded.

Freedom of speech and press Freedom of speech and press indicates the extent of government censorship of communication, including ownership of media outlets. Censorship is any form of restriction placed on freedom of the press, speech, or expression. Expression may be in the form of art or music. There are different degrees of censorship. Complete censorship denies citizens freedom of speech, and does not allow the printing or broadcasting media to express opposing views that challenge the policies of the existing government. In many instances the government owns and operates all forms of press and media. Coders were asked to characterize "Government censorship and/ or ownership of the media (including radio, TV, Internet, and domestic news agencies)" as: complete "0"; some "1"; and none "2."

"Some" censorship means the government places some restrictions yet does allow limited rights to freedom of speech and the press. "No" censorship means the freedom to speak freely and to print opposing opinions without the fear of prosecution. It must be noted that "none" does not mean absolute freedom, as there exists in all countries some restrictions on information and/or communication. Even in democracies there are restrictions placed on freedoms of speech and the press if these rights infringe on the rights of others or in any way endanger the welfare of others.

Free and fair elections Enjoyment of this right means that citizens have both the legal right and the ability in practice to change the laws and officials that govern them through periodic, free, and fair elections held on the basis of universal adult suffrage. After reading the appropriate section of the *Country Reports*, coders were asked to determine whether political participation was: very limited "0"; moderately free and open "1"; and very free and open "2." In a country receiving a score of 2, citizens had the right to self-determination under the law, and exercised this right in practice through periodic, free, and fair elections held on the basis of universal suffrage. The electoral process was transparent and fair. There were no allegations of vote tampering, electoral fraud, and official intimidation of citizens/opposition political parties that could be corroborated by independent election observers. Elections were generally described as free, fair, and open.

In a country receiving a score of 1, citizens had the legal right to self-determination. However, in practice there were some limitations that inhibited citizens from fully exercising this right. One such limitation (among many possibilities) was a lack of transparency in the electoral process. Lack of transparency in the electoral process included voter fraud and electoral irregularities (e.g., biased vote counting and tabulation; use of defective polling machines; government manipulation of voter registration lists). Other electorally based limitations included official intimidation, harassment, physical violence, bribery, or other coercive tactics to prevent citizens from voting in elections or to influence their votes, including government manipulation or control of the media prior to and during elections. Coders were told that instances where government respect for citizens' right to self-determination was described as "somewhat limited," "partial," or "not fully guaranteed," or likewise, also were to be coded as a "1." Similarly, if the USSD report stated that there were limitations on procedural democratic practices, but they were not severe and they did not significantly impinge on citizens' right to self-determination, coders were instructed to code the case as a "1."

In a country receiving a score of "0," the right to self-determination through political participation did not exist either in law, because it was an authoritarian regime, or in practice, because elections were fraudulent. The government systematically retaliated against citizens who sought to exercise this right through intimidation, threats of (or actual) violence, arrest, detention, and other coercive methods of control. In practice, the government severely restricted all or a significant number of citizens' ability to exercise this right. Coders were instructed to code instances where government respect for the right of self-determination was described as "severely restricted," "routinely denied," "systematically repressed," or "significantly curtailed" as a "0." They were also told to code instances where the number of citizens targeted for government restrictions on this right was described as "significant," "many," "numerous," or "a large number" as "0."

Findings

The results presented in Tables 10.3 and 10.4 indicate a consistent positive impact of structural adjustment implementation on government respect for procedural democratic rights. There are two sets of results for each dependent variable included in the analysis. The first column presents the selection corrected results, which should be trusted the most. The second column shows how the analysis would have turned out had we not corrected for the effects of selection. In general, when estimating the cumulative effects of structural adjustment on the development of democracy, selection effects were either positive and insignificant (free and fair elections) or positive and weakly significant at the .05 level of confidence (freedom of assembly and association and freedom of speech) or .10 level of confidence (institutionalized democracy). Thus, selection was either insignificant or tended to favor countries that had higher levels of respect for civil liberties and more democratic institutional development. Our conclusions about the effects of structural adjustment on democracy promotion would have been essentially the same whether or not we had controlled for selection.

The following discussion pertains only to the selection-corrected results. Governments that had spent longer under structural adjustment conditionality had higher levels of respect for institutionalized democracy, freedom of assembly and association, freedom of speech, and respect for free and fair elections. In three of the four models, the length of the period under structural adjustment was significant at the .05 level of confidence or higher. In the fourth, it was significant at the .10 level of confidence. In this case, controlling for the effects of selection had little effect on the relationship between structural adjustment implementation spells and either the degree of democratic institutional development or the degree of respect for civil liberties.

A number of other factors examined also had consistent impacts on the procedural democratic rights measured, indicated by significance in three or more of the four models estimated. The factors that had the most consistent impact included the physical quality of life index, our indicator of government respect for economic and social rights, which consistently improved government respect for all the procedural democratic rights under examination, significant at the .05 level of confidence or greater. Rebellion was also a significant predictor of government respect for procedural democratic rights. Those countries involved in rebellion, our measure of civil conflict, had lower levels of respect for institutionalized democratic rights, freedom of speech, and freedom of

Table 10.3. *The impact of World Bank and IMF structural adjustment agreements on government respect for procedural democratic rights 1981–2003, all developing countries*

	OLS model: respect for institutionalized democracy selection corrected	OLS model: respect for institutionalized democracy selection not corrected	Ordered logit: respect for freedom of assembly and association selection corrected	Ordered logit: respect for freedom of assembly and association selection not corrected
Number of years under a World Bank or IMF SAA	.008^ (.005)	.007^ (.005)	.024* (.011)	.032** (.011)
Economic factors				
GDP per capita	.00001 (.00001)	− 5.42e−06 (6.62e−06)	.0001* (.00005)	−.00002* (.00002)
Change in GDP per capita	.0002 (.0005)	.0003 (.0004)	−.001^ (.001)	−.0005 (.001)
Trade as a proportion of GDP	.0008 (.001)	−.001 (.0006)	−.0002 (.003)	−.003* (.002)
Domestic political factors				
Population density	1.31e−07** (5.54e−08)	8.34e−08 (5.93e−08)	−2.53e−07* (1.40e−07)	−3.07e−07* (1.15e−07)
Physical quality of life index	.007*** (.002)	.008*** (.002)	.01* (.006)	.018*** (.004)
United Kingdom colonial heritage	−.049 (.059)	−.039 (.049)	−.05 (.174)	−.027 (.146)
Conflict proneness				
Interstate conflict	.015 (.132)	−.019 (.089)	.052 (.155)	−.055 (.123)
Rebellion	−.051** (.023)	−.052** (.023)	−.077^ (.053)	−.068^ (.05)
Control variables				
World Bank and IMF selection effects	.232^ (.156)^	–	.631* (.352)	
Lagged dependent variable	.938*** (.011)	.947*** (.009)	2.957*** (.135)	3.098*** (.128)
N	1642	2027	1611	2091
Pseudo R^2	(R-squared).93	(R-squared).93	.44	.46

Note: P>|z .1^ .05*, .01**, .001***
Estimated with robust standard errors, with one-tailed significance tests. The constant in the OLS model is not shown for space limitations but was negative and significant at the .01 level.

Table 10.4. *The impact of World Bank and IMF structural adjustment agreements on government respect for procedural democratic rights 1981–2003, all developing countries (ordered logit)*

	Respect for freedom of speech selection corrected	Respect for freedom of speech selection not corrected	Respect for free and fair elections selection corrected	Respect for free and fair elections selection not corrected
Number of years under a World Bank or IMF SAA	.043*** (.014)	.058*** (.013)	.054*** (.012)	.056*** (.011)
Economic factors				
GDP per capita	.00005 (.00005)	3.38e–06 (.00002)	.0001* (00006)	.0000 (00003)
Change in GDP per capita	.00006 (.0005)	.0006^ (.0005)	–.001* (.0008)	–.0002 (.0006)
Trade as a proportion of GDP	–.001 (.003)	–.004** (.002)	–.001 (.003)	–.002^ (.001)
Domestic political factors				
Population density	–5.51e–07** (1.95e–07)	–6.39e–07*** (1.78e–07)	–6.92e–08 (1.53e–07)	–1.13e–07 (1.59e–07)
Physical quality of life index	.019** (.006)	.0226*** (.005)	.014* (.007)	.024 (.005)
United Kingdom colonial heritage	.049 (.178)	.185^ (.148)	.019 (.18)	–.017 (.15)
Conflict proneness				
Interstate conflict	.115 (.109)	.013 (.102)	.024 (.117)	.012 (.106)
Rebellion	–.193** (.065)	–.178*** (.057)	–.049 (.058)	–.016 (.057)
Control variables				
World Bank and IMF selection effects	.593* (.333)	–	.343 (.372)	–
Lagged dependent variable	2.136*** (.142)	2.147*** (.129)	2.163*** (.125)	2.297*** (.117)
N	1610	2047	1608	2045
Pseudo R^2	.27	.27	.34	.36

Note: P>|z .1^.05*, .01**, .001***
Estimated with robust standard errors, with one-tailed significance tests.

assembly and association, the first two significant at the .01 level and the latter two at the .10 level of confidence. These findings support previous research, which found civil conflict lowered levels of respect for physical integrity rights (Carey 2004; Poe, Tate, and Keith 1999).

A number of other factors were significant but less consistent in their impacts. GDP per capita, our measure of wealth, increased levels of respect for procedural democratic rights in two of the four models: freedom of assembly and association, and free and fair elections, significant at least at the .10 level of confidence. It had a positive but insignificant effect in the remaining models. The impact of wealth also supports the findings of previous research about the beneficial impact of increased wealth on levels of respect for human rights (Poe, Tate, and Keith 1999). Large positive changes in GDP per capita, our measure of economic growth, had a negative impact on respect for freedom of assembly and association and free and fair elections, significant at least at the .10 level of confidence.

Conclusions

After reading the case study literature on the effects of structural adjustment programs, we expected to find that countries under structural adjustment conditionality the longest would be less democratic than similar countries with less exposure to conditionality. To the contrary, the results presented in this chapter showed that countries under structural adjustment conditionality the longest have better-developed democratic institutions, have elections that are more free and fair, have more freedom to form and join organizations, and have more freedom of speech and press than countries with less exposure to structural adjustment conditionality. These things are true even after controlling for the effects of selection.

We did not expect these findings. We tried splitting the period of study into the Cold War and post-Cold War periods. We hypothesized that democracy had been undermined during the Cold War. Perhaps democracy promotion through international lending was something that only came about after the Cold War had ended. We found, instead, that structural adjustment had improved procedural democracy even during the Cold War. We tried different indicators for the independent variables, different mixes of control variables, even different estimation procedures. These findings are robust to all of those variations in research design. Prolonged exposure to structural adjustment has led to greater respect for a variety of important procedural democratic rights. The question is why?

Three answers to this question deserve further investigation. First, the steps towards institutional democracy and respect for civil liberties we have documented may be both meaningful and intended by the Directors of the IMF and the Bank. The second is that this progress towards democracy is meaningful but has been an unintended consequence of structural adjustment conditionality. The final explanation is that, whether the changes have been intentional or unintentional from the viewpoints of the Directors of the IFIs, they are not meaningful, because the democratic process still is not used to make important economic policy decisions in developing countries. These three perspectives are not entirely mutually exclusive. We elaborate on each of them below.

The findings of our study may show that the World Bank and IMF can improve the human rights practices of developing countries if they choose to do so. Advancing the human rights to procedural democracy may have been a priority of the Bank, the Fund, and the major donors to both international financial institutions. Promoting the other human rights examined in the book may not have been a priority. The WTO, which also promotes neoliberal economic reforms, urges member governments to make trade policy more transparent and fair to all interested parties, and these policy changes help support the movement towards democracy in developing countries (Aaronson and Zimmerman forthcoming). This "intentional democracy promotion" explanation is consistent with the fact that the United States government and most other donor countries have bilateral democracy programs. Democracy promotion has been the view of every US administration for a very long time and certainly has been a view espoused by every president of the United States during the period covered by this study. Most of the significant legislation on human rights was passed between 1973 and 1980. A then progressive-minded Congress pushed it on a reluctant executive branch. Among those laws was the International Financial Assistance Act of 1977, which required that the US representatives on the boards of international financial institutions use their voices and votes to advance the cause of human rights (Forsythe 1988).

While there were indications that the Carter administration was concerned about using the weight of US foreign policy to further the full range of human rights, including democratic procedural rights, the Reagan administration quickly redefined "human rights promotion" to mean "democracy promotion" (Cingranelli 1993: 191–205). This emphasis was clear in the Reagan Doctrine, which stated that the US government must stand by its democratic allies in the developing world. The Reagan and first Bush administrations pursued two tracks in the name of human rights. They made a positive effort to export democracy, and they pursued a negative policy of scolding friends and adversaries alike for abusing their citizens' rights to procedural democracy. This executive reinterpretation of US human rights policy has remained largely unchanged by succeeding administrations.

Sen (1999) made the argument in human rights terms, but Milton Friedman, recipient of the 1976 Nobel Prize for Economics, made a similar, though narrower, case about democratic rights as a means to economic growth. In the enormously popular and influential book, written with Rose Friedman, *Free to Choose* (1980), they discussed the complementarities between political and economic freedom. A procedural democracy accompanied by a free-market economy, they contended, was the ideal combination to ensure economic growth and to improve the well-being of average citizens.

A second viewpoint is that democratization was the unintended consequence of structural adjustment policies, because the policies stimulated social movements to resist them. Those social movements or resistance may have been the basis of, or at least contributed to, the further development of democracy in authoritarian or nascent democratic regimes. We have demonstrated that poor people have been hurt by structural adjustment reforms (Chapter 6), and those hardships have been a source of conflict in developing countries (see Chapter 7). Protests against the reforms have been led by civil society groups such as organized labor, the church, students, national and international nongovernmental organizations, and other civil society groups. These groups have also been at the forefront of many democracy movements around the world.

In some cases, the argument against structural adjustment reforms may be one part of a much larger platform of grievances against the regime in power. For example, the Muslim Brotherhood has been using arguments against structural adjustment as part of its larger campaign against the Mubarek-led regime in Egypt (Kienle 2001). In other cases, such as the democracy movement in Bolivia, opposition to structural adjustment policies was the centerpiece of an electoral movement that brought a champion of the poor, indigenous people, Evo Morales, to power. The argument against neoliberal reforms in general, and the IMF and the World Bank in particular, also figured prominently in the election campaigns of left-party candidates in Brazil, Chile, Mexico, and Venezuela.

Yet a third explanation is that institutional and procedural democratic progress may have occurred in the making of some policies, but structural adjustment policies have reduced the voice of the people and their legislatures over the making of fundamental domestic economic policies (Alexander 2006a; SAPRIN 2004). One reason is that the neoliberal reforms promoted by the IFIs shift power and responsibility from governments to firms (Alexander 2006a). Once formerly publicly owned enterprises are privatized, the public has less to say about how they operate. Another reason for what Alexander (2006a) calls "the shrinking policy space" is that the process of negotiating and implementing loans tends to strengthen the executive branch. Popular participation in the design of adjustment loans is not possible, since the provisions of draft structural adjustment agreements are rarely made public. Sometimes, even the final provisions of the agreements are not publicly disclosed (Alexander 2006a). Finally, the loan conditions themselves tend to strengthen the executive branch of recipient governments over the legislative branch. The Ministry of Finance has hegemonic power over other ministries of government and, with the Cabinet, presents bills drafted, often in concert with officials or consultants of the IFIs, to the legislature. Many legislatures have no power to modify proposed laws. Their main responsibility may be to raise the debt ceiling to accommodate the loans (Alexander 2006a). Some conditions require Chief Executives to issue decrees or executive orders and to insist upon the right to an "unassailable presidential veto" to implement policies so unpopular that they would be unlikely to receive majority support from the legislature.

Part IV

Conclusion

11   A human rights-based approach to economic development

Introduction

The findings of our study have ethical and practical implications. Since the passage of the United Nations Universal Declaration of Human Rights in 1948, the promotion of better human rights practices by governments around the world has been one of the most important functions of the United Nations. It is morally wrong for agencies of the United Nations, which include both the World Bank and the International Monetary Fund, to undermine one of their parent organization's most important goals, the promotion of good human rights practices (Clapham 2006; Darrow 2003; Skogly 1993; 2001). The practical implication of our findings is that structural adjustment programs are not producing good economic outcomes mainly because they combine relatively ineffective policies with the undermining of a necessary precondition for economic growth – respect for human rights.

The World Bank and IMF should be pursuing equitable economic development. We have defined equitable economic development as the simultaneous achievement of economic growth and advancement in protections of economic and social rights of citizens. Achieving one element without the other should be considered "development failure." We argue that respect for some human rights will promote equitable development. More precisely, *respect for some physical integrity and civil rights and liberties will lead to faster rates of economic growth and progress in achieving respect for economic and social rights to such things as health care, education, and housing.* This definition captures the essence of Sen's (1999) contention that freedom is both the proper definition of development and the means to achieve it. It also suggests an agenda for empirical tests designed to examine the relationship between respect for particular human rights and economic development. Respect for particular human rights may be related to higher rates of economic growth, improvement in respect for economic and social rights, or both.

The human rights effects of structural adjustment have been (mostly) negative

When we began this research project, we knew that structural adjustment policies had not stimulated much economic growth in most developing countries, and we hypothesized that structural adjustment agreements also encouraged governments to reduce their respect for many types of human rights. Like Vreeland (e.g., 2003), we also considered selection an important issue that had to be addressed before assessing the impact of structural adjustment. There is currently no consensus about which human rights are necessary or conducive to economic development. However, from Kaufmann's work (2004), we knew that respect for some human rights facilitated both economic growth and government respect for economic and social human rights.

We decided to examine whether human rights, some of which had previously been shown to be key instruments in promoting higher levels of economic development, were being undermined by the development strategy employed by the World Bank and IMF – structural adjustment. We found that respect for many of the rights which were shown to facilitate economic development in Kaufmann's work has been undermined by structural adjustment. There is room for further research examining the impact of structural adjustment on additional rights beyond the scope of this particular project. Impacts on women's rights and on the rights of children are prime candidates as foci for future research.

For example, Chapter 8 examining physical integrity rights – the rights of citizens not to be tortured, murdered, disappeared, or politically imprisoned by their government – builds directly upon Kaufmann's (2005) previous research. He found that government respect for these human rights and democratic rights makes it more likely that economic growth will occur in developing countries which in turn leads to greater respect for economic and social rights. We chose to examine the same human rights he found to be important to the achievement of economic growth and progress in achievement of good economic and social rights outcomes. To his list, we added respect for worker rights. We used the same indicators of government respect for human rights, allowing our findings and conclusions to speak directly to this earlier work.

Building upon our reading of the previous literature, the theoretical framework we presented is that structural adjustment policies worsen levels of economic growth that would have occurred without such policies. What's more, the reduced involvement of the state in the economy makes things worse for those people who depend most on the state for protection – the poor. They lose jobs, subsidies for necessities such as oil or bread, and access to education and health care. With privatization, even water may become unaffordable. Respect for social and economic rights of the poorest people either declines or rises slowly relative to states with less exposure to structural adjustment conditions. Mass demonstrations, riots, and rebellions take place more frequently under such circumstances, and governments of developing countries, which are generally weaker and less stable, are likely to respond with increased repression of many types.

The evidence we presented in previous chapters fits this theory in most respects. We showed that the governments of countries that have been under structural adjustment the longest:

- Provide less respect for the economic and social human rights of their citizens (Chapter 6).
- Are more likely to experience violent anti-government rebellion[1] and longer periods of anti-government demonstrations, riots, and rebellion (Chapter 7).
- Torture, politically imprison, disappear, and murder their citizens in greater numbers (Chapter 8).
- And are less likely to respect fundamental worker rights (Chapter 9).

The finding that structural adjustment undermines respect for economic and social rights is especially important, because it demonstrates that structural adjustment erodes one of the two essential definitional characteristics of equitable economic development. This finding should not surprise anyone. It simply adds some weight to the near-unanimous opinions of human rights nongovernmental organizations and scholars who have studied the implementation of structural adjustment in particular countries. Reduced respect for economic and social human rights is also the main reason for the increased civil conflict that occurs in societies undergoing structural adjustment. The increase in civil conflict, in turn, provokes government repression of other human rights. These consequences mean that not only have governments tortured, imprisoned, disappeared, and murdered more of their citizens as a result of structural adjustment, but the consequences of these programs have also reduced the ability of governments to promote economic development of any kind within their societies.

---

[1] When they enter into structural adjustment agreements.

Though it is clear that structural adjustment policies have negative human rights consequences for loan recipients, these bad outcomes probably have been unintended. First, the World Bank has been public in its commitment to good governance, including good human rights practices, as a way to promote economic development (Kaufmann 2005; Kaufmann, Kraay, and Mastruzzi 2005; World Bank 2005b). Second, the selection-stage findings indicated that the Bank and the IMF have been more likely to give loans to governments with relatively good records of protection of physical integrity rights (see Chapter 5). Third, the loan-selection practices of the World Bank were not found to be strongly affected by the political interests of the major donors (Abouharb and Cingranelli 2006). Having an alliance with the United States or another major donor to the Bank had little effect on whether or not a country received a loan. Fourth, elsewhere we have shown that the human rights practices of loan recipients improved during the years new structural adjustment loans were negotiated with the World Bank (Abouharb and Cingranelli 2006). One might infer that these temporary improvements were designed to please World Bank officials, who preferred better human rights practices from loan-recipient governments. Fifth, the findings indicated that democratic governments were not disadvantaged when they sought structural adjustment loans (see Chapter 5). Finally, the findings of this study, discussed in more detail later, showed that countries under structural adjustment the longest had more respect for some procedural democratic rights.

Can structural adjustment agreements be blamed?

Defenders of structural adjustment policies have made several arguments against our findings. First, they claim that structural adjustment has not failed. Rather, in most less developed countries, governments have not really followed through on the policy prescriptions promoted by the Bank and Fund. In a second related argument, critics of global comparative studies like this one do not believe that global, comparative research such as ours really measures whether or not structural adjustment agreements have been implemented. Third, they argue that the Bank and Fund assist many of the worst cases. Thus, any negative findings cannot be attributed to these institutions. Rather, things (including human rights practices) would have been even worse had the Bank and Fund not intervened. Fourth, they contend it is not the fault of the Bank and Fund that the governments of developing countries choose to place hardships on poor people in order to meet the objectives of structural adjustment. Finally, defenders argue that even if previous assessments of these agreements have indicated negative impacts on the societies of developing countries, the Bank and Fund have now recognized these issues and have changed their policies. We consider each of these critiques below.

Structural adjustment prescriptions have been implemented

Many, if not most, governments have liberalized their economies subsequent to negotiations of agreements with the IMF and World Bank. Numerous examples are sprinkled throughout this book. For those who are still skeptical, we recommend reading the excellent study conducted by the Structural Adjustment Participatory Review International Network (SAPRIN 2004). This study details the economic reforms undertaken in Bangladesh, Ecuador, Ghana, Hungary, Mexico, the Philippines, Uganda, and Zimbabwe subsequent to structural adjustment agreements. The report details liberalizing reforms in trade policy, agricultural policy, resource extraction, education policy, in the financial sector, in industrial and labor relations, and in privatization of publicly owned enterprises. The conclusions of the SAPRIN study reinforce conclusions reached in many previous case studies and in other small-scale comparative work. They include the following:

- "Adjustment Policies have contributed to the further impoverishment and marginalization of local populations, while increasing economic inequality" (p. 203).
- "Trade policy and financial sector reforms have destroyed domestic productive capacity, particularly among small and medium-sized enterprises" (p. 204).
- "Trade liberalization and agricultural and other reforms have marginalized the rural poor, reduced cultivation for the local market and undermined food security" (p. 207).
- "Employment has become more precarious and less remunerative with the increase of privatization and the introduction of labour market reforms" (p. 211).

The SAPRIN study's conclusions about the impact of structural adjustment programs on respect for social and economic human rights are especially germane to our argument about negative impacts on this important category of human rights. They include the following:

- "The privatization of public utilities and services has usually resulted in significant price increases for the general public" (p. 214).

- "The elimination of universal subsidies for essential goods and services has negatively affected the poor and their quality of life" (p. 214).
- "Stabilization and structural adjustment programmes have generally led to a sharp deterioration in public spending on social services, often during economic downturns, while debt obligations continue to be paid" (p. 215).
- "The quality of education and healthcare has generally declined as a result of pressures to reduce public expenditures" (p. 216).
- "Cost-sharing schemes have imposed serious constraints on access by poor people to healthcare and education" (p. 216).

Despite the existence of a large body of literature corroborating the SAPRIN study's conclusions, some have criticized developing countries for not "fully implementing" the provisions of structural adjustment agreements (Dollar and Svensson 2000; Killick 1996; Van de Walle 2001). Therefore, the argument goes, poor outcomes, economic or otherwise, cannot be blamed on structural adjustment policies. In his study of structural adjustment in Africa, Van de Walle (2001) illustrated the difficulty of assessing the degree of implementation even for a region. He identified several different common provisions in structural adjustment agreements with African governments, which he divided into two main categories – stabilization and adjustment. Ten economic policies were classified as being part of each main category. He then evaluated the degree to which each of the ten policies had been implemented, on average, for all countries in Africa between 1979–1999 (Van de Walle 2001: 90). He did not attempt to do this for each country in the region for each year of his study. Except for civil service reform, where he rated the degree of implementation as "poor," he concluded that every policy had been implemented to some extent even in Africa, where the average quality of governance is poor.

The question then becomes "how much implementation is required before we agree that the agreement was implemented?" Killick (1996) has conducted the most thorough and comprehensive studies of implementation of structural adjustment programs. He defined a structural adjustment program as incomplete if a country had implemented less than 81 percent of its program conditions. He surveyed 305 IMF agreements in less developed countries, and found that 53 percent had not been completed during the loan period. Though both Van de Walle and Killick criticize developing countries for not fully implementing the provisions of their structural adjustment agreements, both provide ample evidence that the governments of most less developed countries implement many, if not most, of the provisions of their agreements.

Our measure of implementation in each country is reasonable

Those who wish to conduct global, comparative research on the effects of the implementation of structural adjustment policies face a daunting task. An ideal data set would include, for each country in the sample: what provisions were included in each structural adjustment agreement, and which of these provisions was implemented for each year and to what extent. Without access to internal World Bank and IMF files, construction of such a data set would be impossible. Instead, the measure we used to assess the human rights effects of structural adjustment was the number of years each country had been implementing a structural adjustment agreement with either the IMF or the World Bank. We assumed that if a country was under structural adjustment conditionality for more years during the period of our study (1981–2003), then it would have implemented more structural adjustment provisions and would have implemented them more fully. More implementation, measured in this way, would produce greater effects on the human rights practices of governments. The details of constructing this measure are provided in Chapter 4.

This measure is the fairest to date in the debate about the impact of structural adjustment. We take the Bank and Fund at their word concerning the short-term hardships versus the long-term benefits of restructuring developing economies on neoliberal lines. Consistent with this argument, we have measured the cumulative effect of structural adjustment on human rights practices. If the benefits of structural adjustment are over the longer term, which the Bank and Fund insist they are, then measures assessing the impact of structural adjustment should reflect these cumulative consequences. Other studies of the impact of structural adjustment have not considered cumulative effects (Abouharb and Cingranelli 2006; Vreeland 2002; 2003; Keith and Poe 2000; Przeworski and Vreeland 2000). The cumulative measure provides a best-case scenario for defenders of these programs since, during the first few years a country undertakes major reforms of its economy, its government may have to make unpopular decisions. Things may be tough for a while. However, after this period of initial adjustment the economy should benefit, economic growth should increase, and human rights practices should improve. The expectation of defenders of structural adjustment is that the greater the periods of time these countries have been liberalizing their economies the more beneficial will be the outcome. We find this not to be the case.

The negative outcomes can be attributed
to the Bank and Fund

Another argument in defense of structural adjustment programs is that the Bank and Fund assist countries in serious trouble. Without their assistance, human rights and outcomes would be even worse than they are. This type of critique can be used to downplay the results of case study research and small-scale comparative studies. Case studies usually compare the situation in a loan-recipient state before and after it enters into an agreement. Any change in outcomes of interest is attributed to the loan agreement. However, this is an inappropriate conclusion because there may well be a myriad of other factors that effect this change (Harrigan and Mosley 1991: 65).

The research design of this study corrects for the fact that the types of countries that go under structural adjustment most often may be quite different from those that do not. Like others, we have approached discerning the (mostly) economic effects of structural adjustment by controlling for issues of selection (Abouharb and Cingranelli 2004a; 2004b; 2005; 2006; Conway 1994; Khan 1990; Przeworski and Vreeland 2000; Vreeland 2003). The concept of selection refers to the idea that there are factors which make countries candidates for structural adjustment agreements, such as being poor, that are also important factors in affecting the human rights performances of their governments.

Our empirical findings indicate that in eight out of the eleven models presented which included selection effects, the choice of the Bank and Fund was to favor governments that had better human rights records. Thus, at least in terms of human rights practices, on average the Bank and Fund do not work with the worst cases. Nevertheless, despite this selection bias towards governments with good overall levels of respect for human rights, the consequences of these programs have been to generate domestic instability, and reductions in government respect for economic and social rights, physical integrity rights, and worker rights.

It is the Bank and Fund's fault for placing
hardships on the poor

Supporters of the Bank and Fund argue that, if hardships have been placed on the poor in developing countries, it is due to the policy choices of loan-recipient governments, not requirements of the Bank and Fund. After all, structural adjustment agreements are *negotiated*, not imposed. However, leaders of developing countries are in a difficult position.

Their countries need external capital for development and to service debts. Their choices are limited. They can seek bilateral grants from donor countries. Low-income countries can turn to the Bank for grants or loans at concessionary rates of interest. They can seek private loans at higher rates of interest.

If governments turn to the Bank or Fund, they will be expected to make economic policies that produce free-market reforms and end most government intervention in the market. The policies mandated by the Bank and Fund have included privatization of basic services, including water systems, reductions in government spending, and the removal of subsidies and price restrictions for essential goods and services because, according to the Bank and Fund, they can be provided more efficiently by the free market. One common provision in structural adjustment agreements is that the loan recipient adopt a balanced budget (or often a surplus) while continuing to pay debt obligations. Few wealthy countries have balanced budgets. The governments of developing countries have few choices available, so cuts in public employment and reductions in the provision of basic health, education, and welfare services are inevitable.

Structural adjustment conditionality remains fundamental

Finally, defenders argue that even if previous assessments of these agreements have led to some negative impacts on developing countries, the Bank and Fund have now recognized these problems and have changed their policies. Indeed, we have cited language, mostly emanating from the World Bank, that recognizes the issues of respecting human rights, the rights of the poor, and poverty alleviation. Yet, despite the rhetoric, the fundamental approach to promote economic development in poor countries is still structural adjustment. The IFIs require governments to prepare Poverty Reduction Strategy Papers (PRSPs) in order to qualify for assistance, but if they need assistance, governments need to propose the structural adjustment policies that the IFIs will finance. The fundamentals of "less state, more market" remain the same. The Bank and Fund are still wedded to one-size-fits-all, rapid neoliberal structural adjustment as the key tool to promote economic development. The authors of the SAPRIN study (2004) reached the same conclusion.

The positive effects of structural adjustment on respect for procedural democratic rights

Despite the negative impacts of structural adjustment on economic and social, physical integrity, and worker rights we did find that these agreements have had a consistently positive impact on government respect for procedural democratic rights. The critical theoretical perspective of the human rights effects of structural adjustment presented in Chapter 3 suggested that reduced respect for economic and social rights and increased civil conflict in societies would undermine procedural democratic rights. To the contrary, we presented results in Chapter 10 showing that countries under structural adjustment conditionality the longest have better-developed democratic institutions, have more freedom to form and join organizations, have more freedom of speech and press, and have elections that are freer and fairer than countries with less exposure to structural adjustment conditionality. This is true even after controlling for the effects of selection. These findings show that the effects of World Bank and IMF SAAs do not necessarily diminish human rights practices of developing countries.

The steps towards institutional democracy and respect for civil liberties we have documented in this study may be both meaningful and intended by the Directors of the IMF and the Bank. Alternatively, progress towards democracy is meaningful but has been an unintended consequence of structural adjustment conditionality. The final explanation we offered in Chapter 10 was that, whether the changes have been intentional or unintentional (from the viewpoints of the Directors of the IFIs), they are not meaningful, because the democratic process still is not used to make important economic policy decisions in low-income countries. These three perspectives are not entirely mutually exclusive.

Policy implications: towards a human rights-based strategy of economic development

The evidence suggests that there are some preconditions for economic development. Governments must protect certain human rights. Research by others suggests that these rights include the right to participate in free and fair elections, the freedom to form and join organizations, freedom of speech and press, freedom from torture, murder, disappearance, and political imprisonment.[2] We offer an alternative definition of a human rights-based economic development strategy that focuses on human rights-related preconditions. It has four elements:

1) Equitable economic development, defined as the simultaneous achievement of economic growth and advancement in protections

---

[2] There are probably other preconditions including manageable interest payments on debt, and the absence of corruption.

of economic and social rights of citizens, should be the goal of the IMF and the World Bank. Achieving one element without the other should be considered "development failure." Achieving neither element should be considered complete development failure. Both elements should be assessed for every developing country annually so that comparisons among countries will be explicit, and successes and failures can be identified easily.

2) Some minimal level of respect for human rights should be a necessary condition before the World Bank and IMF even enter into negotiations that might result in provision of financial assistance. The World Bank and IMF, as agencies of the United Nations, should try to advance all internationally recognized human rights. At the very least, they should be focused on advancing those rights that have been shown to lead to economic growth and greater respect for economic and social rights. So far, research has shown that respect for some procedural democratic rights and physical integrity rights is associated with both of these beneficial developmental outcomes. Our research indicates that governments which provide higher levels of respect for the physical integrity rights of their citizens, a right shown to promote economic growth, are already being favored by these institutions. Our recommendation would formalize this. In contrast, the other factor shown to promote equitable economic development, democratic regimes, has not been favored by the World Bank and IMF in their loan-selection criteria. The evidence indicates that democracies are more likely to both implement the conditions associated with structural adjustment (Dollar and Svensson 2000) and promote equitable economic development. It seems that these international financial institutions should also be concentrating their efforts in democratic regimes, and for those regimes that are not democratic making democracy a condition of future assistance. Future research almost certainly will point to other human rights that should be added to this list. The minimum level of respect required might also be established through future research. For now, it should be set as "a level of respect that is above the mean for all low-income countries" or for other "benchmark countries."

Democracy should be conceptualized and measured in a way that emphasizes the role of the legislature in making important economic policies. In a public address concerning the unwillingness of the IMF and World Bank to promote this type of "substantive democracy" in low-income countries, Harvard professor Dani Rodrik (2001) suggested that: "The broader the sway of market discipline, the narrower will be the space for democratic governance ... International economic rules must incorporate 'opt-out' or exit clauses [that] allow democracies to reassert their priorities when these priorities clash with obligations to international economic institutions. These must be viewed not as 'derogations' or violations of the rules, but as a generic part of sustainable international economic arrangements."

3) The Bank and Fund should develop and issue regular human rights impact assessments of their activities. To avoid the appearance of conflict of interest, the measures of government human rights practices used should be developed by organizations independent of the Bank and the Fund. The use of measures developed by multiple organizations would be best.

4) The government of every developing country should be expected to make progress (or at least not to regress) in the protection of all human rights and especially those that have been shown to facilitate equitable economic development.

Most insiders will reject this kind of "carrot and stick" approach to the provision of development aid. They would probably argue, like Leite (2001), Assistant Director in the IMF's Office in Europe, that constructive engagement is better than confrontation as a way to change human rights practices of developing countries. However, there is no evidence that working quietly behind the scenes with government leaders is an effective way to resolve abuses over time, and there are advantages in stating noble principles publicly. For these reasons, many European countries have followed the lead of the United States by explicitly including human rights provisions in legislation governing their foreign policy formulation (Donnelly 2003). Even the European Union requires a minimum level of respect for human rights and adoption of democratic institutions as a condition for admittance. The European Union has gone even further by inserting a "human rights clause" in all negotiated bilateral trade and development agreements since 1995 (Decker, McInerney-Lankford, and Sage 2006).

Implications for human rights theory

In Chapter 3, we reviewed the major explanations of global variations in government human rights practices. Those explanations focus on the importance of characteristics of the state, itself, or in the case of interstate war, on the relationships between states. This study adds to the relatively new research emphasis examining the importance of transnational forces such as trade regimes, human rights regimes, and, in the case of this study, the international finance regime. In Chapter 3, we defined a

regime as a set of rights and rules, decision-making procedures or programs that gives rise to social practices, assigns roles to the participants in
these practices, and governs their interactions (Young 1992). Regimes
structure the opportunities of actors interested in a given activity and
they contain the expectation of compliance by their members (Young
1980: 333–342).

Western governments have given responsibility to the World Bank
and International Monetary Fund to determine which developing
countries receive capital and under what conditions. In that sense, the
IMF and the World Bank (along with the WTO) are the gatekeepers to
the global economy. Other work has specifically examined the impact of
international human rights regimes on the levels of respect national
governments provide for their citizens (Landman 2005). These international human rights regimes have had varying degrees of positive
impact in improving levels of government respect for the human rights
of their citizens. Our work then speaks to the differing impact of
international regimes on government respect for human rights. This
study shows that, while some regimes may positively impact human
rights, two important protagonists involved in the international financial
regime, the World Bank and International Monetary Fund, have
negatively impacted the levels of respect governments provide for the
economic, social, and physical integrity rights of their citizens.

The results of this study suggest that existing theories of repression
should be revised to take greater account of the effects of such transnational causal forces on the human rights practices of governments
around the world. The human rights effects of other transnational factors besides participation in international war – such as the degree of
integration into the global economy, sensitivity to international norms,
exposure to transnational corporations, and involvement with international financial institutions – deserve more attention. The positive and
negative human rights effects of other international regimes whose rules
plausibly affect the human rights practices of governments – such as the
bilateral, regional, and multilateral trade agreements and intellectual
property, and labor regimes – also warrant more scrutiny.

Bibliography

Aaronson, Susan and Jamie Zimmerman. Forthcoming. *Trade Imbalance: The Struggle to Weigh Human Rights Concerns in Trade Policymaking.* Cambridge University Press.

Abouharb, M. Rodwan. 2005. "Economic Liberalization and its Impact on Civil War 1870–2000." Ph.D. diss., Binghamton University.

Abouharb, M. Rodwan and David Cingranelli. 2004a. "Human Rights and Structural Adjustment: The Importance of Selection," in Sabine C. Carey and Steven C. Poe (eds.) *Understanding Human Rights Violations: New Systematic Studies.* Burlington, VT: Ashgate, pp. 127–146.

Abouharb, M. Rodwan and David Cingranelli. 2004b. "The Impact of IMF Structural Adjustment Lending on Human Rights, 1981–2000," Paper presented at the 2004 annual meeting of the International Studies Association, Montreal, March.

Abouharb, M. Rodwan and David Cingranelli. 2005. "When the World Bank Says Yes: Determinants of Structural Adjustment Lending," in Gustav Rani and James Raymond Vreeland (eds.) *Impact of Globalization on the Nation-State from Above: The International Monetary Fund and the World Bank.* London: Routledge, pp. 2–65.

Abouharb, M. Rodwan and David Cingranelli. 2006. "The Human Rights Effects of World Bank Structural Adjustment Lending, 1981–2000," *International Studies Quarterly* 50(2): 233–262.

Achen, Christopher H. 1986. *The Statistical Analysis of Quasi Experiments.* Berkeley: University of California Press.

Adams, Roy J. 1993. "Regulating Unions and Collective Bargaining: A Global, Historical Analysis of Determinants and Consequences," *Comparative Labor Law Journal* 14: 272–301.

Adepoju, Aderanti. 1993. "Introduction," in Aderanti Adepoju (ed.) *The Impact of Structural Adjustment on the Population of Africa.* United Nations Population Fund, Portsmouth, NH: Heinemann, pp. 1–6.

Aggarwal, Mita. 1995. "International Trade, Labor Standards, and Labor Market Conditions: An Evaluation of the Linkages," Working Paper 95–96-C. Washington, DC: US International Trade Commission.

Al-Atraqchi, Firas. 2005. December 7. "Cairenes Have Few Illusions over Vote." www.english.aljazeera.net.

Alexander, Nancy. 2001. "The Rebirth, or Second Coming, of Adjustment Lending." Citizens' Network on Essential Services. www.servicesforall.org.

Alexander, Nancy. 2005. "The Roles of the IMF, the World Bank, and the WTO in Liberalization and Privatization of the Water Services Sector." Citizens' Network on Essential Services. www.servicesforall.org.

Alexander, Nancy. 2006a. "Decentralization and Sovereignty: How Policy Space is Eroded." *Social Watch Report 2006: Impossible Architecture*. Uruguay: The Third World Institute.

Alexander, Nancy. 2006b. "Globalization and International Institutions: The International Monetary Fund (IMF), the World Bank, and the World Trade Organization." Citizens' Network on Essential Services. www. servicesforall.org.

Alexander, Nancy. 2006c. "The IMF and the World Bank Group: An Overview of Selected Financial and Accountability Issues." Citizens' Network on Essential Services. www.servicesforall.org.

Alston, Philip and Nehal Bhuta. 2005. "Human Rights and Public Goods: Education as a Fundamental Human Right in India," in Philip Alston and Mary Robinson (eds.) *Human Rights and Development: Towards Mutual Reinforcement*. Oxford University Press, pp. 242–268

Anderson, Sarah, John Cavanagh, and Thea Lee. 2000. *Field Guide to the Global Economy*. New York: The New Press.

Arat, Zehra. 1991. *Democracy and Human Rights in Developing Countries*. Boulder, CO: Lynne Rienner.

Auyero, J. 2001. "Glocal Riots," *International Sociology* 16(1): 33–53.

Ayoob, Mohammed. 1995. *The Third World Security Predicament: State Making, Regional Conflict, and the International System*. Boulder, CO: Lynne Rienner.

Banks, Arthur S. 2002/2005. *Cross-national Time-series Data Archive* [computer file]. Binghamton, NY: Computer Solutions Unlimited.

Banks, Arthur S., Thomas Muller, and William R. Overstreet. 2003. *Political Handbook of the World 2000–2002*. Binghamton, NY: CSA Publications.

Barbieri, Katherine and Rafael Reuveny. 2005. "Economic Globalization and Civil War," *The Journal of Politics* 67(4): 1228–1247.

Barrientos, Stephanie. 1993. "Economic Growth versus Poverty and Inequality in Chile: A Dualist Analysis," Paper Presented to the Development Studies Association Conference, Brighton, UK, September 8.

Bates, Robert. 1981. *Markets and States in Tropical Africa*. Berkeley, CA: University of California Press.

Bates, Robert H. 1993. "Is 'Rational Choice' the Best Choice for Robert Bates – a Reply," *World Development* 21(6): 1077–1081.

Bates, Robert H. 2001. *Prosperity and Violence: The Political Economy of Development*. New York: Norton.

Bayless, M. and S. Bayless. 1982. "Current Quality of Life Indicators: Some Theoretical and Methodological Concerns," *American Journal of Economics and Sociology* 43(1): 185–198.

Beck, Nathaniel, Jonathan N. Katz, and Richard Tucker. 1998. "Taking Time Seriously in Binary Time-Series Cross-Section Analysis," *American Journal of Political Science* 42(4): 1260–1288.

Beer, Linda. 1999. "Income Inequality and Transnational Corporate Penetration," *Journal of World-Systems Research* 5(1): 1–25.

Bello, Walden. 1996. "Structural Adjustment Programs: 'Success' for Whom?," in Jerry Mander and Edward Goldsmith (eds.) *The Case Against the Global Economy*. San Francisco: Sierra Club Book, pp. 285–296.

Bello, Walden F., Shea Cunningham, and Bill Rau. 1994. *Dark Victory: The United States, Structural Adjustment, and Global Poverty*. London: Pluto Press.

Bendat, Alejandro. 2006. "Poverty Reduction Policy Politics in Bolivia." Alternative Information Development Centre. www.aidc.org.za/?q=book/view/141.

Berkeley, Bill. 2001. *The Graves Are Not Yet Full: Race, Tribe and Power in the Heart of Africa*. New York: Basic Books.

Bhagwati, Jagdish. 2002. *Free Trade Today*. Princeton University Press.

Bhagwati, Jagdish. 2004. *In Defense of Globalization*. Oxford University Press.

Bird, G. 1996. "Borrowing from the IMF: The Policy Implications of Recent Empirical Research," *World Development* 24: 1753–1760.

Bjork, J. 1995. "The Uses of Conditionality," *East European Quarterly* 29: 89–124.

Blanchflower, D. G. and R. B. Freeman. 1992. "Going Different Ways: Unionism in the US and other OECD Countries," *Industrial Relations* 31 (1) (Winter): 56–79.

Blanchflower, David G. and Matthew J. Slaughter. 1999. "The Causes and Consequences of Changing Income Inequality," in Albert Fishlow and Karen Parker (eds.) *Growing Apart: The Causes and Consequences of Global Wage Inequality*. New York: Council on Foreign Relations Press.

Blanton, Shannon Lindsey. 2000. "Promoting Human Rights and Democracy in the Developing World: US Rhetoric versus US Arms Exports," *American Journal of Political Science* 44(1): 123–131.

Blanton, Shannon Lindsey. 2005. "Foreign Policy in Transition? US Arms Transfers, Democracy and Human Rights," *International Studies Quarterly* 49(4): 647–667.

Blanton, Shannon Lindsey and Robert G. Blanton. 2007. "What Attracts Foreign Investors? An Examination of Human Rights and Foreign Direct Investment," *Journal of Politics* 69(1) (February): 143–155.

Blasi, Gerald J. and David L. Cingranelli. 1996. "Do Constitutions and Institutions Help Protect Human Rights?," in David Louis Cingranelli (ed.) *Human Rights and Developing Countries*. Greenwich, CT: JAI Press, pp. 223–237.

Blau, Francine D. and Lawrence M. Kahn. 1996. "International Differences in Male Wage Inequality: Institutions versus Market Forces," *Journal of Political Economy* 104(4): 791–837.

Bleicher, Samuel A. 1970. "UN v. IBRD: A Dilemma of Functionalism," *International Organization* 24(1): 31–47.

Blomberg, S. Brock and Gregory D. Hess. 2002. "The Temporal Links between Conflict and Economic Activity," *Journal of Conflict Resolution* 46(1) (February): 74–90.

Boekle, H., V. Rittberger and W. Wagner. 2001. "Constructivist Foreign Policy Theory," in V. Rittberger (ed.) *German Foreign Policy Since Unification*. Manchester University Press, pp. 105–137.

Boix, Carles. 2003. *Democracy and Redistribution.* Cambridge University Press.

Boix, Carles and Susan C. Stokes. 2003. "Endogenous Democratization," *World Politics* 55(4): 517–549.

Bollen, Kenneth A. and Burke Grandjean. 1981. "The Dimension(s) of Democracy: Further Issues in the Measurement and Effects of Political Democracy," *American Sociological Review* 46: 651–659.

Boughton, James M. 2001. *Silent Revolution: The International Monetary Fund, 1979–1989.* Washington, DC: International Monetary Fund.

Boyce, James K. 2004. "Economic Policies and Armed Conflict: Toward a Research Agenda," Remarks at the Social Science Research Council Conference on "The Economic Analysis of Conflict: Problems and Prospects." Washington, DC, April 19–20. www.umass.edu/peri/Calendar/boyce%5B1%5D.final%20text.pdf.

Bradlow, Daniel D. 1996. "The World Bank, the IMF, and Human Rights," *Transnational Law and Contemporary Problems* 6(47): 128–144.

Brady, David and Michael Wallace. 2000. "Spatialization, Foreign Direct Investment, and Labor Outcomes in the American States, 1978–1996," *Social Forces* 79(1): 67–99.

Brodnig, Geront. 2005. "The World Bank and Human Rights: Mission Impossible?" Carr Center for Human Rights Policy Working Paper T–01–05.

Broz, J. Lawrence and Michael Brewster Hawes. 2006a. "Congressional Politics of Financing the IMF," *International Organization* 60(1) (Spring): 367–399.

Broz, J. Lawrence and Michael Brewster Hawes. 2006b. "US Domestic Politics and International Monetary Fund Policy," in Darren G. Hawkins, David A. Lake, Daniel L. Nielson, and Michael J. Tierney (eds.) *Delegation and Agency in International Organizations.* Cambridge University Press, pp. 77–106.

Buchmann, Claudia. 1996. "The Debt Crisis, Structural Adjustment and Women's Education: Implication for Status and Social Development," *International Journal of Comparative Sociology* 37: 5–30.

Bueno de Mesquita, Bruce, Alastair Smith, Randolph M. Siverson, and James D. Morrow. 2003. *The Logic of Political Survival.* Cambridge, MA: MIT Press.

Burgerman, S. D. 1998. "Mobilizing Principles: The Role of Transnational Activists in Promoting Human Rights Principles," *Human Rights Quarterly* 20(4): 905–923.

Burkhart, Ross E. 1997. "Comparative Democracy and Income Distribution: Shape and Direction of the Causal Arrow," *Journal of Politics* 59: 148–164.

Burki, Shahid Javed and Guillermo Perry. 2001. *Beyond the Washington Consensus: Institutions Matter.* Washington, DC: World Bank Group.

Busse, Matthias. 2003. "Do Transnational Corporations Care about Labor Standards?," *Journal of Developing Areas* 36 (Spring): 39–57.

Çağatay, Nilüfer. 1994. "Turkish Women and Structural Adjustment," in Isabella Bakker (ed.) *The Strategic Silence: Gender and Economic Policy.* London: Zed Books.

Callaghy, Thomas. 1990. "Lost Between State and Market: The Politics of Economic Adjustment in Ghana, Zambia, and Nigeria," in Joan Nelson (ed.) *Economic Crisis and Policy Choice: The Politics of Adjustment in the Third World.* Princeton University Press, pp. 257–319.

Callaway, Rhonda. 2001. "Is the Road to Hell Paved With Good Intentions? The Effect of US Foreign Assistance and Economic Policy on Human Rights." Ph.D. diss., University of North Texas.

Callaway, Rhonda L. and Julie Harrelson-Stephens. 2004. "The Path from Trade to Human Rights: The Democracy and Development Detour," in Sabine C. Carey and Steven C. Poe (eds.) *Understanding Human Rights Violations: New Systematic Studies.* Burlington, VT: Ashgate, pp. 87–109.

Camdessus, Michel. 1990. "Statement before the United Nations Economic and Social Council in Geneva July 11th," *IMF Survey* 19: 235–236.

Capdevila, Gustavo. 2001. "IMF Not Taking into Account Human Rights Issues," *Global Policy Forum* (August 13). www.globalpolicy.org.

Carey, Sabine C. 2004. "Domestic Threat and Repression: An Analysis of State Responses to Different Forms of Dissent," in Sabine Carey and Steven C. Poe (eds.) *The Systematic Study of Human Rights.* Burlington, VT: Ashgate, pp. 202–220.

Carleton, David. 1989. "The New International Division of Labor, Export-Oriented Growth, and State Repression in Latin America," in George Lopez and Michael Stohl (eds.) *Dependence, Development, and State Repression.* New York: Greenwood, pp. 211–236.

Cavanagh, John, Sarah Anderson, and Jill Pike. 2005. "Behind the Cloak of Benevolence: World Bank and IMF Policies Hurt Workers at Home and Abroad." www.thirdworldtraveler.com.

Chaudhury, Kiren Aziz. 1994. "Economic Liberalization and the Lineages of the Rentier State," *Comparative Politics* 27(1): 1–25.

Chenery, Hollis B. and A. M. Strout. 1966. "Foreign Assistance and Economic Development," *American Economic Review* 56(4): 679–733.

Chenoweth, E. and J. Teets. 2004. "Constraining US Policy: Adherence to International Norms Post 9/11," Paper presented at the annual meeting of the Western Political Science Association, Portland.

China Daily. 2005. "Forum Examines Impact of Growth," March 21. www.chinadaily.com.

Chipeta, C. 1993. "Malawi," in Aderanti Adepoju (ed.) *The Impact of Structural Adjustment on the Population of Africa.* London: United Nations Population Fund and Heinemann, pp. 105–188.

Chossudovsky, Michel. 1997. *The Globalization of Poverty.* Penang, Malaysia: Third World Books.

Chu, Ke-young, Hamid Davoodi, and Sanjeev Gupta. 2000. "Income Distribution and Tax, and Government Social Spending Policies in Developing Countries," The United Nations University, World Institute for Development Economics Research, Working Papers No. 214, December.

Chua, Amy. 2003. *World on Fire: How Exporting Free Market Democracy Breeds Ethnic Hatred and Global Instability.* New York: Anchor Books.

Cingranelli, David L. 1993. *Ethics, American Foreign Policy, and the Third World.* New York: St. Martin's Press.

Cingranelli, David L. 2002. "Democratization, Economic Globalization, and Workers' Rights," in Edward McMahon and Thomas A. P. Sinclair (eds.) *Democratic Institutional Performance: Research and Policy Perspectives.* Westport, CT: Praeger, pp. 139–158.

Cingranelli, David L. and David L. Richards. 1999a. "Measuring the Level, Pattern, and Sequence of Government Respect for Physical Integrity Rights," *International Studies Quarterly* 43(2): 407–418.

Cingranelli, David L. and David L. Richards. 1999b. "Respect for Human Rights after the End of the Cold War," *Journal of Peace Research* 36(5): 511–534.

Cingranelli, David L. and David L. Richards. 2006. "The Cingranelli and Richards (CIRI) Human Rights Data Project." www.humanrightsdata.org.

Cingranelli, David L. and David L. Richards. Forthcoming. "Measuring Government Effort to Protect Economic and Social Rights: A Peer Benchmark," in Shareen Hertel and Lanse Minkler (eds.) *Economic Rights: Conceptual, Measurement, and Policy Issues.* Cambridge University Press.

Cingranelli, David L. and Chang-Yen Tsai. 2002. "Democracy, Workers' Rights, and Income Equality: A Comparative Cross-National Analysis," Paper presented at the 2002 annual meeting of the American Political Science Association, Boston.

Cingranelli, David L. and Chang-Yen Tsai. 2003. "Democracy, Globalization and Workers' Rights: A Comparative Analysis," Paper presented at the 2003 annual meeting of the American Political Science Association, Philadelphia.

Citizens Network for Essential Services. 2001–2002. "Growing Dangers of Service Apartheid: How the World Bank Group's Private Sector Development (PSD) Strategy Threatens Infrastructure and Basic Service Provision," *News & Notices* 2(5) (Winter). www.servicesforall.org/html/news_notices/winter2002/N &NWinter2002.shtml#OVERVIEW.

Clapham, Andrew. 2006. *Human Rights Obligations of Non-state Actors.* Oxford University Press.

Clark, David and William Reed. 2003. "A Unified Model of War Onset and Outcome," *Journal of Politics* 65(1): 69–91.

Coad, Malcolm. 1985. "Pinochet Lifts 'Siege' after Pressure from Reagan / Martial Law Relaxed in Chile," *The Guardian,* June 18.

Collier, David. 1991. "The Comparative Method: Two Decades of Change," in Dankwart Rustow and Kenneth Erickson (eds.) *Comparative Political Dynamics: Global Research Perspectives.* New York: HarperCollins, pp. 7–31.

Collier, Paul. 2000. "Rebellion as Quasi-Criminal Activity," *Journal of Conflict Resolution* 44(6): 839–853.

Collier, Paul and Anke Hoeffler. 2001. "Greed and Grievance in Civil War," World Bank Policy Research Working Paper no. WPS 2355.

Commonwealth Secretariat. 1989. *Engendering Adjustment for the 1990s: Report of a Commonwealth Expert Group on Women and Structural Adjustment.* London: Commonwealth Secretariat.

Conway, Patrick. 1994. "IMF Lending Programs: Participation and Impact," *Journal of Development Economics* 45: 365–391.

Cornia, Giovanni, Andrea Richard Jolly, and Frances Stewart. 1987. *Adjustment with a Human Face*. Oxford University Press.

Cranston, Maurice. 1964. *What are Human Rights?* New York: Basic Books.

Daddieh, Cyril. 1995. "Structural Adjustment Programs and Regional Integration: Compatible or Mutually Exclusive," in Kidane Mengisteab and B. Ikubolajeh Logan (eds.) *Beyond Economic Liberalization in Africa: Structural Adjustments and the Alternatives*. Capetown: SAPES, pp. 243–271.

Darrow, Mac. 2003. *Between Light and Shadow: The World Bank, the International Monetary Fund and International Human Rights Law*. Portland, OR: Hart Publishing.

Davenport, Christian. 1995. "Multi-Dimensional Threat Perception and State Repression: An Inquiry into Why States Apply Negative Sanctions," *American Journal of Political Science* 39(3): 683–713.

Davenport, Christian. 1996. "Constitutional Promises and Repressive Reality: A Cross National Time Series Investigation of Why Political and Civil Liberties Are Suppressed," *Journal of Politics* 58: 627–654.

Davenport, Christian and David A. Armstrong II. 2004. "Democracy and the Violation of Human Rights: A Statistical Analysis from 1976–1996," *American Journal of Political Science* 48(3): 538–554.

Davidson, J. 2002. "Overcoming Resistance to Change," *Public Management* 84 (11): 20–23.

Davies, James C. 1969. "The J-Curve of Rising and Declining Satisfactions as a Cause of Some Great Revolutions and a Contained Rebellion," in Hugh Davis Graham and Ted Robert Gurr (eds.) *Violence in America: Historical and Comparative Perspectives*. Washington, DC: National Commission on the Causes and Prevention of Violence: US Government Printing Office, pp. 547–576.

Davies, John L. and Ted Robert Gurr. 1998. "Preventive Measures: An Overview," in John L. Davies and Ted Robert Gurr (eds.) *Preventive Measures: Building Risk Assessment and Crisis Early Warning Systems*. Lanham, MD: Rowman & Littlefield, pp. 1–14.

Decker, Klaus, Siobhan McInerney-Lankford, and Caroline Sage. 2006. "Human Rights and Equitable Development: 'Ideals,' Issues and Implications," World Bank Working Paper. http://siteresources.worldbank.org/ INTWDR2006\Resources/4773831118673432908/Human_Rightsand_ Equitable_Development_Ideals_Issues_and_Implications.pdf.

Democracy Now. 2006. "Evo Morales Sworn in as Bolivia's First Indigenous President, Hails Election as End of 'Colonial and Neo-Liberal Era,'" Monday, January 23, 2006. www.democracynow.org/article.

DeNardo, James. 1985. *Power in Numbers: The Political Strategy of Protest and Rebellion*. Princeton University Press.

Dennis, Carolyne. 1992. "The Christian Churches and Women's Experience of Structural Adjustment in Nigeria," in Haleh Afshar and Carolyne Dennis (eds.). *Women and Adjustment Policies in the Third World*. New York: St. Martin's Press.

DeSoto, Hernando. 2000. *The Mystery of Capital: Why Capitalism Triumphs in the West and Fails Everywhere Else*. New York: Basic Books and London: Bantam Press/Random House.

De Soysa, Indra. 2004. "Globalization, Social Insurance, and Civil Conflict, 1975–2002," Paper prepared for presentation at Barcelona, Spain meeting of the "Polarization and Conflict" research group sponsored by the European Union, December 10–12.

Di John, Jonathan. 2005. "Economic Liberalization, Political Instability, and State Capacity in Venezuela," *International Political Science Review* 26(1): 107–124.

DiNardo, John E., Nichole M. Fortin and Thomas Lemieux. 1996. "Labor Market Institutions and the Distribution of Wages, 1973–1992: A Semiparametric Approach," *Econometrica* 64(5) (September): 1001–1004.

Dixit, A. K. 1996. *The Making of Economic Policy: A Transaction-Cost Perspective*. Cambridge, MA: MIT Press.

Dollar, David and Jakob Svensson. 2000. "What Explains the Success or Failure of Structural Adjustment Programmes?," *Economic Journal* 110 (October): 894–917.

Domar, E. 1946. "Capital Expansion, Rate of Growth and Employment," *Econometrica* 14: 137–147.

Donnelly, Jack. 2003. *Universal Human Rights in Theory and Practice*, 2nd edn. Ithaca, NY: Cornell University Press.

Dorosh, Paul, B. Essama-Nssah, and Ousmane Samba-Manadou. 1996. "Terms of Trade and the Real Exchange Rate in the CFA Zone: Implications for Income Distribution in Niger," in David E. Sahn (ed.) *Economic Reform and the Poor in Africa*. Oxford University Press, pp. 147–182.

Drazen, Allen. 2002. "Conditionality and Ownership in IMF Lending: A Political Economy Approach," *IMF Staff Papers* 49 (November): 36–67.

Dreher, Axel. 2006. "IMF and Economic Growth: The Effects of Programs, Loans, and Compliance with Conditionality," *World Development* 34(5): 769–788.

Dreher, Axel and Nathan M. Jensen. 2007. "Independent Actor or Agent? An Empirical Analysis of the Impact of US Interests on IMF Conditions," *Journal of Law and Economics* 50(1).

Dreher, Axel and Jan-Egbert Sturm. 2006. "Do IMF and World Bank Influence Voting in the UN General Assembly?," KOF Working Paper 137, ETH Zurich.

Dreher, Axel, Jan-Egbert Sturm, and James Vreeland. 2006. "Does Membership on the UN Security Council Influence IMF Decisions? Evidence from Panel Data," Mimeo.

Dubofsky, Melvyn. 1994. *The State and Labor in Modern America*. Chapel Hill: University of North Carolina Press.

Durbin, Richard J., Joseph R. Biden, Jr., Byron L. Dorgan, Christopher Dodd, Paul S. Sarbanes, and Daniel K. Akaka. 2006. "6 US Senators Condemn Bank's Publication 'Doing Business Report 2007' for Labor Standard Violations" (October 13), *50 Years*. www.50years.org\cms\update\story\342.

Dymski, Gary A. and Manuel Pastor, Jr. 1990. "Bank Lending, Misleading Signals, and the Latin American Debt Crisis," *The International Trade Journal* 6: 151–192.

Easton, David. 1965. *A Systems Analysis of Political Life.* New York: John Wiley and Sons.

Edwards, S. and J. A. Santaella. 1993. "Devaluation Controversies in the Developing Countries: Lessons from the Bretton Woods Era," in M. D. Bordo and B. Eichengreen (eds.) *A Retrospective on the Bretton Woods System.* University of Chicago Press, pp. 405–455.

Eiras, Ana I. 2003. "IMF and World Bank Intervention: A Problem, Not a Solution," Backgrounder. Heritage Foundation Paper No. 1689. September 17. www.heritage.org/research.

Eliott, Josie W. 1993. "Sierra Leone," in Aderanti Adepoju (ed.) *The Impact of Structural Adjustment on the Population of Africa.* Portsmouth, NH: Heinemann and United Nations Population Fund, pp. 40–59.

Eller J. D. 1999. *From Culture to Ethnicity to Conflict.* Ann Arbor: University of Michigan Press.

Elliott, Kimberly Ann and Richard B. Freeman. 2001. "White Hats or Don Quixotes? Human Rights Vigilantes in the Global Economy," NBER Working Paper 8102.

Elson, Diane. 1990. "Male Bias in Macro-economics: The Case of Structural Adjustment," in Diane Elson (ed.) *Male Bias in the Developmental Process.* Manchester University Press, pp. 1–28.

Enke, Stephen. 1963. *Economics for Development.* Englewood Cliffs, NJ: Prentice-Hall.

Estache, Antonio. 2005. "PPI Partnerships versus PPI Divorces in Developing Countries," World Bank and Université Libre de Bruxelles, January.

Esty, Daniel C., Jack A. Goldstone, Ted R. Gurr, Barbara Harff, Marc Levy, Geoffrey D. Dabelko, Pamela T. Surko, and Alan N. Unger. 1998. *State Failure Task Force Report: Phase II Findings.* McLean, VA: Science Applications International Corporation.

European Centre for Conflict Prevention. 2006. "Ghana." www.conflict-prevention.net\index.html.

Farnsworth, Clyde H. 1984. "US Votes NO at World Bank More Often Under Reagan," *The New York Times* November 26, p. A1.

Fearon, James D. 2005. "Primary Commodity Exports and Civil War," *Journal of Conflict Resolution* 49(4): 483–507.

Fearon, James D. and David Laitin. 2003. "Ethnicity, Insurgency, and Civil War," *American Political Science Review* 97(1): 75–90.

Feierabend, Ivo K. and Rosalind L. Feierabend. 1966. "Aggressive Behavior within Polities 1948–1962: A Cross-national Study," *Journal of Conflict Resolution* 10: 249–271.

Fein, Helen. 1995. "More Murder in the Middle: Life-Integrity Violations and Democracy in the World, 1987," *Human Rights Quarterly* 17 (Winter): 170–191.

Fields, A. Belden. 2003. *Rethinking Human Rights for the New Millennium.* New York: Palgrave Macmillan.

Fording, Richard. 2001. "The Political Response to Black Insurgency: A Critical Test of Competing Theories of the State," *American Political Science Review* 95(1): 115–130.

Forsythe, David P. 1987. "Congress and Human Rights in US Foreign Policy: The Fate of General Legislation," *Human Rights Quarterly* 9: 391–411.

Forsythe, David P. 1988. *Human Rights and US Foreign Policy*. Gainesville, FL: University Press of Florida.

Fortin, Nichole M. and Thomas Lemieux. 1996. "Institutional Changes and Rising Wage Inequality," *American Economic Review* 86(2) (May): 240–245.

Francisco, Ronald A. 1995. "The Relationship between Coercion and Protest: An Empirical Evaluation in Three Coercive States," *Journal of Conflict Resolution* 39(2): 263–282.

Franklin, James. 1997. "IMF Conditionality, Threat Perception, and Political Repression: A Cross-National Analysis," *Comparative Political Studies* 30: 576–606.

Frausum, Yves Van and David E. Sahn. 1996. "Perpetuating Poverty for Malawi's Smallholders: External Shocks and Policy Distortions," in David E. Sahn (ed.) *Economic Reform and the Poor in Africa*. Oxford University Press, pp. 311–338.

Frey, Bruno S. and Friedrich Schneider. 1986. "Competing Models of International Lending Activity," *Journal of Development Economics* 20: 225–245.

Friedman, Milton. 1962. *Capitalism and Freedom*. University of Chicago Press.

Friedman, Milton and Rose D. Friedman. 1980. *Free to Choose: A Personal Statement*. New York: Harcourt Brace Jovanovich.

Friedman, Thomas L. 2000. *The Lexus and the Olive Tree*. New York: Anchor Books.

Garcia-Johnson, R. 2000. *Exporting Environmentalism: US Multinational Chemical Corporations in Brazil and Mexico*. Boston: MIT Press.

Gartner, Scott Sigmund and Patrick M. Regan. 1996. "Threat and Repression: The Non-Linear Relationship Between Government and Opposition Violence," *Journal of Peace Research* 33(3): 273–287.

Garuda, Gopal. 2000. "The Distributional Effects of IMF Programs: A Cross-Country Analysis," *World Development* 28: 1031–1051.

Gasiorowski, Mark J. 1998. "Macroeconomic Conditions and Political Instability: An Empirical Analysis," *Studies in Comparative International Development* 33(3): 3–17.

Geddes, Barbara. 1999. "What Do We Know about Democratization after Twenty Years?," *Annual Review of Political Science* 2: 115–144.

Gereffi, Gary and Miguel Korzeniewicz (eds.). 1994. *Commodity Chains and Global Capitalism*. New York: Praeger.

Gibney, Mark and Matthew Dalton. 1996. "The Political Terror Scale," in David L. Cingranelli (ed.) *Human Rights and Developing Countries*. Greenwich, CT: JAI Press, pp. 124–156.

Gleditsch, Kristian S. and Michael D. Ward. 1997. "Double Take: A Reexamination of Democracy and Autocracy in Modern Polities," *Journal of Conflict Resolution* 41(3) (June): 361–383.

Gleditsch, Nils Petter, Peter Wallensteen, Mikael Eriksson, Margareta Sollenberg, and Håvard Strand. 2002. "Armed Conflict 1946–2001: A New Dataset," *Journal of Peace Research* 39(5): 615–637.

Goering, Curt. 2007. "Amnesty International and Economic, Social, and Cultural Rights," in Daniel A. Bell and Jean-Marc Coicaud (eds.) *Ethics in Action: The Ethical Challenges of International Human Rights Nongovernmental Organizations*. Cambridge University Press, pp. 204–217.

Goldstein, J. 1985. "Basic Human Needs: The Plateau Curve," *World Development* 13: 595–609.

Goldstein, Morris and Peter Montiel. 1986. "Evaluating Fund Stabilization Programs with Multicountry Data: Some Methodological Pitfalls," *IMF Staff Papers* 33: 304–344.

Goldstein, Robert Justin. 2001. *Political Repression in Modern America: From 1870–1976.* Urbana, IL: University of Illinois Press.

Goodwin, Jeff and Theda Skocpol. 1989. "Explaining Revolutions in the Contemporary World," *Politics and Society* 17 (December): 489–509.

Green, Robert T. 1972. "Political Instability as a Determinant of US Foreign Investment," *Studies in Marketing* no. 17. The University of Texas at Austin: Bureau of Business Research Graduate School of Business.

Greene, William H. 2003. *Econometric Analysis*, 5th edn. Upper Saddle River, NJ: Prentice Hall.

Grove, A. 2001. "The Intra-national Struggle to Define 'Us': External Involvement as a Two-way Street," *International Studies Quarterly* 45(3): 357–388.

Grusky, Sara. 2001. "IMF Forces Water Privatization on Poor Countries," Globalization Challenge Initiative. www.ige.org.

Gujarati, Damodar. 1995. *Basic Econometrics*, 3rd edn. New York: McGraw Hill.

Gurr, Ted Robert. 1968. "Psychological Factors in Civil Violence," *World Politics* 20(2): 245–278.

Gurr, Ted Robert. 1970. *Why Men Rebel.* Princeton University Press.

Gurr, Ted Robert. 1986. "The Political Origins of State Violence and Terror: A Theoretical Analysis," in Michael Stohl and George Lopez (eds.) *Government Violence and Repression: An Agenda for Research.* Westport, CT: Greenwood Press, pp. 45–71.

Gurr, Ted Robert. 2000. *People Versus States: Minorities at Risk in the New Century.* Washington, DC: United Institutes of Peace.

Gylfason, T. 1987. "Credit Policy and Economic Activity in Developing Countries with IMF Stabilization Programs," *Princeton Studies in International Finance* 60.

Haggard, Stephan. 1995. "Democracy and Economic Growth," in Daniel M. Schydlowsky (ed.) *Structural Adjustment: Retrospect and Prospect.* Wesport, CT: Praeger, pp. 199–219.

Handa, Sudhanshu and Damien King. 1997. "Structural Adjustment Policies, Income Distribution and Poverty: A Review of the Jamaican Experience," *World Development* 25(6): 915–930.

Harrelson-Stephens, J. and Rhonda Callaway. 2003. "Does Trade Openness Promote Security Rights in Developing Countries? Examining the Liberal Perspective," *International Interactions* 29(2): 143–158.

Harrelson-Stephens, J. and Rhonda Callaway. 2004. "The Path from Trade to Human Rights: The Democracy and Development Detour," in Sabine C. Carey and Steven C. Poe (eds.) *Understanding Human Rights Violations: New Systematic Studies*. Aldershot, UK: Ashgate, pp. 85–105.

Harrigan, Jane and Paul Mosley. 1991. "Assessing the Impact of World Bank Structural Development Lending 1980–1987," *Journal of Development Studies* 27(3): 63–94.

Harrod, R. 1939. "An Essay in Dynamic Theory," *Economic Journal* 49: 14–33.

Hathaway, O. 2002. "Do Treaties Make a Difference? Human Rights Treaties and the Problem of Compliance," *Yale Law Journal* 111: 1932–2042.

Hauge, Wenche and Tanja Ellingsen. 1998. "Beyond Environmental Scarcity: Causal Pathways to Conflict," *Journal of Peace Research* 35(3): 299–317.

Hayek, Frederich A. 1984. "Principles and Expedience," in Chiaki Nishiyama and Kurt R. Leube (eds.) *The Essence of Hayek*. Stanford, CA: Hoover Institution Press, pp. 299–317.

Heath, J. A., T. D. Mason, W. T. Smith, and J. P. Weingarten. 2000. "The Calculus of Fear: Revolution, Repression, and the Rational Peasant," *Social Science Quarterly* 81(2) (June): 622–633.

Heckman, J. J. 1988. "The Microeconomic Evaluation of Social Programs and Economic Institutions," in *Chung-Hua Series of Lectures by Invited Eminent Economists*. No. 14. Taipei: The Institute of Economics Academia Sinica.

Hegre, Håvard, Tanja Ellingsen, Scott Gates, and Nils Petter Gleditsch. 2001. "Towards a Democratic Civil Peace? Opportunity, Grievance, and Civil War 1816–1992," *American Political Science Review* 95(1): 33–48.

Hegre, Håvard, Ranveig Gissinger, and Nils Petter Gleditsch. 2003. "Liberalization and Internal Conflict," in Gerald Schneider, Katherine Barbieri, and Nils Petter Gleditsch (eds.) *Globalization and Armed Conflict*. Boulder, CO: Rowman and Littlefield, pp. 251–276.

Held, David, Anthony McGrew, David Goldblatt, and Jonathan Perraton. 1999. *Global Transformation: Politics, Economics, and Culture*. Stanford University Press.

Henderson, Conway. 1993. "Population Pressures and Political Repression," *Social Science Quarterly* 74: 322–333.

Heredia, Carlos and Mary Purcell. 1996. "Structural Adjustment and the Polarization of Mexican Society," in Jerry Mander and Edward Goldsmith (eds.) *The Case Against the Global Economy*. San Francisco: Sierra Club Books, pp. 273–284.

Herman, Edward S. and Frank Brodhead. 1984. *Demonstration Elections*. Boston: South End Press.

Hibbs, Douglas A. 1973. *Mass Political Violence*. New York: Wiley.

Hicks, N. and Streeten, P. 1979. "Indicators of Development: The Search for a Basic Needs Yardstick," *World Development* 7: 567–580.

Horowitz, Donald L. 1985. *Ethnic Groups in Conflict*. Berkeley, CA: University of California Press.

Huang, Chang-Ling. 2000. "Learning the New Game: Labor Politics in the Newly Democratized South Korea and Taiwan," Paper presented at the

2000 annual meeting of the American Political Science Association. Washington, DC.

Human Rights Watch. 2001. *World Report 2001. Peru*. www.hrw.org.

Human Rights Watch. 2003. "Bolivia: Strengthen Investigation into Protest Deaths," *Human Rights News*. http://hrw.org.

Human Security Centre. 2006. *Human Security Report 2005*. Oxford University Press.

Huntington, Samuel P. 1984. "Will More Countries Become Democratic?," *Political Science Quarterly* 99(2): 193–218.

Ikenberry, G. John. 1999. *American Foreign Policy: Theoretical Essays*, 3rd edn. New York: Longman.

ILO (International Labour Organization). 1998a. *Child Labour: Targeting the Intolerable*. Geneva: ILO.

ILO (International Labour Organization). 1998b. *International Labour Standards*. Geneva: International Labour Office.

ILO (International Labour Organization). 2003. *Fundamental Rights at Work and International Labour Standards*. Geneva: International Labour Office.

IMF (International Monetary Fund). 2004. Articles of Agreement of the International Monetary Fund: Article I – Purposes. www.imf.org/external/pubs/ft/aa/aa01.htm.

Innes, Judith Eleanor. 1992. "Human Rights Reporting as a Policy Tool," in Thomas B. Jabine and Richard P. Claude (eds.) *Human Rights and Statistics: Getting the Record Straight*. Philadelphia: University of Pennsylvania Press, pp. 235–257.

International Finance Corporation. 2006. "IFC Adopts New Environmental and Social Standards." www.ifc.org/.

Inter-Parliamentary Union. 1994. *Declaration on Criteria for Free and Fair Elections*, Paris, March 26. www.ipu.org/cnl-e/154-free.htm.

Isham, Jonathan, Daniel Kaufmann, and Lant H. Pritchett. 1997. "Civil Liberties, Democracy, and the Performance of Government Projects," *World Bank Economic Review* 11(2): 219–242.

ITUC. 2006. "Action by World Bank's IFC on Workers' Rights a Major Step Forward." www.icftu.org/.

Jackman, Robert W. 1973. "On the Relation of Economic Development to Democratic Performance," *American Journal of Political Science* 17: 611–621.

Jackman, Robert W. 1974. "Political Democracy and Social Equality: A Comparative Analysis," *American Sociological Review* 39: 29–45.

Jacobs, Antoine. 1986. "Collective Self-Regulation," in Bob Hepple (ed.) *The Making of Labor Law in Europe: A Comparative Study of Nine Countries up to 1945*. New York: Mansell.

Jayarajah, Carl A. B., William H. Branson, and Binayak Sen. 1996. *Social Dimensions of Adjustment: World Bank Experience, 1980–1993*. A World Bank Operations Evaluation Study. Washington, DC: World Bank.

Job, Brian L. 1992. "The Insecurity Dilemma: National, Regime, and State Securities in the Third World," in Brian L. Job (ed.) *The Insecurity*

Dilemma: National Security in Third World States. Boulder, CO: Lynne Rienner, pp. 3–22.

Johnson, O. and J. Salop. 1980. "Distributional Aspects of Stabilization Programs in Developing Countries," *IMF Staff Papers* 27: 1–23.

Joyce, Joseph P. 1992. "The Economic Characteristics of IMF Program Countries," *Economics Letters* 38: 237–242.

Kane, Karamoko. 1993. "Senegal," in Aderanti Adepoju (ed.) *The Impact of Structural Adjustment on the Population of Africa.* London: United Nations Population Fund and Heinemann, pp. 60–68.

Kanji, Nazneen and Niki Jazdowska. 1995. "Gender, Structural Adjustment and Employment in Urban Zimbabwe," *Third World Planning Review* 17(2): 133–154.

Kapoor, Kapil. 2001. "Comments on the Draft Synthesis Report on the Bangladesh SAPRI Research," World Bank Office, Dhaka, Bangladesh, April 22. www.worldbank.org/research/sapri/SAPRI_Bangladesh.pdf.

Kapur, Devesh and Richard Webb. 2006. "Beyond the IMF – Working Paper 99," Center for Global Development. www.cgdev.org/content/publications/detail/10246/.

Kaufmann, Daniel. 2005. "Human Rights and Governance: The Empirical Challenge," in Philip Alston and Mary Robinson (eds.) *Human Rights and Development: Towards Mutual Reinforcement.* Oxford University Press, pp. 352–402.

Kaufmann, Daniel, Aart Kraay, and Massimo Mastruzzi. 2005. "Governance Matters IV: Governance Indicators for 1996–2004," World Bank Policy Research Department Working Paper. www.worldbank.org/wbi/governance/pubs/govmatters4.html.

Kaufmann, Daniel, Massimo Mastruzzi, and D. Zavaleta. 2003. "Sustained Macroeconomic Reforms, Tepid Growth: A Governance Puzzle in Bolivia?," in Dani Rodrik (ed.) *In Search of Prosperity.* Princeton University Press, pp. 1–52.

Kaufmann, Daniel and L. Pritchett. 1998. "Civil Liberties, Democracy and the Performance of Government Projects," *Finance and Development.* International Development and the World Bank. Washington, DC, March.

Keck, Margaret E. and Kathryn Sikkink. 1998. *Activists Beyond Borders: Advocacy Networks in International Politics.* Ithaca, NY: Cornell University Press.

Keen, David. 2005. "Liberalization and Conflict," *International Political Science Review* 26(1): 73–89.

Keith, Linda. 1999. "The United Nations International Covenant on Civil and Political Rights: Does it Make a Difference in Human Rights Behavior?," *Journal of Peace Research* 36(1): 95–118.

Keith, Linda. 2002a. "Constitutional Provisions for Individual Human Rights (1976–1996): Are They More than Mere Window Dressing?," *Political Research Quarterly* 55: 111–143.

Keith, Linda. 2002b. "International Principles for Formal Judicial Independence: Trends in National Constitutions and their Impact (1976 to 1996)," *Judicature* 85: 194–200.

Keith, Linda. 2004. "National Constitutions and Human Rights Practices," in Sabine Carey and Steven C. Poe (eds.) *Understanding Human Rights Violations: New Systematic Studies.* Burlington, VT: Ashgate, pp. 162–180.

Keith, Linda and Steven C. Poe. 2000. "The United States, the IMF, and Human Rights," in David F. Forsythe (ed.) *The United States and Human Rights.* Lincoln, NE: University of Nebraska Press, pp. 273–299.

Keohane, Robert O. and Lisa L. Martin. 1995. "The Promise of Institutionalist Theory," *International Security* 20(1) (Summer): 39–51.

Khan, M., I. P. Montie and H. Haque. 1990. "Adjustment with Growth," *Journal of Development Economics* 32: 155–179.

Kienle, Eberhard. 2001. *A Grand Delusion: Democracy and Economic Reform in Egypt.* London: I. B. Tauris.

Killick, Tony. 1989. *A Reaction Too Far: Economic Theory and the Role of the State in Developing Countries.* London: Overseas Development Institute.

Killick, Tony. 1996. *IMF Programmes in Developing Countries: Design and Impact.* London: Overseas Development Institute.

King, Gary, Robert O. Keohane, and Sidney Verba. 1994. *Designing Social Inquiry: Scientific Inference in Qualitative Research.* Princeton University Press.

King, Lawrence. 2002. "The Emperor Exposed: Neoliberal Theory and De-modernization in Postcommunist Society." Yale University.

Klak, Thomas. 1996. "Distributional Impacts of the 'Free Zone' Component of Structural Adjustment: The Jamaican Experience," *Growth and Change* 27 (Summer): 352–387.

Knack, Stephen and Phillip Keefer. 1997. "Does Social Capital Have an Economic Payoff? A Cross-Country Investigation," *Quarterly Journal of Economics* 112(4) (March): 1251–1288.

Knight, M. and J. A. Santaella. 1997. "Economic Determinants of Fund Financial Arrangements," *Journal of Development Economics* 54: 405–436.

Köhler, Horst. 2000. "Concluding Remarks by Horst Köhler," Chairman of the Executive Board and Managing Director of the International Monetary Fund at the Closing Joint Session, Prague, September 27. www.imf.org/external/np/speeches/2000/092700.htm.

Konadu-Agyemang, K. 2001. "Structural Adjustment Programs and Housing Affordability in Accra Ghana," *Canadian Geographer* 45(4) (Winter): 528–544.

Krasner, Stephen D. (ed.). 1983. *International Regimes.* Ithaca, NY: Cornell University Press.

Krasner, Stephen D. 1999. *Organized Hypocrisy.* Princeton University Press.

Krueger, Anne O., Constantine Michalopoulos, and Vernon W. Ruttan (eds.). 1989. *Aid and Development.* Baltimore: The Johns Hopkins University Press.

Krueger, Anne O. and Vernon W. Ruttan. 1989. "Assistance to Korea," in Anne O. Krueger, Constantine Michalopoulos, and Vernon W. Ruttan (eds.). 1989. *Aid and Development.* Baltimore: The Johns Hopkins University Press, pp. 226–249.

Kwame, Boafo-Arthur. 1999. "Structural Adjustment Programs (SAPS) in Ghana: Interrogating PNDC's Implementation," *West Africa Review* 1(1): 1–19.

Landman, Todd. 2005. *Protecting Human Rights: A Comparative Study*. Washington, DC: Georgetown University Press.

Lasswell, Harold. 1936. *Politics: Who Gets What, When, How*. New York: McGraw-Hill.

Leary, Virginia A. 1996. "The Paradox of Workers' Rights as Human Rights," in Lance A. Compa and Stephen F. Diamond (eds.) *Human Rights, Labor Rights, and International Trade*. Philadelphia: University of Pennsylvania Press.

Lebovic, James H. and Erik Voeten. 2006. "The Cost of Shame: International Organizations, Foreign Aid, and Human Rights Norms Enforcement," Paper presented at the 2006 annual International Studies Association Conference, San Diego, CA.

Leeds, Brett Ashley. 1999. "Domestic Political Institutions, Credible Commitments and International Co-operation," *American Journal of Political Science* 43(4): 979–1002.

Legro, J. 1997. "Which Norms Matter? Revisiting the 'Failure' of Internationalism," *International Organization* 51: 31–63.

Leite, Sérgio Pereira. 2001. "Human Rights and the IMF," *Finance and Development* 38(4). www.imf.org.

Lele, Uma. 1991. "The Gendered Impacts of Structural Adjustment Programs in Africa," *American Journal of Agricultural Economics* (December): 1452–1455.

Lensink, R. 1996. *Structural Adjustment in Sub-Saharan Africa*. London: Longman.

Lindblom, Charles E. 1965. *The Intelligence of Democracy*. New York: The Free Press.

Lindstrom, Ronny and Will H. Moore. 1995. "Deprived, Rational or Both? 'Why Minorities Rebel' Revisited," *Journal of Political & Military Sociology* 23(2): 167–190.

Lipset, Seymour Martin. 1959. "Some Social Requisites of Democracy: Economic Development and Political Legitimacy," *American Political Science Review* 53(1): 69–105.

Lloyd, Vincent and Robert Weissman. 2001. "Against the Workers: How IMF and World Bank Policies Undermine Labor Power and Rights," *Multinational Monitor* (September). www.globalpolicy.org.

Long, J. Scott. 1997. *Regression Models for Categorical and Limited Dependent Variables*. Thousand Oaks, CA: Sage Publications.

Lubeck, Paul M. 2000. "The Islamic Revival: Antinomies of Islamic Movements under Globalization," in R. Cohen and S. Rai (eds.) *Global Social Movements*. London/New Brunswick, NJ: Athlone Press, pp. 1–20.

McCormick, James and Neil Mitchell. 1997. "Human Rights Violations, Umbrella Concepts, and Empirical Analysis," *World Politics* 49(4): 510–525.

McLaren, Lauren M. 1998. "The Effect of IMF Austerity Programs on Human Rights Violations: An Exploratory Analysis of Peru, Argentina, and Brazil," Paper presented at the 1998 meeting of the Midwest Political Science Association.

Martin, Lisa L. 2000. *Democratic Commitments: Legislatures and International Cooperation*. Princeton University Press.

Mason, T. D. 2004. *Caught in the Crossfire: Revolutions, Repression, and the Rational Peasant*. New York: Rowman and Littlefield.

Mazmanian, Daniel and Paul Sabatier. 1989. *Implementing Public Policy: Governance in Theory and Practice*. Lanham, MD: University Press of America.

Mehra, Rekha. 1991. "Can Structural Adjustment Work for Women Farmers?," *American Journal of Agricultural Economics* (December): 1440–1447.

Meier, G. M. 1993. "The New Political Economy and Policy Reform," *Journal of International Development* 5: 381–389.

Meilink, Henk. 2003. "Structural Adjustment Programmes on the African Continent: The Theoretical Foundations of IMF/World Bank Reform Policies," ASC Working Paper no. 53 (December). http://asc.leidenuniv.nl/pdf/workingpaper53.pdf.

Meyer, William H. 1996. "Human Rights and MNCs: Theory versus Quantitative Analysis," *Human Rights Quarterly* 18: 368–397.

Meyer, William H. 1998. *Human Rights and International Political Economy in Third World Nations*. Westport, CT: Praeger.

Millard Jr., Charles. 1986. "Reagan: Put the Pressure on Pinochet," *Christian Science Monitor*, July 18, p. 14.

Milner, Helen V. 1997. *Interests, Institutions, and Information: Domestic Politics and International Relations*. Princeton University Press.

Milner, Wesley T. 2000. "Economic Freedom, Globalizations and Human Rights: Can We Have it All?," *Journal of Private Enterprise* 15(2): 35–61.

Milner, Wesley T., Steven C. Poe, and David Leblang. 1999. "Security Rights, Subsistence Rights, and Liberties: A Theoretical Survey of the Empirical Landscape," *Human Rights Quarterly* 21(2): 403–443.

Mitchell, Neil and James McCormick. 1988. "Economic and Political Explanations of Human Rights Violations," *World Politics* 40(4): 476–498.

Monshipouri, Mahmood and Claude E. Welch. 2001. "The Search for International Human Rights and Justice: Coming to Terms with the New Global Realities," *Human Rights Quarterly* 23(2): 370–401.

Moon, Bruce E. 1991. *The Political Economy of Basic Human Needs*. Ithaca, NY: Cornell University Press.

Moon, Bruce E. and William J. Dixon. 1985. "Politics, the State, and Basic Human Needs: A Cross-National Study," *American Journal of Political Science* 29: 661–694.

Moore, Barrington. 1966. *Social Origins of Dictatorship and Democracy: Lord and Peasant in the Making of the Modern World*. Boston: Beacon Press.

Moore, Will H. 1998. "Repression and Dissent: Substitution, Context and Timing," *American Journal of Political Science* 42(3): 851–873.

Moran, Theodore H. 2002. *Beyond Sweatshops: Foreign Direct Investment and Globalization in Developing Countries*. Washington, DC: Brookings Institution Press.

Morris, Morris David. 1979. *Measuring the Condition of the World's Poor: The Physical Quality of Life Index*. New York: Pergamon.

Morris, David Morris. 1996. "Measuring the Changing Condition of the World's Poor: The Physical Quality of Life Index (1960–1990)," Working Paper. The Thomas J. Watson Institute for International Studies, Brown University.

Moses, Jonathon W. 2000. "Love It or Leave It: Exit, Voice and Loyalty with Global Labor Mobility," Paper presented at the annual meeting of the American Political Science Association, Washington, DC.

Mosley, Layna. 2002. "Racing to the Bottom or Climbing to the Top? Foreign Direct Investment and Human Rights," Paper presented at the annual meeting of the American Political Science Association, Boston.

Mosley, Layna. 2006. "Varieties of Capitalists? Economic Globalization and Labor Rights in the Developing World," Paper presented at the 2006 annual meeting of the Southern Political Science Association, Atlanta, GA.

Mosley, Layna and Saika Uno. 2007. "Racing to the Bottom or Climbing to the Top? Economic Globalization and Collective Labor Rights," *Comparative Political Studies* (August).

Mosley, Paul, Jane Harrigan, and John Toye. 1995. *Aid and Power: The World Bank and Policy Based Lending*, vol. I: *Analysis and Policy Proposals*, 2nd edn. London: Routledge.

Most, Benjamin A. and Harvey Starr. 1989. *Inquiry, Logic, and International Politics*. Columbia, SC: University of South Carolina Press.

Mousseau, D. Y. 2001. "Democratizing with Ethnic Divisions: A Source of Conflict?," *Journal of Peace Research* 38(5): 547–567.

Moyo, S. 2001. "The Land Occupation Movement and Democratisation in Zimbabwe: Contradictions of Neoliberalism," *Millennium Journal of International Studies* 30(2): 311–330.

Muller, Edward N. 1988. "Democracy, Economic Development, and Income Inequality," *American Sociological Review* 53: 50–68.

Muller, Edward N. and Erich Weede. 1990. "Cross-national Variations in Political Violence: A Rational Action Approach," *Journal of Conflict Resolution* 34(4): 624–651.

Munck, Ronaldo. 1994. "Workers, Structural Adjustment, and *Concertacion-Social* in Latin-America," *Latin American Perspectives* 21(3): 90–103.

Murillo, M. Victoria and Andrew Schrank. 2005. "With a Little Help from my Friends? Partisan Politics, Transnational Alliances, and Labor Rights in Latin America," *Comparative Political Studies* 38: 971–999.

Murrell, Peter. 1992. "Evolutionary and Radical Approaches to Economic Reform," *Economics of Planning* 25(1): 79–95.

Muuka, Gerry Nkombo. 1998. "In Defense of World Bank and IMF Conditionality in Structural Adjustment Programs," *Journal of Business in Developing Nations*. www.jbdn.org.

Mwanawina, I. 1993. "Zambia," in Aderanti Adepoju (ed.) *The Impact of Structural Adjustment on the Population of Africa*. Portsmouth, NH: Heinemann and United Nations Population Fund, pp. 69–77.

Navia P. and T. D. Zweifel. 2003. "Democracy, Dictatorship, and Infant Mortality Revisited," *Journal of Democracy* 14(3): 90–103.

Ndongko, Wilfred A. 1993. "Cameroon," in Aderanti Adepoju (ed.) *The Impact of Structural Adjustment on the Population of Africa*. Portsmouth, NH: Heinemann and United Nations Population Fund, pp. 119–129.

Nelson, P. 2000. "Whose Civil Society? Whose Governance? Decision-Making and Practice in the New Agenda at the Inter-American Development Bank and the World Bank," *Global Governance* 6(4): 405–431.

Ness, Immanuel. 2005. *Immigrants, Unions, and the New US Labor Market*. Philadelphia: Temple University Press.

Neumayer, Eric and Indra de Soysa. 2006. "Globalization and the Right to Free Association and Collective Bargaining: An Empirical Analysis," *World Development* 34(1): 31–49.

Nwosu, Aloysius C. 1992. *Structural Adjustment and Nigerian Agriculture: An Initial Assessment*. Washington, DC: United States Department of Agriculture.

Oatley, Thomas and Jason Yackee. 2004. "American Interests and IMF Lending," *International Politics* 41(3): 415–429.

Office of the UN High Commissioner for Human Rights. 2002. "Declaration on the Right to Development": Adopted by General Assembly Resolution 41/128 of 4 December 1986. www.unhchr.ch\html\menu3\b\74.htm.

Olson, Mancur. 1963. "Rapid Growth as a Destabilizing Force," *Journal of Economic History* 23: 529–552.

Omang, Joanne. 1985. "US Supports World Bank Loan for Chile," *The Washington Post*, June 19, A 28.

Organisation for Economic Co-operation and Development. 1996. *Trade, Employment and Labour Standards: A Study of Core Workers' Rights and International Trade*. Paris: OECD Publishing.

Organisation for Economic Co-operation and Development. 2000. *International Trade and Core Labour Standards*. Paris: OECD Publishing.

OSCE (Organization for Security and Co-operation in Europe). 1990. *International Standards of Elections*, Document of the Copenhagen Meeting of the Conference on the Human Dimension of the CSCE, June 29, at www.osce.org/documents/odihr/1990/06/1704_en.html?PHPSESSID= d0a43b96bae871253a5fb68e4de076ee.

OSCE (Organization for Security and Co-operation in Europe). 2003. *Existing Commitments for Democratic Elections in OSCE Participating States*. Warsaw, at www.osce.org/documents/odihr/2003/10/772_en.pdf?PHPSESSID= d0a43b96bae871253a5fb68e4de076ee.

Palast, Greg. 2003. *The Best Democracy Money Can Buy: An Investigative Reporter Exposes the Truth about Globalization, Corporate Cons and High Finance Fraudsters*. New York: Penguin.

Parenti, Michael. 1989. *The Sword and the Dollar*. New York: St. Martin's Press.

Parfitt, Trevor W. 1995. "Adjustment for Stabilization or Growth? Ghana and The Gambia," *African Review of Political Economy* 22(63) (March): 55–72.

Park, Han S. 1987. "Correlates of Human Rights: Global Tendencies," *Human Rights Quarterly* 9: 405–413.

Pastor, Manuel. 1987a. "The Effects of IMF Programs in the Third World: Debate and Evidence from Latin America," *World Development* 15(2): 365–391.

Pastor, Manuel. 1987b. *The International Monetary Fund and Latin America: Economic Stabilization and Class Conflict.* Boulder, CO: Westview Press.

Paul, Jim. 1981. "Riots in Morocco," *MERIP Reports*, No. 99, Land and Labor (September): 30–31.

Petersen, Roger D. 2002. *Understanding Ethnic Conflict.* Cambridge University Press.

Pettifor, Ann. 2001. "Global Economic Justice: Human Rights for Debtor Nations," *Journal of Human Development* 2(1): 47–51.

Pion-Berlin, David. 1983. "Political Repression and Economic Doctrines," *Comparative Political Studies* 16: 37–66.

Pion-Berlin, David. 1984. "The Political Economy of State Repression in Argentina," in Michael Stohl and George A. Lopez (eds.) *The State as Terrorist: The Dynamics of Governmental Violence and Repression.* Westport, CT: Greenwood Press, pp. 99–123.

Pion-Berlin, David. 1989. *The Ideology of State Terror: Economic Doctrine and Political Repression in Argentina and Peru.* Boulder, CO: Lynne Rienner.

Pion-Berlin, David. 1991. "Between Confrontation and Accommodation: Military and Government Policy in Democratic Argentina," *Journal of Latin American Studies* 23: 543–566.

Pion-Berlin, David. 1997. *Through Corridors of Power: Institutions and Civil–Military Relations in Argentina.* University Park, PA: Pennsylvania State University Press.

Pion-Berlin, David. 2001. *Civil–Military Relations in Latin America: New Analytical Perspectives.* Chapel Hill: University of North Carolina Press.

Pion-Berlin, David and George Lopez. 1991. "Of Victims and Executioners: Argentine State Terror, 1975–1979," *International Studies Quarterly* 35 (March): 63–86.

Piven, Frances Fox and Richard A. Cloward. 1993. *Regulating the Poor: The Functions of Public Welfare.* New York: Vintage Books.

Platteau, Jean-Philippe. 1994. "Behind the Market State where Real Societies Exist," *Journal of Development Studies* 30: 533–577 and 753–817.

Poe, Steven C. 2004. "The Decision to Repress: An Integrative Theoretical Approach to the Research on Human Rights and Repression," in Sabine C. Carey and Steven C. Poe (eds.) *Understanding Human Rights Violations.* Burlington, VT: Ashgate, pp. 16–38.

Poe, Steven C., Sabine C. Carey, and Tanya C. Vazquez. 2001. "How are these Pictures Different? A Quantitave Comparison of the US State Department and Amnesty International Human Rights Reports, 1976–1995," *Human Rights Quarterly* 23(3) (August): 650–677.

Poe, Steven, Wesley Milner, David Leblang, and Kara Smith. 2004. "Providing Subsistence Rights: Do States Make a Difference?," in Sabine Carey and Steven Poe (eds.) *Understanding Human Rights Violations: New Systematic Studies.* London: Ashgate, pp. 110–124.

Poe, Steven C. and C. Neal Tate. 1994. "Repression of Physical Integrity in the 1980s: A Global Analysis," *American Political Science Review* 88(4): 853–872.

Poe, Steven C., C. Neal Tate, and Linda Keith. 1999. "Repression of the Human Right to Physical Integrity Revisited: A Global Cross-National Study Covering the Years 1976–1993," *International Studies Quarterly* 43: 291–313.

Pogge, Thomas. 2007. "Moral Priorities for International Human Rights NGOs," in Daniel A. Bell and Jean-Marc Coicaud (eds.) *Ethics in Action: The Ethical Challenges of International Human Rights Nongovernmental Organizations.* Cambridge University Press, pp. 218–256.

Polak, J. J. 1957. "Monetary Analysis of Income Formation and Payments Problems," *IMF Staff Papers* 6(1): 1–50.

Polanyi, Karl. 1957. *The Great Transformation: The Political and Economic Origins of our Time.* Boston: Beacon Press.

Policzer, Pablo. 2004. "How Organizations Shape Human Rights Violations," in Sabine C. Carey and Steven C. Poe (eds.) *Understanding Human Rights Violations.* Burlington, VT: Ashgate, pp. 221–238.

Powell, G. Bingham and Guy Whitten. 1993. "A Cross-National Analysis of Economic Voting," *American Journal of Political Science* 37 (May): 11–30.

Przeworski, Adam, Michael E. Alverez, José Antonio Cheibub, and Fernando Limongi. 2000. *Democracy and Development: Political Institutions and Well Being in the World, 1950–1990.* Cambridge University Press.

Przeworski, Adam and Henry Teune. 1970. *The Logic of Comparative Social Inquiry.* Malabar, FL: Krieger Publishing Company.

Przeworski, Adam and James Raymond Vreeland. 2000. "The Effects of IMF Programs on Economic Growth," *Journal of Development Economics* 62: 385–421.

Putnam, Robert D. 1988. "Diplomacy and Domestic Politics: The Logic of Two-Level Games," *International Organization* 42(3): 427–460.

Quinn, Dennis P. and John T. Woolley. 2001. "Democracy and National Economic Performance: The Preference for Stability," *American Journal of Political Science* 45 (July): 634–657.

Raja, Kanaga. 2002. "New IMF Loan Conditions Will Raise Water Fees in Ghana," *Third World Network* 276 (March). www.twinside.org.

Rapley, John. 1996. *Understanding Development: Theory and Practice in the Third World.* Boulder, CO: Lynne Rienner.

Rapley, John. 2004. *Globalization and Inequality: Neoliberalism's Downward Spiral.* Boulder, CO: Lynne Rienner.

Ratner, S. 2004. "Overcoming Temptations to Violate Human Dignity in Times of Crisis: On the Possibilities for Meaningful Self-Restraint," *Theoretical Inquiries in Law* 5: 81–107.

Ray, Debraj. 1998. *Development Economics.* Princeton University Press.

Raymond, G. A. 1997. "Problems and Prospects in the Study of International Norms," *Mershon International Studies Review*, Supplement 2, 41: 205–245.

Regan, Patrick. 2005. "Helmets, Swords and Half Forgotten Things: Civil Wars in Our Time." Unpublished manuscript.

Regan, Patrick and Errol Henderson. 2002. "Democracy, Threats and Political Repression in Developing Countries: Are Democracies Internally Less Violent?," *Third World Quarterly* 23(1): 119–136.

Regan, Patrick M. and Daniel Norton. 2005. "Greed, Grievance, and Mobilization: The Onset of Protest, Rebellion, and Civil War," *Journal of Conflict Resolution* 49(3): 319–336.

Remmer, K. L. 1986. "The Politics of Economic Stabilization, IMF Standby Programs in Latin America, 1954–1984," *Comparative Politics* 19: 1–24.

Richards, David L. 1999. "Death Takes a Holiday: National Elections, Political Parties and Government Respect for Human Rights." Ph.D. diss., State University of New York at Binghamton.

Richards, David L. and Ronald D. Gelleny. 2003. "Is It a Small World After All? Economic Globalization and Human Rights in Developing Countries," in Steven Chan and James Scarritt (eds.) *Coping with Globalization*. London: Frank Cass Press.

Richards, David L., Ronald D. Gelleny, and David H. Sacko. 2001. "Money with a Mean Streak? Foreign Economic Penetration and Government Respect for Human Rights in Developing Countries," *International Studies Quarterly* 45(2): 219–239.

Rimlinger, Gaston. 1977. "Labor and the Government: A Comparative Historical Perspective," *Journal of Economic History* 37: 210–225.

Riphenburg, Claudia. 1997. "Women's Status and Cultural Expression: Changing Gender Relations and Structural Adjustment in Zimbabwe," *Africa Today* 44(1) (January–March): 33–49.

Risse, T. 2000. "Transnational Actors and World Politics," in W. Carlsnaes, T. Risse, and B. Simmons (eds.) *Handbook of International Relations*. London: Sage, pp. 255–274.

Risse, T., S. C. Ropp, and Katherine Sikkink. 1999. *The Power of Human Rights: International Norms and Domestic Change*. Cambridge University Press.

Rodrik, Dani. 1998. "Democracies Pay Higher Wages," National Bureau of Economic Research Working Paper 6364: 1–9.

Rodrik, Dani. 2001. "Four Simple Principles for Democratic Governance of Globalization," Transcript of an interview. Harvard University, May 12. ksghome.harvard.edu.

Rodrik, Dani. 2005. "Real Economic Success Stories not Explained by 'Trade and Aid,'" *Taipei Times*, August 8, p. 9. www.taipeitimes.com.

Rogoff, Kenneth. 2003. "The IMF Strikes Back," *Foreign Policy* 134: 39–46.

Rosh, Robert. 1986. "The Impact of Third World Defense Burdens on Basic Human Needs," *Policy Studies Journal* 15: 135–146.

Ross, Marc Howard. 1993. *The Culture of Conflict: Interpretations and Interests in Comparative Perspective*. New Haven: Yale University Press.

Rueda, David. 2005. "Insider–Outsider Politics in Industrialized Democracies: The Challenge to Social Democratic Parties," *American Political Science Review* 99 (February): 61–74.

Sachs, Jeffrey. 2005. *The End of Poverty: Economic Possibilities for our Time*. New York: Penguin Press.

Sadasivam, B. 1997. "The Impact of Structural Adjustment on Women: A Governance and Human Rights Agenda," *Human Rights Quarterly* 19(3): 630–655.

Sahin, Yossi and Juan J. Linz. 1995. *Between States: Interim Governments and Democratic Transitions.* Cambridge University Press.

Sahn, David E. 1996. "Economic Reform and Poverty: An Overview," in David E. Sahn (ed.) *Economic Reform and the Poor in Africa.* Oxford University Press.

Sahn, David E. and Lawrence Haddad. 1991. "The Gendered Impacts of Structural Adjustment Programs in Africa: Discussion," *American Journal of Agricultural Economics* (December): 1448–1451.

Salter, Frank. 2001. "A Defense and an Extension of Pierre van den Berghe's Theory of Ethnic Nepotism," in Patrick James and David Goetze (eds.) *Evolutionary Theory and Ethnic Conflict.* Westport, CT: Greenwood Publishing Group.

Sambanis, Nicholas. 2004a. "Do Ethnic and Nonethnic Civil Wars Have the Same Causes? A Theoretical and Empirical Inquiry (Part 1)," *Journal of Conflict Resolution* 45(3): 259–282.

Sambanis, Nicholas. 2004b. "What Is Civil War? Conceptual and Empirical Complexities of an Operational Definition," *Journal of Conflict Resolution* 48(6): 814–858.

SAPRIN (Structural Adjustment Participatory Review International Network). 2004. *Structural Adjustment: The SAPRIN Report: The Policy Roots of Economic Crisis, Poverty, and Inequality.* London: Zed Books.

Schelling, Thomas C. 1960. *The Strategy of Conflict.* Cambridge, MA: Harvard University Press.

Schleifer, Andrei and Robert Vishny. 1997. "A Survey of Corporate Governance," *Journal of Finance* 52(2) (June): 737–783.

Schultz, Kenneth A. 2001. *Democracy and Coercive Diplomacy.* Cambridge University Press.

Schumpeter, Joseph A. 1942. *Capitalism, Socialism and Democracy.* London: Harper and Brothers.

Scott, James C. 1976. *The Moral Economy of the Peasant.* New Haven: Yale University Press.

Sen, Amartya. 1999. *Development as Freedom.* New York: Anchor Books.

Sensor, Robert. 2003. "Getting the World Bank to Move," *Human Rights for Workers* 8(8): 4–5.

Sensor, Robert. 2005. "World Bank's Rare Positive Note on Unions," *Human Rights for Workers* 10(10) (October). www.sensor.com.

Shannon, V. P. 2000. "Norms Are What States Make of Them: The Political Psychology of Norm Violation," *International Studies Quarterly* 44: 293–316.

Shue, Henry. 1980. *Basic Rights: Subsistence, Affluence, and US Foreign Policy.* Princeton University Press.

Shultz, Jim. 2000. "Bolivia's Protesters Win War Over Water," *The Democracy Center.* www.democracyctr.org/waterwar/#win.

Sidell, Scott. 1988. *The IMF and Third-World Political Instability: Is There a Connection?* New York: St. Martin's Press.

Silver, Beverly J. 2003. *Forces of Labor: Workers' Movements and Globalization since 1870.* Cambridge University Press.

Simon, M. V. and Harvey Starr. 1996. "Extraction, Allocation and the Rise and Decline of States: A Simulation Analysis of Two-Level Security Management," *Journal of Conflict Resolution* 40(2): 272–297.

Simpson, Miles. 1990. "Political Rights and Income Inequality: A Cross-National Test," *American Sociological Review* 55: 682–693.

Sisson, C. A. 1986. "Fund-Supported Programs and Income Distribution in LDC's," *Finance and Development* 23: 30–32.

Skocpol, Theda. 1979. *States and Social Revolutions: A Comparative Analysis of France, Russia, and China.* Cambridge University Press.

Skogly, Sigrun. 1993. "Structural Adjustment and Development: Human Rights – an Agenda for Change?," *Human Rights Quarterly* 15.

Skogly, Sigrun. 2001. *The Human Rights Obligations of the World Bank and the International Monetary Fund.* London: Cavendish Publications.

Snyder, David and Charles Tilly. 1972. "Hardship and Collective Violence in France, 1830 to 1960," *American Sociological Review* 37(5): 520–532.

Sobek, David, M. Rodwan Abouharb, and Christopher G. Ingram. 2006. "The Human Rights Peace: How the Respect for Human Rights at Home Leads to Peace Abroad," *Journal of Politics* 68(3) (August): 519–529.

Sowa, Nii Kwaku. 1993. "Ghana," in Aderanti Adepoju (ed.) *The Impact of Structural Adjustment on the Population of Africa.* Portsmouth, NH: Heinemann, pp. 7–24.

Spalding, Nancy. 1986. "Providing for Economic Human Rights: The Case of the Third World," *Policy Studies Journal* 15(1): 123–135.

Spar, Debora L. 1998. "The Spotlight and the Bottom Line: How Multinationals Export Human Rights," *Foreign Affairs* 77(2): 7–12.

Starr, Harvey. 1994. "Revolution and War: Rethinking the Linkage between Internal and External Conflict," *Political Research Quarterly* 47(3): 481–507.

Stein, H. 1992. "Economic Policy and the IMF in Tanzania: Conditionality, Conflict, and Convergence," in H. Campbell and H. Stein (eds.) *Tanzania and the IMF: The Dynamics of Liberalization.* Boulder, CO: Westview, pp. 59–83.

Stewart, Frances. 1985. "The Fragile Foundations of the Neoclassical Approach to Development," *Journal of Development Studies* 21: 282–292.

Stiglitz, Joseph E. 1999. "The World Bank at the Millennium," *Economic Journal* (November): F577–F597.

Stiglitz, Joseph. 2002. *Globalization and its Discontents.* New York: W. W. Norton.

Stiglitz, Joseph E. and Lyn Squire. 1998. "International Development: Is it Possible?," *Foreign Policy* 110 (Spring): 138–151.

Stone, Randall W. 2002. *Lending Credibility: The International Monetary Fund and the Post-Communist Transition.* Princeton University Press.

Stone, Randall. 2004. "The Political Economy of IMF Lending in Africa," *American Political Science Review* 98(4): 577–592.

Strand, Håvard, Lars Wilhelmsen, and Nils Petter Gleditsch. 2002. "Armed Conflict Dataset Codebook," Version 1.1, September 9. www.prio.no/cwp/ArmedConflict/.

Strand, Håvard, Lars Wilhelmsen, and Nils Petter Gleditsch. 2005. "Armed Conflict Dataset Codebook," Version 3.2, September 9. www.prio.no/cwp/ArmedConflict/.

Strange, Susan. 1988. *States and Markets*. London: Blackwell.

Stryker, J. Dirck and Hasan A. Tuluy. 1989. "Assistance to Ghana and the Ivory Coast," in Anne O. Krueger, Constantine Michalopoulos, and Vernon W. Ruttan (eds.) *Aid and Development*. Baltimore: The Johns Hopkins University Press, pp. 269–302.

Subramanian, Shankar. 1996. "Vulnerability to Price Shocks under Alternative Policies in Cameroon," in David E. Sahn (ed.) *Economic Reform and the Poor in Africa*. Oxford University Press.

Sukhamte, Vasant. 1989. "Assistance to India," in Anne O. Krueger, Constantine Michalopoulos, and Vernon W. Ruttan (eds.) *Aid and Development*. Baltimore: The Johns Hopkins University Press, pp. 203–225.

Tanski, Janet M. 1994. "The Impact of Crisis, Stabilization and Structural Adjustment on Women in Lima, Peru," *World Development* 22: 1627–1642.

Tarnoff, Curt and Larry Nowels. 2001. "Foreign Aid: An Introductory Overview of US Programs and Policy," Congressional Research Service: The Library of Congress (April 6) Order Code 98–916 F.

Tarp, F. 1993. *Stabilization and Structural Adjustment: Macroeconomic Frameworks for Analysing the Crisis in Sub-Saharan Africa*. London: Routledge.

Tarrow, Sidney. 1994. *Power in Movement: Social Movements, Collective Action and Politics*. Cambridge University Press.

Thacker, Strom C. 1999. "The High Politics of IMF Lending," *World Politics* 52(1): 38–75.

Tilly, Charles. 1978. *From Modernization to Revolution*. Reading, MA: Addison Wesley.

Tockman, Jason. 2005. "Bolivia Pulls Back from Civil War," *ZNET*. www.zmag.org.

Tomasevski, K. 1993. *Development Aid and Human Rights Revisited*. New York: St. Martin's Press.

Tonelson, Alan. 2002. *The Race to the Bottom*. Boulder, CO: Westview Press.

Tucker, Lee. 1997. "Child Labor in Modern India: The Bonded Labor Problem," *Human Rights Quarterly* 19: 572–629.

Union Network International. 2006. "World Bank Takes Major Step on Labour Standards." www.union-network.org. United Nations Committee on Economic, Social, and Cultural Rights, 2001, Statement on Poverty and the International Covenant on Economic, Social, and Cultural Rights, May 4. www.unhchr.ch/tbs/doc.nsf/(Symbol)/E.C.12.2001.10.En.

United Nations Development Programme. 2004. *Human Development Report 2004: Cultural Liberty in Today's Diverse World*. New York: UNDP.

United Nations Economic Commission for Africa. 1989. *African Alternative Framework to Structural Adjustment Programmes for Socio-Economic Recovery and Transformation (AAF-SAP)*. Addis Ababa: UNECA.

US Central Intelligence Agency. 2005. *The World Factbook*. www.cia.gov/cia/publications/factbook/index.html.

US Department of State. 2005. *Country Reports on Human Rights Practices for 2004: Ghana*. Washington, DC: Government Printing Office.

Van den Berghe, Pierre. 1978. *Man: A Biosocial View*. New York: Elsevier.

Van de Laar, Aart. 1980. *The World Bank and the Poor*. Boston: Nijhoff.

Van der Lijn, N. 1995. "Measuring Well-being with Social Indicators, HDI, PQLI, and BWI for 133 Countries for 1975, 1980, 1985, 1988, and 1992." Research Memorandum No. 704, Tilburg University, Faculty of Economics and Business Administration. http://econpapers.repec.org/paper/dgrkubrem/1995704.htm.

Van de Walle, Nicolas. 2001. *African Economies and the Politics of Permanent Crisis, 1979–1999*. Cambridge University Press.

Van Dijck, Pitou (ed.). 1998. *The Bolivian Experiment: Structural Adjustment and Poverty Alleviation*. Amsterdam: Center for Latin American Research and Documentation.

Vanhanen, Tatu. 1999. "Domestic Ethnic Conflict and Ethnic Nepotism," *Journal of Peace Research* 36(1): 55–73.

Vaubel, R. 1986. "A Public Choice Approach to International Organization," *Public* 51: 39–57.

Vreeland, James Raymond. 1999. "The IMF: Lender of Last Resort or Scapegoat?," Paper presented at the annual meeting of the International Studies Association Conference, Washington, DC.

Vreeland, James Raymond. 2001. "Institutional Determinants of IMF Agreements." http://pantheon.yale.edu/jrv9/Veto.pdf.

Vreeland, James Raymond. 2002. "The Effect of IMF Programs on Labor," *World Development* 30(1): 21–39.

Vreeland, James Raymond. 2003. *The IMF and Economic Development*. Cambridge University Press.

Vuorela, Ulla. 1991. "The Informal Sector, Social Reproduction and the Impact of Economic Crisis on Women," in Horace Campbell and Howard Stein (eds.) *Tanzania and the IMF: Dynamics of Liberalization*. Harare, Zimbabwe: Southern Africa Political Economy Series Trust.

Walton, J. and D. Seddon (eds.). 1994. *Free Markets and Food Riots: The Politics of Global Adjustment*. Oxford: Blackwell.

Weisband, Edward and Christopher J. Colvin. 2000. "An Empirical Analysis of International Confederation of Free Trade Unions (ICFTU) Annual Surveys," *Human Rights Quarterly* 22(1): 167–186.

Weisbrot, Mark, Dean Baker, Egor Kraev, and Judy Chen. 2001. "The Scorecard on Globalization: 1980–2000: Twenty Years of Diminished Progress." Center for Economic and Policy Research. www.cepr.net.

Welch, Claude. 1995. *Protecting Human Rights in Africa: Roles and Strategies of Nongovernmental Organizations*. Philadelphia: University of Pennsylvania Press.

Williams, Marc. 1994. *International Economic Organizations and the Third World*. Hemel Hempstead: Harvester Wheatsheaf.

Williamson, J. 1990. "The Debt Crisis at the Turn of the Decade," *Institute of Development Studies Bulletin* 21(2): 4–6.

Wolfensohn, James D. 2004. "Closing Remarks at the Shanghai Conference on Scaling Up Poverty Reduction by James D. Wolfensohn President The World Bank Group Shanghai, China, May 27, 2004," http://web. worldbank.org/WBSITE/EXTERNAL/EXTABOUTUS/ORGANIZA-TION/PRESIDENTEXTERNAL/0,,contentMDK:20207692~menuPK: 232083~pagePK:159837~piPK:159808~theSitePK:227585,00.html.

World Bank. 1989. IBRD Articles of Agreement: Article I. http://web.worldbank.org/WBSITE/EXTERNAL/EXTABOUTUS/0,, contentMDK:20049563~pagePK:43912menuPK:58863piPK:36602,00. html#I1.

World Bank. 1992. *The World Bank Operational Manual: Operational Directive Adjustment Lending Policy* (OD 8.60) http://wbln0018.worldbank.org \institutional\manuals\opmanual.nsf.

World Bank. 1998. *Development and Human Rights: The Role of the World Bank.* Washington, DC: World Bank.

World Bank. 2004. "Joint Statement by the General Secretary of the World Council of Churches, President of the World Bank, and Deputy Managing Director of the International Monetary Fund." http://web.worldbank.org/ WBSITE\EXTERNAL/TOPICS/EXTPOVERTY/0,,con-tentMDK:20270913menuPK:337038pagePK:64020865piPK:149114the-SitePK:336992,00.html.

World Bank. 2005a. *World Development Report 2006: Equity and Development.* http://siteresources.worldbank.org/INTWDR2006/Resources/477383-1127230817535/082136412x.pdf.

World Bank. 2005b. "Human Rights." *FAQs.* http://web.worldbank.org/ WBSITE/EXTERNAL/EXTSITETOOLS/0, contentMDK:20749693pagePK:98400piPK:98424theSite PK:95474,00.html.

World Bank. 2005c. *Voice for the World's Poor: Selected Speeches and Writings of World Bank President James D. Wolfensohn, 1995–2005.* Washington, DC: World Bank.

World Bank. 2006a. *Doing Business 2007: How to Reform.* Washington, DC: World Bank.

World Bank. 2006b. *World Bank Annual Report.* Washington, DC: World Bank.

Young, O. R. 1980. "International Regimes: Problems of Concept Formation," *World Politics* 32(3): 331–356.

Young, O. R. 1992. "The Effectiveness of International Institutions: Hard Cases and Critical Variables," in J. N. Rosenau and E. Czempiel (eds.) *Governance without Governments: Order and Change in World Politics.* Cambridge University Press, pp. 160–194.

Zack-Williams, Alfred B. 2000. "Social Consequences of Structural Adjustment," in Giles Mohan, Ed. Brown, Bob Milward, and Alfred B. Zack-Williams (eds.) *Structural Adjustment: Theory, Practice and Impacts.* London: Routledge, pp. 59–74.

Zakaria, Fareed. 1997. "The Rise of Illiberal Democracy," *Foreign Affairs* 76(6): 22–43.

Zanger, Sabine C. 2000. "A Global Analysis of the Effect of Political Regime Changes on Life Integrity Violations, 1977–93," *Journal of Peace Research* 37: 213–233.

Zweifel, Thomas D. and Patricio Navia. 2000. "Democracy, Dictatorship, and Infant Mortality," *Journal of Democracy* 11(2): 99–114.

Author index

Subject index